Adrift

POSTMODERNISM IN THE CHURCH

Phil Sanders

Adrift

POSTMODERNISM IN THE CHURCH

GOSPEL ADVOCATE COMPANY
P.O. BOX 150
NASHVILLE, TENNESSEE 37202

Published by Gospel Advocate Co.
P.O. Box 150, Nashville, TN 37202
www.gospeladvocate.com

ISBN 0-89225-382-7

Dedication

Because their mother, Jackie, my beloved wife, and I have invested our lives in them and because the future belongs to them, it is with deepest love and greatest hope, this book is dedicated to our four beautiful daughters: Christa Marie, Chara Elizabeth, Tara Dawn and Laura Lynn Sanders.

Acknowledgments

Ten years ago at Oklahoma Christian University of Science and Arts, Dr. William E. Jones in an Old Testament Theology class planted the seeds of this book. From him I learned a different view of our changing world, a view that opened my eyes to the forces working in the minds of people today. I am deeply grateful to him for the many lessons he has taught me over these last three decades. I count him a friend and a mentor.

Mack Lyon and Jimmy Jividen have been priceless "sons of encouragement" to me. I owe much to both men who have urged me to write. Such men have proved worthy of respect for their unfailing loyalty to our Lord Jesus and their uncompromising love for truth. Both are soul winners, as well as preachers and scholars. I only hope to imitate their faith.

I give my deep thanks to the elders and members of Concord Road Church of Christ, who have encouraged me and endured my writing of this book. I am especially grateful to the two church secretaries, Nancy Smith and Helen Zimmel, for their patience and support.

To Greg Tidwell, my friend, my brother, my editor and my co-conspirator, I owe deep gratitude. This simple, midwestern preacher of the gospel has taught me much and given me a wonderful friendship. Greg is one of the best friends I have ever had. His assistance, along with Gospel Advocate, has made this project a pleasure. To my dear wife and children, I will always be grateful. Their support and love have gone with me through each step and hurdle. For 25 years Jackie has stood with me; she is my dearest friend and God's gift as my helper. My four daughters, each attending a Christian college and serving the Lord, provided the drive and need to write this book.

To my Lord Jesus, from whom are all things, I can only lift up my deepest thanks and praise. He is my Light, my life, and my joy. I am so thankful to know Him.

Table of Contents

Preface

The postmodern mindset at the close of the second millennium sets an individual adrift on a sea of uncertainty,
not having a north star to guide him, a rudder to steer him,
or an anchor to secure him. He does not know where he has
been, where he is now, or where he is going; and he will not
let anyone else tell him. He is insulted if anyone questions his
right to drift. He may affirm his own plans as right and good
but will not allow anyone to criticize or deny them. He will
not judge anything as right or wrong, nor will he tolerate any
intolerance. This is a commitment to absolute moral and doctrinal freedom. He has set himself adrift on a sea without the
eternal foundation of God.

CHAPTER 1

Why Is the World Turned Upside Down?

THE MINDSET OF CONFUSION

What makes Christians act as if they never knew God? What turns values upside down as if God had never spoken about right and wrong? What makes it wrong to speak against sin? Why do people think they can make up their own religion? Why is it that regardless of what people say, everybody thinks it is all right? How can everybody be right?

Why is it some people in the church do not understand basic Bible teachings? It is clear that baptism is essential to salvation. It is clear that there is only one church. Why is it some are calling important things non-issues? Why are choirs singing in churches? Why are some churches using instruments of music? Why are women now leading in worship? Why is it the world we have known in churches of Christ has turned upside down?

These questions are easier to ask than they are to answer. The winds of change seem to be blowing us away from our moorings. The things of God, which are so familiar, vaguely appear behind us. We are moving into uncharted waters that confuse, surprise and alarm us. What was familiar is no longer. The rules are changed, and we are not sure what the new ones are. The Bible seems outmoded, and a way of thinking without any foundations seems to dominate our society.

It should not surprise us that the mindset of the world does not match the mindset of God as it is presented in the Scriptures. The world, after all, is worldly; and God is not! Isaiah said so many years ago:

"For My thoughts are not your thoughts,
Neither are your ways My ways," declares the Lord.
"For as the heavens are higher than the earth,
So are My ways higher than your ways,
And My thoughts than your thoughts" (Isaiah 55:8-9).

It should not surprise us that the world will not accept the thinking or judgments of God. The world serves the god of this world who is hostile in mind to God and Christ. John reminds us that whatever is evil hates the light (John 3:19-21). The devil has been in a struggle with God for ages to do all that he can to defeat goodness, righteousness, truth and love. The world simply does not know God; it is determined to operate by its own designs.

Throughout the history of the world, the devil has come up with schemes in an effort to diminish the influence of God and to steal the hearts of men from God. Eve was seduced to sin, and Adam fell in with the transgression. By the time of Noah, "the Lord saw that the wickedness of man was great on the earth, and that every intent of the thoughts of his heart was only evil continually" (Genesis 6:5). God wiped that world clean through the flood, but the desire for sin remained in men. The Old Testament tells us the stories of idolatry, immorality, rebellion and anarchy. Many of these stories reflect a culture very much like our own today. The Jewish nation was monotheistic (believing in one God) in a world that was polytheistic (believing in many gods). The war between the one true God and the countless idols produced by men dominates Jewish history.

Occasionally we fool ourselves into thinking that we do not have those kinds of struggles. Really there is only one struggle – that between two masters. Will we serve God, or will we serve the evil one? The Bible presents us with a picture of only two ways (Matthew 7:13-14) and two destinies. John observed, "We know that we are of God, and the whole world lies in the power of the evil one" (1 John 5:19). There is no mixed-up, middle ground where we can play with both sides and still maintain a right relationship with God. James said, "You adulteresses, do you not know that friendship with the world is hostility toward God? Therefore whoever wishes to be a friend of the world makes himself an enemy of God" (James 4:4). Salvation in any terms is leaving the "domain of darkness" and

14

entering the "kingdom of His beloved Son, in whom we have re-demption, the forgiveness of sins" (Colossians 1:13-14). The plea of God is that we "come out from their midst and be separate." The Lord says, "[D]o not touch what is unclean; And I will welcome you" (2 Corinthians 6:17). God is not content to have His people unequally bound to those who are outside of Jesus Christ. Paul further confirms this:

> I urge you therefore, brethren, by the mercies of God, to present your bodies a living and holy sacrifice, accept-able to God, which is your spiritual service of worship. And do not be conformed to this world, but be trans-formed by the renewing of your mind, that you may prove what the will of God is, that which is good and accept-able and perfect (Romans 12:1-2).

It is this exclusiveness that is so objectionable to the postmodern mindset; yet God has called us to a mind transformed from such worldliness to His good, acceptable and perfect will.

No substitute exists for that perfect will, but men are forgetful and gullible. The devil has for centuries promised people the world – only to steal their souls. He is cunning, deceitful and masterful at his art of seducing God's people away from the truth. Satan arrays himself as an angel of light (2 Corinthians 11:14) in order to sug-gest he has a better way than that perfect will. With glitz and glam-our, speaking to our selfish inner selves, Satan seductively sells his "successful" improvements on God's will. Worldly people listen. Some have tried the devil's way and found that by it they can attract a crowd. Fooled by what appears successful, Christians fool them-selves, thinking there is a better way than God's and fall headlong into the old error. What is called successful is not successful for God but for the devil. What is called successful may not be good nor ac-ceptable nor perfect. It is no substitute for God's perfect will.

Astoundingly we are unaware that there is a serious conflict with Satan in our midst. In Romans 13:11 Paul said of the church in Rome that they knew "the times in which we are living."[1] I question whether this can be said of us. We keep ardent watch of the latest media news, are constantly bombarded with the latest polls, and talk our-selves silly over the latest events. Meanwhile, subtly and surely,

Satan wages a war of mindset and ideology, threatening to turn our whole society upside down. This we do not seem to understand. We know things have changed, but we are at a loss to explain what is happening or what we should do. In 1990 George Barna noted this dullness to our times among Christians. Citing some challenges to the church, Barna said,

> The first challenge we must rise to meet is the need to awaken the Christian community to America's spiritual crisis. Incredibly most Christians do not perceive the Church to be in the midst of the most severe struggle it has faced in centuries. Perhaps we have simply become accustomed to hearing gloom and doom preaching, or reading books about the impending decline of civilization. Just as the general public have been anesthetized to the gospel, maybe we have been inoculated against cries alerting us to the present danger.[2]

If modernism and liberalism were threats to the church in the 20th century, we can be sure that the devil will make an even stronger threat in the 21st century. There are times when we seem totally unaware that the tolerance of sin has any affect on our everyday lives and upon our children. We see moral evil and are afraid to speak, lest we are ostracized. Meanwhile, step by step, Satan takes another foothold.

Somehow our conviction, our faith in Jesus Christ, has not made the firm impact on our lives that it needs to make. David F. Wells in his book *God in the Wasteland* calls this the weightlessness of God:

> We have turned to a God that we can use rather than to a God we must obey; we have turned to a God who will fulfill our needs rather than to a God before whom we must surrender our rights to ourselves. He is a God for us, for our satisfaction – not because we have learned to think of him in this way through Christ but because we have learned to think of him this way through the marketplace. In the marketplace, everything is for us, for our pleasure, for our satisfaction, and we have come to assume that it must be so in the church as well. And so we transform the God of mercy into a God who is at our

mercy. We imagine that He is benign, that he will acquiesce as we toy with his reality and to co-opt him in the promotion of our ventures and careers. Thus do we presume to restrain him in a Weberian "iron cage" of this-worldly preoccupation. Thus we do tighten our grip upon him. And if the sunshine of his benign grace fails to warm us as we expect, if he fails to shower prosperity and success on us, we will find ourselves unable to believe in him anymore.[3]

In these days man dares to sit above God and judge Him. We dare to tell God what we desire and then go about molding God into that form. I sometimes think some really want a genie in a bottle more than they want the cross of Jesus Christ.

Churches today are less and less likely to ask, "What does the Bible say?" and more and more likely to ask, "What does the community want?" We often hear about congregations taking community surveys to determine what their neighbors think a church should be. We are not critical of looking for ways to serve the community as long as we remember who our Lord is. The church does not belong to the community; it belongs to the Lord. The church is uniquely His and was designed to be His servant to take His gospel to a lost and dying world. The community may influence our methods, but it must never change our message. The community may help us understand what our tasks are, but we must never forget who our Master is or that our primary task is evangelism. A satisfied community that never hears the gospel is not a saved community. What does it profit a church if it gains the whole community but loses its own souls?

Christians today are clamoring for more and more grace from God, but they want less and less accountability. Some people seem to think that the grace of God removes from us any need to be responsible or accountable. If we misunderstand the truth on some matter, so what? If we do not take time to know the facts, if we act hastily, if we are wrongly informed, no fear – the grace of God will cover us. The idea is that since we do not have to know everything before we obey, we can be uninformed or misinformed and still please God. Why is it that we are hearing this kind of reasoning more and more? The changes in our culture prompt us to want to justify everything we can and condemn as little as we can. The cost of such a popular and pseudo-comforting religion is that it is weak and worldly.

Such presuming upon God's grace is a far cry from David's prayer, "[K]eep back Your servant from presumptuous sins; Let them not rule over me; Then I shall be blameless, And I shall be acquitted of great transgression" (Psalm 19:13). David did not want to take it upon himself that he had permission to do whatever he wanted. Nadab and Abihu thought they could make an impromptu incense offering using a strange fire but found God does not accept what He does not instruct (Leviticus 10:1-2). Saul thought he could make burnt and peace offerings at Gilgal to keep the people of Israel from deserting him before the battle with the Philistines, but God took the kingdom from Saul for his presumption (1 Samuel 10:8; 13:8-14). David thought he could transport the ark from Kiriath-jearim by using an oxcart but found God's wrath striking out against Uzza, because David did not follow God's instructions for moving the ark (1 Chronicles 13:7-13; 15:2,13-15). Although David became angry at God for His outburst, he learned that self-designed obedience is irreverence (2 Samuel 6:7). We cannot presume upon the grace of God by accepting every view. The fact is that what we believe and what we do matters to God.

Why Is the Church Changing So Much?

A few years ago, my family of six traveled to a metropolis where Chara, one of our four daughters, was to receive a national award for high academic achievement. Since I had no duties in the pulpit that Sunday night, we left as soon as morning services were finished so that we could worship in the city. We were not prepared for what we witnessed.

When the church began singing, the sound was quite unusual. It was much louder and fuller than the sparse attendance suggested. On the front row sat four men and four women, each holding a microphone. They were the "worship team." We thought everyone was supposed to worship together. While we enjoyed many of the contemporary songs we sang, we noticed that a few of the songs were known only to the worship team. It was a time for them to showcase their talents rather than for us to worship God.

18

After a lengthy song service, the preacher arose. He began his sermon, confessing to his speculations on the text. He knew there was no scriptural basis for what he was to preach, but he believed it accurate anyway. His pulpit small and his papers many, he had little room for his Bible. Noting this to the congregation, he tossed his Bible on the floor so he would have more room for his papers. Jackie, our daughters and I sat in utter shock!

Tara asked quietly, "Is this a church of Christ?"

As soon as we returned to the car, each of the four girls began to assess our experience.

No one knew what was "wrong" with what we had witnessed, but we were sure it was not what we had practiced through the years. Immediately Christa, our debater, noted that the worship team was little more than a disguised choir. Chara wondered why the preacher threw aside his Bible to preach his opinions. Tara wondered why only the worship team should get a microphone. The girls felt unclean as they left the worship that night; and Laura echoed the question, "Dad, are you sure this is a church of Christ?"

The questions stung, because they demanded explanations for the alarming changes among us. The questions were more difficult because they were strange; we were facing problems unlike those we had faced before. We knew something was wrong; we just could not lay a finger on what. We only knew we were unsettled with this progressive experience. We began searching the Scriptures and asking what the will of God is.

At the same time, churches began advertising their desire for unity with denominations and their intention to swap pulpits with nearby churches – churches other than churches of Christ. Other congregations began offering concerts with instrumental music in place of Wednesday classes. Controversies over who is a Christian and who we are to fellowship have grown sharp. Those who have held to traditional views have found themselves polarized from those who call themselves progressive.

A conversation with my wife's brother revealed to me the dilemma many churches face. He told about the nightmare his congregation has faced in finding a youth minister. He said many of the applicants, graduates of universities associated with churches of Christ, could not give scriptural answers to the most basic doctrinal questions. Some could not say whether baptism preceded salvation or followed it. Many believed that instrumental music was a non-issue and could not give a scriptural reason for the church not using it. One applicant was dating a girl who attended a denomination and saw nothing wrong with what it taught or how it worshiped.

It is frightening to see what the future holds. Our Christian colleges and universities have fewer and fewer men who are training to preach the gospel. One university boasts large numbers of youth ministers in the Bible department but very few who want to preach. Youth ministry, counseling and foreign missions dominate the Bible majors in some places. Some youth ministry students see the day when they will leave ministry altogether to pursue another career; they have no desire to be preachers. Many churches are already finding it difficult to find a man sound in faith, doctrine, ethics and morals. In years to come churches of Christ will realize a serious shortage of well-trained men to fill their pulpits. As the place of doctrine diminishes among us, one wonders where the preachers will arise in the next century.

Dramatic Changes All Around

The world is going through tumultuous cultural changes. No wonder many people feel disillusioned, displaced, apprehensive or confused. They are afraid to speak anything with conviction. They know what they believe and are willing to profess a faith, but in postmodern America many people are unwilling to speak against what they believe is wrong. Bullied by those who are politically correct, they are not sure whether they have a right to express a loyalty to anything that puts down something else.

Many people are a little like the man in a strange town who has lost his sense of direction. He is not sure whether he is facing north, south, east or west. For him, what ought to be and what he is seeing are worlds apart. He is hesitant to do anything because he does not know what to do or which way to go. People are hesitant to make ethical, moral or theological stances because they have lost their frame of reference. Having taken the view that every view is right – except an intolerant one – postmodern society moves with whatever idea is fashionable at the time. Who knows what is next?

The strange town is even more confusing considering the fact that what was once familiar has now been changed. Everything seems to have been renamed and reconstructed, and nothing is much like it used to be. They have renamed sinful lifestyles to make them sound more respectable. They now laugh at the prudish and mock the fundamentalist. They cannot tolerate those who are intolerant of their freedom to view anything as they wish. For them, truth is not so much what one finds as it is what one makes it out to be.

The person who has settled convictions is not simply in culture shock – his whole world seems out of balance. To him, God seems to have been replaced with something that looks like religion but is awfully man-centered. For him, what once was a Christian nation has become everything but Christian. What once was considered the divine authority of the Bible has become a socially constructed theology among many theologies.

The church itself is not immune to the unsettled mindset of our times. Although some may think that the church is the haven of truth wherein the Word of God rules and the faith was once for all time delivered, today one finds the church to be a place filled with market ploys designed to meet the felt needs of the populace and to make them feel good about themselves. What happens in the world has always profoundly affected the church; today is no different. The subtle mindsets affecting many other aspects of our lives also shape how we perceive and practice our faith. In a society that wants to reinvent government and rewrite history, it should not be surprising that some might want to reconstruct their faith.

Consequently, many people, with no ill intentions, have subtly come to believe that the church must become more like the world in order to survive. The church can no longer be content to be what it has always been or do what it has always done. It must be more focused on meeting felt needs and less focused on theology. It must be more focused on practical things and less focused on doctrine. If the church is to survive, it is going to have to be more focused on positive things and less focused on anything negative.

In today's society the one thing the church must never do is judge anyone. It must become more tolerant of the religious diversity of our time. God, after all, is in the saving business, not the condemning business. In this multicultural society, it is politically incorrect

21

to put down anyone's lifestyle or ideas or especially to say anything is sinful. It could seriously injure someone's self-esteem if he thought the church did not approve of him. The church is supposed to love everybody no matter what. The church's job is to win people to God's love and not get involved with every aspect of other people's lives.

The mood of our times tells us that mossback churches are irrelevant in our culture. Mossback churches still talk about sin, still talk about repentance, and still think there is a hell. Mossback churches believe there is only one Savior and only one church. They continue to bore their audiences with their traditional worship formats and topical sermons. For them, Christianity, with its belief that it is the only way to heaven, can no longer speak meaningfully in a world that is determined to recognize all views as valid. As long as Christians maintain an exclusive mindset, they can never be taken seriously in the postmodern world. With the back of a hand, exclusive Christianity will be dismissed.

Our purpose here is to awaken America and specifically churches of Christ. The postmodern mindset has made a profound impact upon our thinking, our morality, and even our theology. We must be like the sons of Issachar: "men who understood the times, with knowledge of what Israel should do" (1 Chronicles 12:32). We need faith in God's Word, courage to stand for the truth, and a willingness to take up crosses. We must understand that we are in that transitional period from one era to another and that this transition is temporary. As the world continues to race toward an anti-foundational point of view, we must show why we are sure our foundation cannot be removed.

This book attempts to explain the current, cultural megashifts affecting churches of Christ and how we can respond to them. Chapters 2 and 3 will attempt to illustrate the mindset and consequences of postmodernism. Our world has seemed to turn upside down, and we remain confused as to why people are thinking so strangely. Immorality remains rampant, and no one cares. People no longer respect God, the Bible does not have the power to influence that it once had, and we cannot say that anything is wrong anymore.

Chapters 4-12 suggest our need to respond to this mindset in nine crucial categories: absolute truth, authority, the Restoration Plea, an unashamed commitment, the nature of the church, worship, obedience, right attitudes, and evangelism. In chapter 13 this book presents an optimistic view for the future of churches of Christ. We must face the future with an unshakable faith in the past, an inexhaustible love in the present, and an enduring hope for the future.

I can only pray that this information will help elders, preachers, teachers, and loving Christians understand our unique place as stewards of an eternal truth in an ever-changing world. It is written with the belief that we can buy the truth, and the attempt to possess the truth is worth the struggle. Jesus in His prayer to the Father said, "Your Word is truth" (John 17:17). Jesus said of Himself that He is the truth (14:6) and that He came to bear witness to the truth (18:36). Christians in the heritage of the last 2000 years believe in truth; postmodernists do not. Though postmodern ideology would try to remove the foundations upon which such statements are made, the simple fact is that Jesus still said it. What He said has stood the test of time, and when another two millennia have passed, men will still be reading Him. Whatever is in the Bible stands written, and even the devil knows that. Ignoring the foundations does not remove them.

Discussion Questions

1. What schemes in the Old Testament did the devil design to lead the people of Israel away from the truth?

2. How serious a struggle do you believe the church is facing today? List the struggles you believe could lead the church astray.

3. According to David Wells, how have people in our times treated God?

4. Why is it important to understand our times?

5. What changes have you seen in the church in the last 20 years?

CHAPTER 2

Adrift on the Sea of Uncertainty
THE LOSS OF OUR FOUNDATIONS

Postmodernism calls into question all traditional ideas about truth, about reality and about foundational beliefs – the structures of knowledge itself. The truths on which Christians rely have been uprooted. In their place have been planted human preference and subjectivity. In the mind of a postmodernist, there is no such thing as absolute truth. D. Martin Fields insightfully says,

> So where did this come from? For many of us the notion that there is no objective truth seems silly, and yet this notion is becoming more and more entrenched. After all, who would question the scientific truth that light travels at 186,282 miles per second or that the law of non-contradiction is a fundamental rule of logic? Better yet, who would question that "2 + 2 = 4," or that interpretation of John 14:6 that says Jesus is the only way to the Father? Answer: more and more people. Those beliefs may be true for some people, but not necessarily all. What we are seeing today is a shift; a shift in worldview. We are seeing the shift from the Modern to the Postmodern.[1]

This radical change profoundly affects the way our postmodern society views Christianity. During the 20th century modernists and liberals denied the existence of God, the historicity or divinity of Jesus, the inspiration of the Scriptures, and the reality of miracles. All has changed. Today postmodernists do not make arguments against Christianity; they simply dismiss it as one option among many in a sea of beliefs and ideas. Gene Veith in *Postmodern Times* argues that Christians must be aware of the postmodern attitude toward the foundations of their faith:

> [M]odernists would argue in various ways that Christianity is not true. One hardly hears this objection any more. Today the most common critique is that "Christians think they have the only truth." The claims of Christianity are not denied; they are rejected because they purport to be true. Those who believe "there are no absolutes" will dismiss those who reject relativism as "intolerant," as trying to force their beliefs on other people. Postmodernists reject Christianity on the same grounds that they reject modernism, with its scientific rationalism. Both Christians and modernists believe in truth. Postmodernists do not.[2]

The thinking of the day is not so much to deny the reality of truth as it is to dismiss it with the back of the hand. Truth becomes trivial, irrelevant. It must not be taken so seriously as to say that anyone or anything is wrong or untrue. Whatever is said may be taken back so that it may not offend. Truth must be made to become uncertain so that no solid foundation will have control over our lives; no one group can ever dominate again.

George Will once wryly commented that there is nothing too vulgar in our experience that would prevent us from flying a professor in from somewhere to defend it. It seems that every view is as valid as every other view in the minds of modern America. The fact is that 70 percent of Americans now believe that there is no such thing as absolute truth.[3] In the June 27, 1997, edition of *The Chronicle of Higher Education*, Robert L. Simon, professor of philosophy at Hamilton College, related this news about his students:

> Although groups denying the reality of the Holocaust have raised controversies ... I have recently seen an increasing number of students who, although well-meaning, hold almost as troubling a view. ... They accept the reality of the Holocaust, but they believe themselves unable morally to condemn it, or indeed to make any moral

judgments whatsoever. Such students typically comment that they themselves deplore the Holocaust and other great evils, but then they wind up by suspending moral judgment.

In an increasingly multicultural society, it is not surprising that many students believe that criticizing the codes of conduct of other groups and cultures is either unwise or prohibitive. They equate such criticism with intolerance and the coercive imposition of a powerful culture's norms on the less powerful.[4]

Professor Simon calls this "absolutophobia." In another article in the same issue of *The Chronicle*, Kay Haugaard, an instructor of creative writing at Pasadena City College, was dismayed with students over the issue of human sacrifice: "No one in the whole class of more than 20 ostensibly intelligent individuals would go out on a limb and take a stand against human sacrifice."

Fyodor Dostoyevsky said, "Without God, all things are permissible." Without the foundation of Christian morality, there is only amorality. When amorality is the order of the day, immorality will increase and soon will dominate. The removal of foundations means a loss of any law and any boundaries. The immoral person, who can dismiss every restraint, does as he pleases. Anti-foundationalism means each one can become a law to himself, a morality to himself. Each person's subjective morality is further subject to the whims of the moment and the frailties of human nature itself. This self-made morality reminds one of the days of the judges of old: "In those days there was no king in Israel; everyone did what was right in his own eyes" (Judges 21:25).

The sea of uncertainty can have no order, no purpose and no design. It can only clash against itself irrationally, filled with countless contradictions. Since there is no North Star, there can be no unfailing frame of reference. What is dependable one moment is confused the next. Such hopeless insecurity can only lead to utter despair and disorientation. Such a sea leaves its citizens bewildered at what comes next; the people can never find peace. Consequently, we remain children, "tossed here and there by waves and carried about by every wind of doctrine, by trickery of men, by craftiness in deceitful scheming" (Ephesians 4:14). Children do not know better; they cannot by themselves discern what is or is not moral. They need a parent to guide them and help them grow up successfully. On the other hand, mature Christians "because of practice have their senses trained to discern good and evil" (Hebrews 5:14). The postmodern mindset, while claiming maturity, is inconsistent. It wants to be understood as more advanced than previous mindsets yet acts like Peter Pan, refusing to grow up. It wants the respect of adulthood but will not make mature decisions about morality. It cannot decide what is right and wrong; and when it finally does speak, it takes back what it says so as not to offend.

Postmodern America seems plagued with constant navel-gazing. We poll ourselves continuously to see what we believe and think. The persistent reporting of a variety of opinions on all sorts of matters leads many to conclude that a variety of opinions implies there is no settled truth. The data from the Roper Poll on abortion is a good case in point.[5] Here are the responses to the question "Which of the following statements best reflects your view of abortion?":

- 19 percent believed abortion is wrong under any circumstances.
- 7 percent believed abortion is wrong except to save the life of the mother.
- 18 percent believed abortion is wrong except to save the life of the mother and in cases of rape or incest.
- 11 percent believed abortion is wrong except in instances of rape or incest; to save the life of the mother; or in case of infant deformity, disease or retardation.
- 11 percent believed abortion is wrong, except in instances of rape or incest; to save the life of the mother; in case of infant deformity, disease or retardation; and where the child is unwanted and will not have a good quality of life.

- 9 percent believed abortion was permissible for any reason the woman chooses until the fetus can survive outside the womb.
- 4 percent believed abortion is permissible for any reason, except as a way to select the sex of a child.
- 7 percent believed abortion is permissible for any reason the woman chooses at any time during pregnancy; and no legal restrictions should be imposed, including parental notification or delay for informed consent.
- 6 percent believed that abortion is permissible for any reason the woman chooses at any time during the pregnancy; there should be no legal restrictions of any kind; and the government should pay for the procedure if a woman cannot afford the expense.
- 8 percent do not know what they believe about abortion.

The poll also revealed that 60 percent of women and 52 percent of men identified with a more pro-life position. At least 84 percent of women approved of some restrictions on abortion.

This Roper Poll provided a variety of views on a controversial topic. Such polls are informative about what people think, but they are not designed either to tell us why or to make ethical judgments on the results. If we allow what we find in opinion polls to be the basis of our beliefs, any view is as good as another. No view really dominates, so every view is both right and wrong. At least, this is the conclusion some people make. These people hold the right to choose any view about abortion as a more sacred right than the right of life to the child. For them, rights have a more valid place in deciding morality than doing or believing what is right.

The subject of partial-birth abortions brought this misplacement of morality particularly into focus a few years ago. Although the majority of Americans opposed partial-birth abortions and both houses of Congress passed legislation against it, the president refused to sign the legislation because it would deny the mother's right to choose. Freedom to choose became the deciding factor, dismissing long-held foundations concerning the right to life. No matter how gory, how unjustified, how unnecessary, how contradictory, how cruel, or how sinful partial-birth abortion is, choosing is a more precious right than the infant's life. Of course, no one holding that view regards the right of the infant to choose. We have abandoned the foundations of morality in order to drift in a sea of selfish freedom.

Since the sea of uncertainty has no rudder, it cannot determine which direction to go. We may drift wherever we please, but we may not make moral judgments. No one may impose any morality on anyone else so choosing one true direction over another is impossible. The thinking of the time suggests we must allow going in many directions at once; every alternative is all right. The words of the theme song from *Mahogany* ask, "Do you know where you're going to?" The postmodernist cannot say. He may know what he has ceased to be, but he has cut all ties to the past. He is not so sure what he is right now and really does not know what he is becoming. He cannot say what he is becoming because he cannot determine with any finality where he is going. Since he is committed to remaining free from determining where he is going, he will not allow anyone to tell him. It is the worst of postmodern sins to decide and point. Again, the ultimate commitment is absolute moral and theological freedom.

In addition to the lack of a North Star and a rudder, this ship lacks an anchor. Although it may seek to anchor itself to tolerance or to freedom, such an anchor is a delusion at best. There is no ultimate freedom to being absolutely tolerant. While the postmodernist boasts tolerance, he himself is often intolerant of people with convictions. He will tolerate anyone except the person who says there is only one true way. The Christian, of course, affirms the statement of Jesus, "I am the way, and the truth, and the life; no one comes to the Father, but through Me" (John 14:6). The postmodern rejection of any foundation requires that he be intolerant of this basic Christian affirmation.

The postmodernist can tolerate the compromising Christian, but he will reject the uncompromising one. The postmodernist would love to hear Christians say, "I believe in my God, and you believe in your god. Basically they're all good and the same God. We'll see each other in heaven." Of course, faithfulness to God will not allow a Christian to make that kind of statement. An uncompromising Christian's message leads idolaters to put away their idols and turn to the true and living God (1 Thessalonians 1:9). The Lord demands that His people say no to sin and no to the devil.

The crucial point of the postmodernist is not truth or convictions. The point of the postmodernist view is power. He is unwilling to allow anyone the right to press one religious conviction over any other. He wants all religious views to be equivalent – all correct. Because he regards Christianity to be socially constructed, or man-made, the postmodernist does not see Christianity as better than any other religion. Even if he agrees with all the credible evidence for Christianity, he will dismiss its superiority because he also sees credible evidence supporting all other religions. Postmodernism is committed to a diversity of truths rather than to the one truth. Consequently, the postmodernist will not allow any one religion to be exclusively right. Gene Veith, in *Postmodern Times*, observed,

> Those who do not believe in truth are more likely, I believe, to lie. Those who believe that moral values are nothing more than the imposition of power may be more likely to use power to suppress their opposition, whether in enforcing politically correct postures in academia or, when they have political power, in acts of tyranny.[6]

When anti-foundationalism becomes the norm and power becomes the goal, those with a postmodernist agenda will not withhold any effort to press their influence on others. Interestingly the politically correct or better, theologically correct, have exalted themselves as judges ruling against anyone not holding their point of view. Postmodernists fearlessly make declarations of how the world should be. In the same way those pressing for a progressive inclusivism have become quite intolerant of anyone who might disagree with them. Among churches of Christ, they have, unfortunately, pushed the issue to the division of many congregations. In all of this, they claim to be more loving and pious, more compassionate and understanding than others in the Lord's church.

The Uncertainty Among Churches of Christ

The present mood of uncertainty among churches of Christ contrasts starkly with the boldness of the apostles and the courage and sacrifice of early Christians who would not bow to Caesar. Early Christians believed Jesus was the Lord, the Christ, and the Son of the living God. They were willing to rest all their hope in Him and to die for Him. They were committed to the one gospel and placed an anathema on anyone who would preach any other gospel. They knew but one church and one baptism.

Today, some people in churches of Christ suffer an identity crisis simply because they back away from the only firm foundation, the Word of God. It is not uncommon to hear a brother or sister state what the church believes about some matter but qualify the comment with the disclaimer that he or she is not sure why.

Some leaders within churches of Christ hold views about baptism that back away from the teachings of the Scriptures. Although most people have steadfastly held the view of baptism as immersion in water of a penitent believer to wash away sins, some now suggest that other views, such as sprinkling, are as valid as immersion; any good reason for baptism is sufficient to secure the blessing; and baptism is important but not necessary for one to be saved. They affirm that they believe and teach "church-of-Christ" tradition about baptism, but they will not refuse to recognize as a brother someone who was baptized differently or with a different understanding of baptism than the church of Christ has. Such statements confuse at best and contradict at worst.

How can one truly believe baptism washes away sins but accept a baptism that affirms one's sins are already washed away? Can one be obedient to the Lord in baptism when one is practicing a kind of baptism that denies what the Lord in the Scriptures affirms? Can baptism be "for the forgiveness of sins" and "because of the forgiveness of sins" at the same time? This view abandons theological truth in order to fellowship one who has not been scripturally baptized. It sacrifices truth to avoid offense.

Many church members oppose instrumental music in worship but do not know why. Because they do not know why, they are not sure that the use of the instrument is wrong. "Not sure" is a terrible indictment against preachers, teachers and elders who have never taken the time to explain the reasons. Church leaders can no longer assume the people in the pew have heard and understand many fundamental teachings of Christ. It is also a terrible indictment against many otherwise faithful Christians who have never taken the time to study the issue. When we hear "a cappella music is just a church-of-Christ tradition," "music in worship is not a salvation issue," or "there is not any passage that says instrumental music is a sin," we see clearly that the speaker does not understand the issues.

In some cases such controversies among us lead some people to say, "Well, there is enough doubt in my mind about baptism to believe that none of us can ever really know the truth. How do we know that everyone was baptized in water? How do we know that baptism is for the remission of sins? We cannot afford to get into the judging business." When someone says such things, that person should listen to himself and think of the implications of what he has said. Are the Scriptures really so unclear that we cannot understand them? Does God really mean what He says? Do we have any obligation to warn those who are in error?

The Scriptures affirm that we not only can know the truth but that we will know it (John 8:31-32). There is but one baptism that saves in Christianity (Ephesians 4:4-5). Peter on Pentecost called for the people to repent and be baptized "every one of you" (Acts 2:38). Apparently, all 3,000 who were baptized understood Peter alike (v. 41). Paul rhetorically asked, "Or do you not know that all of us who have been baptized into Christ Jesus have been baptized into His death?" (Romans 6:3). His question implies that Paul expected a uniformity to the true, doctrinal understanding of baptism. He is appalled that they might think anything else. Paul expected their thinking to conform to God's.

Occasionally someone says, "We're supposed to love everybody, and I do not think we can make immersion in water for the remission of sins the one and only test of who is a Christian." That we are to love everybody is certainly the teaching of the Scriptures, but our responsibility to love others does not determine what the truth is. Only God can determine what He desires, and He has told us what He wills in His Word, the Bible. Our loving someone does not change what God has spoken in His Word. Our loving someone does not excuse error or rebellion toward God. Real love is bound to the truth. Real love does not leave another person in error. Real love takes the time to show someone the error of his ways so that he may leave that error before it is too late.

> Brethren, even if a man is caught in any trespass, you who are spiritual, restore such a one in a spirit of gentleness; each one looking to yourself, lest you too be tempted (Galatians 6:1).

> And the Lord's bond-servant must not be quarrelsome, but be kind to all, able to teach, patient when wronged, with gentleness correcting those who are in opposition, if perhaps God may grant them repentance leading to the knowledge of the truth, and they may come to their senses and escape from the snare of the devil, having been held captive by him to do his will (2 Timothy 2:24-26).

> My brethren, if any among you strays from the truth, and one turns him back, let him know that he who turns a sinner from the error of his way will save his soul from death, and will cover a multitude of sins (James 5:19-20).

The fact is that churches of Christ have never made immersion in water for remission of sins the one and only test of who is a Christian. Without a doubt, baptism can never substitute for genuine faith or repentance. A baptized unbeliever is merely wet. A baptized but impenitent person is only fooling himself if he thinks he is a Christian. Both have gone to the water, but neither has been born again. It takes both the right heart and the right act to be obedient (Romans 6:16-18). God is not satisfied with half-hearted obedience any more than He is with man-made rituals. God wants our all.

The effort among some to compromise the Bible's teaching on baptism in order to fellowship those in denominational groups has arisen in recent years because of the influence of postmodern thinking. Although most brethren do not accept the radical views of liberal postmodernists, some think that a unity derived from theological freedom is more important than the requirements of truth. For them, truth is expendable if it gets in the way of maintaining a relationship with someone they love or admire. It actually becomes more important for them to please those whom they hope to influence for Christ than it is to please Christ Himself. Such thinking sets one adrift, forsaking the sure foundation of the Word of God. It can only lead to destruction.

One individual said, "People are more important than laws." No one doubts the value of a soul; each soul is worth more than all the world. No one should give lip service to the value of a soul, but God gave laws because He valued souls so highly. Moses could boast of the God of heaven as a good God because of His Law:

> For what great nation is there that has a god so near to it as is the Lord our God whenever we call on Him? Or what great nation is there that has statutes and judgments as righteous as this whole law which I am setting before you today? (Deuteronomy 4:7-8).

The Lord gave the Law to bless Israel, not to curse it. David knew this and delighted in the law:

> How blessed is the man who does not walk in the
>   counsel of the wicked,
> Nor stand in the path of sinners,
> Nor sit in the seat of scoffers!
> But his delight is in the law of the Lord,
> And in His law he meditates day and night.
>   (Psalm 1:1-2)

The Law is not merely law; it is God's law. Because it is God's law, we are subject to it; and it is not subject to us. Sin transgresses the law (1 John 3:4). The sin of breaking God's law is that it is a transgression against Him. The law is important because God is important. Jesus said at one point, "And why do you call Me, 'Lord, Lord,' and do not do what I say?" (Luke 6:46). Joseph would not give in to Potiphar's wife because he could not "do this great evil, and sin against God" (Genesis 39:9). All sin is sin against God.

The point of the postmodern view in churches of Christ is the power to do as one pleases. Postmodernists want to throw aside the doctrines and practices they consider objectionable by redesigning them as mere traditions, so they can feel free to pursue their own agendas. Ultimately, what they desire is that traditional, undenominational churches of Christ be replaced with an ecumenical, progressive denomination. They are unwilling to leave the churches of Christ for denominations more to their liking. Rather they are intent on gaining places of power whereby they can bring about the changes they think the church must have to survive in the postmodern age.

Frankly, many postmodernist Christians are ashamed of the churches of Christ. They are tired and bored with the no-frills approach to worship and prefer a more exciting and entertaining format. They are embarrassed that churches of Christ might think that there is but one gospel and one path of obedience. Such arrogance, they charge, is offensive to our religious neighbors, so we must rid ourselves of anything offensive. Ashamed of the name "church of Christ," they have adopted names such as "community church." They put the emphasis more on people and less on the Lord. Embarrassed by the archaic view of limiting the woman's role in the church, they have gone beyond the cultural biases of the past and exalted their sisters to new heights of leadership.

Those with a postmodern mindset claim they are smarter and more honest than their fathers, admitting their cultural biases. They understand why traditional churches of Christ are so rigid and have rejected that firmness as socially constructed. They believe that we are what we are because we were raised that way and that we are naive as to our traditions and institutions. They wonder why everyone does not admit his cultural biases. Churches of Christ, to them, did not arrive at their beliefs through a study of the revealed will of

God but have blindly accepted the rationalistic views of another era. They claim the church today is out of touch and in desperate need of reinvention under a new hermeneutic of their design.

Postmodernists assume nothing is quite as settled as it seems. There is, after all, for them no absolute truth. Of course, the Bible teaches that God has settled His Word in heaven, that the words of Jesus will last longer than the heavens and the earth, and that the faith is once for all time delivered to the saints. Consequently, the battle rages between loyalty to the one truth revealed for all time and a culturally determined, progressive attitude of nonjudmentalism. They prefer to set the church, like the rest of society, adrift on a sea of uncertainty.

Christians, living in a postmodern world, must remember that the sacred message is relevant for our time and culture, just as it has always been. When Peter preached on Pentecost, there were Jews present "from every nation under heaven" (Acts 2:5). The apostles, baptized in the Holy Spirit, spoke the wonders of God in the tongues of at least 15 nations. Jesus sent the apostles into every nation and every culture with only one gospel (1:8; Mark 16:15). We should remember there was in those days as much diversity of thought and culture as there is in our own day. Peter and the others lifted their voices in that day to libertines and legalists, to young and old, to patriots and compromisers, and to liberals and conservatives. They spoke the same message to everybody, just as we must do today. Gene Veith commented,

> What it means, among other things, is that the gospel is for the whole human race in all of its diversity, that through the Word preached by the apostles the Holy Spirit communicates faith to people of every language and culture. Far from being some unintelligible utterance, the tongues of Pentecost were uniquely intelligible – to everyone, no matter what their native language."[7]

The idea that because some culture has a logic of its own, it ought to have a gospel of its own flies in the face of the teaching of the Scripture. We are not speaking about a methodology here; we are speaking about a message. Paul, the original cross-cultural missionary, teaches the need to accommodate himself to the culture in which he lives; but he also recalls he is "under the law of Christ" (1 Corinthians 9:21). He will not change the message of the gospel and contends that there is but one gospel. It gets so serious to Paul that he would condemn anyone who preaches any other gospel (Galatians 1:6-9).

The Christian must not be conformed to this world but be transformed, so he may "prove what the will of God is, that which is good and acceptable and perfect" (Romans 12:1-2). Anytime culture and the gospel come into conflict, the gospel is to win out with the Christian. He should embody what God's will is. The church is to be the salt that influences the world rather than allowing the world to influence the church (Matthew 5:13-16). Paul said, "We are destroying speculations and every lofty thing raised up against the knowledge of God, and we are taking every thought captive to the obedience of Christ" (2 Corinthians 10:5). Preaching the gospel was and is an act of persuasion to bring people to act obediently to the one and only faith. The Christian begins his work assuming that God's Word is both right and authoritative. He realizes the urgency and the compulsory nature of gospel obedience. He preaches with the fear of the Lord (5:11) and the love of the Lord (Ephesians 4:15). The gospel should penetrate the lives of those who are unbelievers, so they may come to a knowledge of the truth and be saved (1 Timothy 2:3-4).

The gospel derives its power from the story of the cross. Nothing must diminish that compelling story. Nothing must take away from its passion, its ugliness and its beauty, its hatred and its love, its injustice and its justification. It is a powerful message because it is filled with conviction, with truth and with love. There is no other message that can save the souls of men; it is unique.

To water down the gospel story mocks the great lengths to which God went to save mankind. To downplay or dismiss sin scorns the blood which Jesus so freely shed for our sake. To obscure obedience ignores the cross Jesus demands that each of us carry. To suggest there are other saviors is to blaspheme the once-for-all sacrifice of our Savior. To consider other churches than the one for which

Jesus died renders His purchase unnecessary. The postmodern mind-set stands in utter disrespect for Jesus Christ, for it suggests that there are other lords and saviors just as good and just as valid.

When we say that we are adrift in this postmodern age, we cast a strong indictment. God has made in no uncertain terms a statement and a demonstration of His unfailing love for us through the gift of His Son. He has acted while we were sinners and enemies and while we were helpless (Romans 5:6-8). Further, He has powerfully declared Jesus to be His Son by raising Him from the dead (1:4). To suggest that our risen Lord should be put on a par with the animism of native Africans or the philosophies of Confucius blasphemes the Name which is above every name. It is rebellion to imagine that helpless humans can manufacture a belief as valid as the one that came down from heaven. In reality, the new postmodernism is as old as ancient paganism. Each individual becomes his own god. Like Eve, man today has come to believe the old lie of the devil that he can become like God and make his own rules. We want King Jesus as long as He does not make rules in our lives. We want Him to be our Lord as long as we do not have to be His slave.

The gospel of the grace of God is our foundation. We may wish to be set free from its rule, but we must understand there is a price to pay for such liberation. If we reject Jesus as Lord, we also lose Him as our Savior. The Savior of the body is also the head of the church (Ephesians 5:23). We cannot accept one part of Him and not the other; both come as a package deal. If we do not bear His cross, we cannot wear His crown. A change in our culture will not change His utter rule nor will a change in our mindset change His place in heaven. There is no paradigm that can remove the Lordship of Jesus Christ. We can pretend there are no foundations and trash traditions, but we cannot imagine away the one and only Son of God. We may sit in judgment of Him and decide His teachings are not binding upon us today, but one day He will return with the Book in His hand. What a surprise it will be to some people to learn that the universal and eternal message will be the standard of our judgment!

The sea of uncertainty is one of our own making. Some have imagined it and called their imaginations the reality of our times. Although culture is rapidly accepting the lie, Christians do not have to. We can awaken to the reality that has stood the test of time and will survive this latest challenge. That reality is the one true and living God, who has spoken to us in these last days through His Son. To find the foundation, all we need to do is listen, trust and obey.

Discussion Questions

1. How do Americans with a postmodern mindset view absolute truth, God and the Bible?

2. Why have many Americans rejected any attempt in making moral judgments?

3. Why do you suppose churches of Christ may be facing an identity crisis?

4. What factors are essential in determining who is a Christian?

5. What kind of unity does God desire in the church?

CHAPTER 3

What Is Postmodernism?
SECULARIZATION, PRIVATIZATION, PLURALIZATION, RELATIVIZATION

The term "postmodern" refers more to a period of time rather than to a distinct ideology. Until the end of the 19th century, the Western world thought itself capable of arriving at truth in all arenas through scientific inquiry. We believed some truths were absolute. Believing we could know those truths, we also believed men could reason about reality. This mindset describes the modern world. Many people still consider themselves to be living in the modern world. Yet that modern world has given way to postmodernity.

Postmodernism describes a dislocating human condition that arose in the final years of the 20th century. It is dislocating because it throws people out of their traditionally held worldviews. Without our understanding what was happening, all the things upon which we have relied seem to have vanished.

Postmodernism refers to a new set of assumptions about reality, going far beyond mere relativism. It impacts our literature, our dress, our art, our architecture, our music, our sense of right and wrong, our self-identity, and our theology. Postmodernism tends to view human experience as incoherent, lacking absolutes in the area of truth and meaning. Life and meaning are assigned to endless browsing of possible alternatives without the possibility of settling on any one as the rock-solid truth.

Many postmodernists assume that either no rational structures exist or that we cannot know them. In fact, their view is no one can know anything for sure – except, of course, we cannot know anything for sure. Amazingly we are told we can know that "we do not know anything." Just how we can know this one fact, but nothing else, remains unsolved.

Defining postmodernism is a little like trying to put toothpaste back in the tube; though you may be somewhat successful, you will likely make a mess of it. Postmodernism is not so much a doctrine as it is a mindset or a mood. It does not want the restraints of what has been handed down through what is called a "metanarrative." A metanarrative, according to postmodernism, is "a religious tradition or philosophical system that commits acts of cultural tyranny by promoting the fiction that all knowledge reduces to a set of universally applicable truths."[1] Of course, the Bible fits the postmodern definition of a metanarrative. Advocates of postmodernism are unwilling to let a singular set of religious truths or the one faith "tyrannize" their worldview or morality. Jesus can be "a way" but not "the only way." Jesus can be a great moral teacher as long as His views are not imposed on those who might believe something different. It seems odd that postmodernists become the very kind of tyrant they despise. They want the complete obliteration of Christian absolutes only to replace it with the absolutes of pluralism.

The goal of abolishing metanarratives is not to find the truth; the goal is to take away the power and authority from the Bible and from other religious sources. No one system can dominate. There can be no foundational religion. Postmodernists believe the evangelistic nature of Christianity destroys culture. Of course, there is a sense in which that is true. Wherever the truth goes, error is exposed and often forsaken.

When the truth was preached in Ephesus, the people brought their magic books together and burned them in sight of everyone (Acts 19:18-20). The "word of the Lord was growing mightily and prevailing." This is precisely what postmodernists are opposing. They do not want any one belief system to prevail over any other so as not to destroy any culture. Feeling the threat of God, whose Word is settled in heaven (Psalm 119:89), and Jesus, whose teachings will judge mankind in the last days (John 12:48), postmodernists must find a way to render Christianity impotent. Modern attacks denying the truth of Christianity have somewhat failed, so postmodernists have chosen rather to dismiss Christianity with the wave of a hand.

Questions about truth and right are not asked by postmodernists. Such questions are dismissed as trivial and irrelevant. For them, the issue is power. They are unwilling to let men dominate women, heterosexuals dominate homosexuals, or Christianity dominate other faiths. Postmodernists say they oppose tyranny, and they consider Christian values and morality to be religious and moral tyranny. They want no system that demands repentance. For every view to be right, no one view can demand that all the others fall into its line. Consequently, they tyrannize and devalue any belief system that gets in the way.

The plan of postmodernists is to deconstruct the metanarratives. They do this by attesting that all belief systems are socially constructed by cultures; they are merely relative truths affirmed by particular cultures and uniquely belonging to that culture. Since the Jewish metanarrative, the Bible, represents only one belief system among many, then the Bible should not be considered as a higher authority than other metanarratives.

Postmodernists deconstruct the metanarratives by supposedly uncovering the author's culturally determined biases. They say that an author expressed his favored ideas because of his social context and used God to strengthen his point. Paul's male bias as a Jew, for instance, is what caused him to tell women to be silent in church. Postmodernists are not really interested in understanding what Paul said about women or why. They are opposed to the restriction and must find a way to render the "tyrannical" passages powerless. They must show Paul's passages to be a subjective product, relative to that time and culture, and not applicable to our culture today.

The silent-women view grows out of first-century Jewish culture, and, to postmodernists, Paul was merely expressing his belief in his own time. If he had grown up in postmodern America, Paul would have expressed the biases of this time and place. He would not have had his first-century, male-dominated biases. Such a view makes it painfully clear that the role of the Holy Spirit inspiring Paul is not considered a possibility. Inspiration is ignored, and a context of universality is never contemplated. The historical reality of a Jewish man speaking cross-culturally to a Greek and Roman society has been ignored. For them, truth is relative, so there can never be a universal application of any metanarrative. Consequently, the silent-women view is not to be applied outside the first century, so today's woman may do as she pleases.

This cultural argument has become quite popular in recent years. Applied to any biblical view that is out of step with popular beliefs, the cultural argument attempts to negate the universality of the "faith once for all delivered to the saints." Postmodernists say that many commandments of the Bible are limited to the first century culture and not applicable to any other culture or time. They argue that biblical writers were only addressing circumstances related to their own time, and these circumstances are quite different from ours today. They suggest the writers never addressed the questions of our times; they were only dealing with the behaviors of their times.

The classical statement of the cultural argument is not any clearer today than in the way homosexuals justify their lifestyle apart from repentance. In 1955 the late Sherwin Bailey argued that the sin of Sodom was not sexual but a lack of hospitality.[2] More recently Letha Scanzoni and Virginia Mollenkott argued in their book, *Is the Homosexual My Neighbor?*, that the New Testament passages dealing with homosexuality did not argue against a committed, loving relationship. They said,

> The Bible clearly condemns certain kinds of homosexual practice (… gang rape, idolatry, and lustful promiscuity). However, it appears to be silent on certain other aspects of homosexuality – both the "homosexual orientation" and "a committed love-relationship" analogous to heterosexual monogamy.[3]

Unwilling to accept the idea that homosexuality framed in their own terms could be sin, postmodernists suggested the term "alternative." They wanted to remove the paradigm of a universal right and wrong and replace it with a paradigm of many alternative rights and scarcely any wrongs. Robert Williams has probably done the best job of showing how the cultural argument reflects the mindset of postmodernists when he says,

> The point is not really whether or not some passage in the Bible condemns homosexual acts; the point is that you cannot allow your moral and ethical decisions to be determined by the literature of a people whose culture and history are so far removed from your own. You must dare to be iconoclastic enough to say, "So what if the Bible does say it? Who cares?"[4]

As the religious belief system of the Jewish culture, the Bible is regarded by postmodernists as humanly constructed myths to explain and to affirm why Jews and Christians are what they are. They consider it fine to express the beliefs of one's heritage as long as one does not assume that one can press it on anyone else or deny any other view. They reason that Jewish culture is not any better than any other; why should its beliefs prevail over some other culture? Such views willfully ignore the idea of a universal God who will judge all mankind according to His Word. They dismiss God as a culturally designed Being. "If you wish to believe in Him, okay, but do not impose Him or His morals on anyone else."

In postmodernism God is dismissed with the wave of the hand. He is excused from duty; there are plenty of other gods who deserve equal time. There is not much difference between the postmodern mindset toward God and the idolatry of ancient times. Christianity is a bothersome menace, which must be stamped out. The attack of liberalism on Christianity in the last century was to deny the existence of God, to deny the resurrection, to deny miracles, and to deny the inspiration of the Scriptures. The postmodern mindset is to ignore God, to dismiss Him, and to regard His teachings as irrelevant. They are willing to admit that much about Christianity has a truth to it, but they still look at it as a socially constructed religion and not *the* truth. God's first commandment was that man have no other gods before Him. Postmodern man has forgotten that He is the one and only God.

Four trends have come into play to create the postmodern mindset: secularization, privatization, pluralization and relativization. These trends have taken decades to gain the momentum they now enjoy, but the persistent pushing of these agendas have made a profound impact on every aspect of our civilization.[5]

Secularization: Throw God Out

Simply stated, secularization is the process whereby God is replaced with man. From the days of the philosopher Friedrich Nietzsche (1844-1900), there has been the prediction that "God is dead."[6] What many meant by that is that the thought of traditional beliefs in God and Christ is now obsolete. Corliss Lamont describes the beliefs of secular humanism this way:

> There is no place in the Humanist worldview for either immortality or God in the valid meanings of those terms. Humanism contends that instead of the gods creating the cosmos, the cosmos, in the individualized form of human beings giving reign to their imagination, created the gods.[7]

For Lamont, there is no room for Divine providence. The secular humanist believes man is not under the control or guidance of any supernatural Being, rather he has to rely on himself and his own powers. It is not that God made man but that man dreamed up God. The consequence is man no longer needs God to control his life or to provide for his needs. The secular humanist considers man quite capable of taking care of himself, making belief in God obsolete.

Kicking God out of His place as the Divine Sovereign and provider does not come cheap. With the loss of God comes the loss also of the blessings and security He provides morally, ethically and spiritually. The postmodern mindset replaces faith in God with an uncertain cynicism, a bitterness and hopelessness in life. Generation X is one of the most pessimistic generations of all time; they have been robbed of their hope that life can get any better. There is no heaven for them, and this life pretty much stinks. Constantly fed a diet of dark and cruel movies, they have retreated into a world skeptical of others. Surrounded by fear, they never talk to strangers. It should not come as a surprise that barbarism is increasing, along with racial tensions. The new openness and tolerance for diversity has not removed the racism on all sides.

When one no longer respects God, respect for others and everything else goes too. America is rapidly becoming a profane society where all authority is suspect and the sacred is to be mocked. The smart aleck cartoon *The Simpsons* portrays the mindset that parents utterly lack any merit worthy of respect. Roseanne, the queen of comedy in the early '90s, weekly trashed traditional ideas and morality. MTV introduced Beavis and Butthead, two obnoxious teens who smoked, loved fire, took God's name in vain, and had their minds on sex continuously. In more recent days Ellen Degeneres has come out of the closet to champion the lesbian agenda on prime time television. Even the president of the United States recently has been willing to embrace the homosexual agenda and establish job quotas for them.

If you think this desire to kick God out is not serious, perhaps you should be aware that there is a movement now to change the way we record our years. Until now we have used the initials B.C. ("before Christ") and A.D. (Latin *Anno Domini*, "in the year of our Lord") to mark our dates. There is now an effort to change these matters to a more politically correct BCE ("before the Common Era") and CE (Common Era). The desire here is to be more politically correct and inclusive of people who are outside the Christian tradition. One scholar, Harold Bloom of Yale University, recently said, "Every scholar I know uses BCE and shuns A.D."[8]

The secularism of the world should not surprise Christians. The world has always been worldly. What is shocking is how much secularism has infected religion in our country and how much it is affecting the churches of Christ. Many Christians live today as if God did not exist, as if God did not mean what He said in His Word. For the Christian who has forgotten God or will not listen to God, God is as good as dead. For the person who thinks that the Bible needs updating to fit current cultures, God and His Word have become irrelevant.

Privatization: Replace God with Yourself

Some people propose the deconstruction of religion so that they may reinvent their faith. Unwilling to live within the boundaries of a faith passed down to them, they seek to establish their own brand of Christianity, blended from the values of their own invention. Religion for them is do-it-yourself. They can design their own God. They can pick and choose the kind of Christianity they like and reject the rest. They have a smorgasbord of sacred ideas from which to customize their beliefs and practices. They reason like Micah of the hill country of Ephraim who figured God would prosper him despite his idolatrous worship because he had a Levite for a priest (Judges 17:13). Those were the days when there was no king over Israel, and every man did what was right in his own eyes (18:1; 21:25). William Jones, professor emeritus of Oklahoma Christian University, describes religious America today as a laissez-faire eclecticism, i.e., "it is my own business if I design my personal religion to include elements from many faiths."[9] People want to live and let live, never mind the truth. They want to invent their own faith and allow others the same privilege. No one is to judge anyone about religion because all religion is true.

With privatization, true and false, or right and wrong, give way to likes and dislikes. Personal preferences serve to validate individual behavior. Personalized religion has become epidemic; as a result ethics have become more complex than ever. "Rather than people simply siding with the good against forces of evil, they now juxtapose multiple concepts of the good and situationalize these concepts in a way that makes all of them relativistic."[10] Things are wrong, then, only to the person who thinks that they are wrong; but they "may not be wrong for me."

David F. Wells, in his book *God in the Wasteland*, presents the problems with the demand for privatization being faced by evangelical religious institutions. He observes:

> The right of each individual to his or her own private thoughts and beliefs is held to be both axiomatic and inviolable. So it is that the particularities of evangelical

faith – the things that make it different – are dissolved. Modern culture grants me absolute freedom to believe whatever I want to believe – so long as I keep these beliefs from infringing on the consciousness or behavior of anyone else, especially on points of controversy. So it is, as John Cuddihy has suggested, that civil religion is always a religion of civility: the edges of faith are rounded off, the angles softened.[11]

America is a free country; our democracy ensures that every voice and every view has a right to be heard. Many men have died to preserve the freedom of religion in America, but the nation of America and the kingdom of God are not identical. In the church, the kingdom of God, only the King has the right to make the rules. Citizens are to be in subjection to His will and to deny themselves. Christians are expected to bring their thinking in line with the teaching of Jesus in the New Testament. Jesus said, "If you abide in My word, then you are truly disciples of Mine; and you shall know the truth, and the truth shall make you free" (John 8:31-32). Abiding in the words of Jesus in order to be a true disciple is incompatible with the notion of privatization. Jesus is the source of truth, and our beliefs must remain within His sayings. Privatization is neither the denial of self nor the following of Him and can never approve one as His disciple.

In the end, privatization is doing what Eve wanted to do so long ago – become a god. Privatization means that I become my own god and fashion my own religion to my own tastes and likes. I make my own laws and my own rules, which are subject to my changes. My perceptions are always correct, even when they change, for I myself am the source of my truth. You may believe as you please, but my truth is untouchable by anyone but me. This process leaves little room for a God outside my own thinking or will.

Enslaved to their own desires, such relativists never can know the freedom of the truth. Since they cannot find truth outside themselves in any independent, absolute sense, they settle for an enslaving spiritual system of their own making. Privatization is hardly different from idolatry. In the process they have abandoned the one and only truth that can make one free – the truth that comes from Jesus Christ. There is a high price to privatizing and customizing our faith.

Since postmodernists have come to regard Christianity as irrelevant, they seek to reinvent it so that it is more palatable and comfortable. They want Jesus as Savior but want to reinvent His place as Lord. After all, He is a rebel going against the grain of tradition. They want the compassionate forgiveness and grace He offers, but they do not want to bear a cross with Him. They feel the need to rewrite and edit His Word, so they will not be ashamed of it in front of their disagreeing friends. They love Jesus when He loves sinners, but they dismiss as irrelevant His call to repentance. They want a Christianity that does not confront anyone's private faith.

George Barna has his fictional Jeff Brown saying, "Religion is a private matter. What you believe, how your pursue those beliefs and relationships, and what one's faith looks like is nobody else's business."[12] Such privatizing of faith was never the intent of the Great Commission to preach the gospel to every creature. It ignores the constant stress in Scripture that there is one gospel, one faith, one Lord, and one body or church (e.g., Galatians 1:6-9; Ephesians 4:4-6). It denies the faith, which was once delivered for all the saints (Jude 3).

Pluralization: Recognize Everyone's Beliefs

Pluralization, according to Os Guinness, is "the process by which the number of options in the private sphere of modern society rapidly multiplies at all levels, especially at the level of world views, faiths and ideologies."[13]

This view holds that "all convictions about values are of equal validity, which says in effect that no convictions about values have any validity."[14] We are living in times like the paganism of the first few centuries – the Semite god was one god among many. Christians were rejected in the early centuries because they did not approve of the gods around them. They were unwilling to recognize an equal place for a plurality of gods. Polycarp, for instance, was condemned as an atheist for his disbelief of the Greek and Roman gods, especially the emperor. His faith for 80 years in the one true and living

God led him to deny all others. Postmodernists want the absolute freedom of belief in all the religions within and without Christianity. They are not willing to consider the contradictory and conflicting views that pluralism demands. Banishing distinctives, ignoring the evidence, postmodernism would have all religions to be alike.

The press for political correctness has certainly found its way to religion. Those who believe one way is right and another is wrong have been labeled as inflexible, mean-spirited and politically incorrect. Conviction that there is an absolute God who has spoken with finality can never be compatible with the pluralism of our times. The notion of pluralism must ever be opposed to New Testament Christianity, which cries out, "There is one body, ... one Lord, one faith, one baptism!"

Relativization: Abandon Your Absolutes

"Truth is relative." Seven in 10 Americans now believe that there is no such thing as absolute truth. According to most people, there is no set of truths that can be unquestionably relied upon in every circumstance in every place and time. Situationism, truth according to the circumstances, has captured the thinking of most people and has booted out the belief that we can be absolutely certain about anything. While some things are situation-dependent (as Romans 14 points out), the idea that no truth can be absolute is an illusion.

George Barna describes the way of life where all standards are transient and personal. He notes that in the world of relativism, "two conflicting and irreconcilable views may exist – but neither is allowed to be rejected, because that would infer the existence of an absolute." In relativism, two conflicting and irreconcilable views can both be correct and equally valid. This makes truth hopelessly confused and insane. Barna argues that this mindset has left America "emotionally, morally, and ethically paralyzed" by a seriously flawed philosophy. He argues that our time may be represented by the phrase "Because I said so."

In the relativist scheme of life, everything is subjective. Morality is a matter of personal preference. Ethics vary from situation to situation. Covenants and agreements may be changed on a whim. Values shift from day to day, as we experience unforeseen consequences, encounter novel concepts, or realize that our existing values stand in the way of enjoying a greater degree of satisfaction. People demand rights but ignore the corresponding responsibilities.

The outcomes of a system riddled with internal conflict are obvious. People often become frustrated and angry because they cannot get their own way. Nobody listens to anyone else because the opinions of other people do not really matter and there's nothing of value to learn from others. Arguments based on facts are refuted because we can choose not to accept the veracity of the underlying data. In fact, data are comparatively useless since all ideas are equally valid, regardless of the supporting statistics. Arguments based on intuition, however, cannot be refuted because you cannot challenge someone else's feelings; all feelings are similarly valid.[15]

J. Richard Middleton and Brian J. Walsh in their book, *Truth Is Stranger Than It Used to Be*, state openly their rejection of the notion of absolute truth. Embracing relativism, they argue:

Since all worldviews in a postmodern reading are merely human inventions, decisively conditioned by the social context in which they occur, and certainly not given to us by either nature or revelation, any "truth" we claim for our cherished positions must be kept strictly in quotation marks.[16]

Sadly we are experiencing, on a rather large scale, a subjectivism that betrays its weakened hold on the objective truth and reality of Christianity by its neglect or even renunciation of its distinctive objective character. Nowadays men cheerfully abandon the whole substance of Christianity, but they will hardly be persuaded to surrender the name. They really wish a creedless Christianity. "Creeds," they shout, "are divisive things; away with them!" If there must be such things, at least let us prune all their distinctive features away and give ourselves a genial and unpolemic Christianity, one in which all the "stress is laid on life, not dogma."

An undogmatic Christianity, however, is no Christianity at all. We are often told that "Christianity is a person, not a doctrine." How true! Christianity is centered on the person of Jesus Christ; but we must grant that Christianity, precisely because it is essentially a person, is also a body of facts and ideas. We cannot divorce Jesus Christ from what He did or what He taught; otherwise, to exalt Him is meaningless. It is the worst kind of hypocrisy to exalt the person of Christ and dismiss His teaching. When Paul declared, "I determined to know nothing among you except Jesus Christ, and Him crucified" (1 Corinthians 2:2), he was defining a special doctrine of Jesus as the essence of Christianity.

Elmer J. Thiessen, in his article "Truth in a Pluralist World," helps us to put into perspective what has happened in our quest for truth:

> Postmodern relativism rests on a fundamental confusion – a failure to distinguish between truth and our search for the truth. It is obvious that our search for truth is subjective and relative. We often find that we have to change our minds about what we believe and even about what we have claimed to know. But this in no way suggests that truth itself is relative. Indeed, we change our minds precisely because we realize that we hadn't got the truth the first time.
>
> There is a famous Persian story of some blind men, each describing an elephant from his limited perspective. One man feels the tail and thinks the elephant is long and thin like a rope. Another grabs hold of a leg and concludes the elephant is round and thick like a tree trunk. This story is often used to illustrate the subjectivity and relativity of truth. But we forget that the story is told from the point of view of the king and his courtiers who are not blind and who can therefore see that the blind men are unable to grasp the full reality of the elephant. The story only makes sense if there is a real elephant which someone can see and describe more fully. Partial truth only

makes sense in the light of some notion of full truth. The recognition of error presupposes truth with a capital "T."[17]

Conclusion

These four trends – secularism, privatization, pluralization and relativization – have made a profound impact upon American religion and the churches of Christ. George Barna said,

> [S]yncretism is in full blossom. Syncretism is the condition in which people pick and choose the elements they approve of from different, irreconcilable faith systems and then piece those elements together in a unique, idiosyncratic, customized faith system. The prevailing concern of people is no longer "Is my faith pure and true?" The dominant concern today is "Does my faith make me feel good and help me understand the world in a way I find reassuring and personally beneficial?"[18]

While postmodern America can tolerate a warm and fuzzy faith that judges little and accepts all, it can hardly live with the bold convictions of a New Testament Christianity. The mindset of the day does not want the serious challenge of the cross, and many people are completely unwilling to deny themselves. There is an utter reluctance to be uncomfortable or to make anyone else uncomfortable. There is the unwritten creed that the honest assessment of anyone's beliefs is utterly arrogant, rude and unreasonable. Inside the hearts of many Christians is a ready willingness to affirm basic truths, but there is an unwillingness to stand firm against any error. They will speak up for what they believe but will not speak out against sin or deceit.

Christianity is in a serious conflict with the postmodern mindset. As time goes by, Christians may expect a more hostile attitude in a world that neither understands nor respects them any more. The Jews were plagued with idolatry in ancient times, and we are no less plagued today. Those who held fast to idols persecuted the faithful Jews, so much so that in the days of Elijah he supposed that he was the only one left (1 Kings 19:14). As we read the history of Israel we find that idolatry was ever present; and though there were periods of restoration, the fatal folly of dumb idols had a way of recurring again and again.

Isaiah wonders how a man could use two pieces of wood from the same tree to make an idol and to make a fire (Isaiah 44:15). What good is this block of wood? We readily see the folly of a home-made, wooden god but miss the folly of self-made, individualized religion. We are not bowing at the feet of gilded wood; we bow at the feet of the idol of individualism. We bow before "Me." We serve our own desires. The fact is we have the same religion as the idol-aters but without a crafted, wooden image. Idolatry was so attractive in ancient times because one could tell the image what his belief was. If one served God, God determined the terms and rules. If one served a dumb idol, one could determine for himself what he believed. Idolatry meant that one could be his own god, could do what he wished, could believe what he wished, and did not have to give an account to anybody.

Individualized Christianity is so attractive today because we become the judge and arbiter of our religion. I may decide how I interpret Scripture. I may have my subjective faith. I can speak of my experiences with Christ and the Holy Spirit. I can define what I believe in terms of my experience and culture. When people disagree I can merely reply, "Well, that's your interpretation. I can let people have a right to their own faith, and I can have a right to mine. I do not judge them, and I will not let them judge me. I refuse to let any church doctrine or tradition tell me what to believe or practice." Such people are so busy listening to themselves that they hardly hear God.

When a person serves at the altar of individualized religion, he grants himself the privilege to set aside the commands of God that he does not favor and to establish his own traditions. The person who privatizes his faith in Jesus is not much different from the Pharisee who separates himself from common religion to practice his new and improved form. Jesus charged the Pharisees with "lawlessness" (Matthew 23:28). Lawlessness (*anomia* in the Greek) is the frame of mind of one who despises the law or thinks he is above the law.[19] In either case the lawless person is unwilling to be in subjection to God's will. He is willing to set aside God's commands for the sake of his own manufactured tradition (15:6). Jesus might very well say to those who are so quick to make their own faith, "You hypocrites, rightly did Isaiah prophesy of you, saying, 'This people honors Me with their lips, But their heart is far away from Me. But in vain do they worship Me, teaching as doctrines the precepts of men' " (vv. 7-9). Privatized faith leads one away from God not toward Him. There is not room in our hearts for God Himself if we are busy stylizing our own beliefs and practices. When God looks down on one who is worshiping Him and sees a heart that is crafting its own religion, God sees that worship as futile. Such songs and prayers never get above the ceiling.

What is postmodernism? It is rebellion toward God. The postmodern mindset arrogantly dares to treat God as a trivial non-issue. With the wave of the back of a hand, it dismisses the Creator and Lord. It robes itself with self-made laws, values and religion. It grants all others the right to design their own faiths. It is willing to entertain any notion except an absolute truth. It is willing to believe in anything, as long as no view wins out over any other. Postmodernism loves the freedom to be adrift in the sea of uncertainty. It wants no port and will never know the true and living God.

Discussion Questions

1. What things have been "dislocated by postmodernism"?
2. What is the "cultural argument," and how do homosexuals use this argument?
3. What are the consequences of no longer believing or respecting God?
4. How has privatization affected people's view of truth?
5. How does pluralization compare with biblical teaching on unity?
6. How has individualized Christianity affected the church?

Recognizing the North Star
ABSOLUTE TRUTH, INSPIRATION
AND INERRANCY

Absolute truth – true for all people in all places for all time – rises above any one culture; it is true for all cultures. For any truth to be absolute, it must come from a supernatural source transcending the local scene. The God who created this world created all people. All cultures must find their ultimate source of truth in Him and are accountable to His laws. Finite man is not the source of absolute truth; God must reveal it either by natural or by supernatural means. Since God is universal and changeless, then universal and changeless teachings and laws must come from Him. Such universal and changeless truths are, of necessity, absolute. To challenge the existence of any absolute truth is not really a challenge to truth but a challenge to the character of God.

A recent poll indicates that 72 percent of Americans 18-25 years old do not believe in absolute truth.[1] They think truth is relative, varying with time and circumstance. It is not surprising today to hear, "You cannot say that something is true for everybody! How do you know? Just because something is true for you does not mean it's true for everybody else." Such statements not only reflect what the speaker thinks about truth but also, more importantly, what he thinks about God. These statements raise some questions: Can God speak universally, immutably and with finality? Does God have an eternal covenant made with all men? Has He spoken at any time to all people of all cultures a message that cannot be changed? The answer to each of these questions is yes, and the gospel fits these categories. Three factors make the gospel an absolute message:

1. The gospel is universal. Jesus said,

> Go therefore and make disciples of all the nations, bap-
> tizing them in the name of the Father and the Son and
> the Holy Spirit, teaching them to observe all that I com-
> manded you; and lo, I am with you always, even to the
> end of the age (Matthew 28:19-20).

Paul tells his audience, "Therefore having overlooked the times
of ignorance, God is now declaring to men that all everywhere should
repent" (Acts 17:30). The Lord's church is commissioned to appeal
to every culture in every land until the end of time. The gospel was
not merely a message for ancient Palestine; it is also a message for
postmodern America.

2. The gospel is final. "Heaven and earth will pass away," Jesus
promised, "but My words shall not pass away" (Matthew 24:35).
Likewise, He told the apostles,

> I have many more things to say to you, but you cannot
> bear them now. But when He, the Spirit of truth, comes,
> He will guide you into all the truth; for He will not
> speak on His own initiative, but whatever He hears, He
> will speak; and He will disclose to you what is to come
> (John 16:12-13).

Jude, in his epistle, mentions "faith which was once for all delivered to the saints" (Jude 3). This faith was to be delivered only
once for all time. The idea that the gospel would need reinventing
for the whims of each culture is not contemplated in Scripture. Every
culture was to conform to the gospel. The gospel was given to change
the sinful things in every culture so that it might conform to the will
of God. The delivered faith is once for all just as the sacrifice of
Christ was once for all to bear our sins (Hebrews 9:28).

3. The gospel is unchangeable. Paul warns the Galatians:

> I am amazed that you are so quickly deserting Him who
> called you by the grace of Christ, for a different gospel;
> which is really not another; only there are some who are

disturbing you, and want to distort the gospel of Christ. But even though we, or an angel from heaven, should preach to you a gospel contrary to that which we have preached to you, let him be accursed (Galatians 1:6-8).

The wise man of the Old Testament wrote, "Every word of God is tested; He is a shield to those who take refuge in Him. Do not add to His words Lest He reprove you, and you be proved a liar" (Proverbs 30:5-6). The most serious consequences are directed toward anyone who would dare to change or edit the gospel. Anything that is unchangeable is, in that sense, absolute.

These three characteristics, derived from an absolute God, make the gospel absolute truth. Those who espouse Christianity have very little to say or to offer if the gospel they believe and preach is not settled in heaven. It is a great offense to God to suggest that somehow the death of Jesus was somehow not enough so that its message is not universal, final and unchangeable. Paul argued that if the resurrection of Jesus from the dead was not true, then our faith is in vain and our preaching is in vain (1 Corinthians 15:14). If Jesus is not raised, we are still in our sins (v. 15). If the resurrection were not a settled and eternal truth, undeniable and unchangeable, then we are of all men most to be pitied (v. 19).

These historical events, the death and resurrection of Jesus, have such an eternal and universal message that one can hardly imagine how they could be made relative and still maintain any ability to influence the world. Jesus either died for our sins or He did not. He is either a sacrifice for sins or He is not. Jesus either bodily arose from the dead or He did not. The idea that we can hold both options (Jesus died for our sins or Jesus did not die for our sins) as true and correct at the same time casts us into complete confusion and nonsense. If both are true, how can we ever believe that we really have forgiveness of sins? If the bodily resurrection is true and untrue at the same time, how can we ever face death with confidence at the grave of a loved one? Truth matters in our practical lives. The notion that truth is relative means that we must take back everything we believe simply because we cannot know anything.

The Consequences of Making Truth Relative

The person who believes that truth is relative must argue that truth can never be reduced to a single point of view. For him, there must be a plurality of views. There can be no foundational worldview to which all people can appeal, because all worldviews, though contradictory, are equally true and valid. One person's morality is as good as another's; one person's beliefs are as good as another's. There are no wrong views, only different views. Reason or logic cannot be used to determine what the truth is, because each worldview has its own logic as well as its own truth.[2]

The idea is that since every truth is culturally determined by ways of reasoning unique to that culture, then there can be no universal logic or absolute truth. There can be no universal God for all mankind, because each culture has its own views and logic through which they perceive God. For the postmodernist, truth is always the product of the human mind. Because there are many minds in this world, there must be diversities of truth.

In the postmodern world the reality of any truth does not exist apart from human reasoning. People do not perceive the truth as it is; they manufacture it. Walter Truett Anderson in his book *The Truth about the Truth* quotes philosopher Richard Rorty, saying, "truth is made rather than found."[3]

Even religious truths are not to be "found" in Scripture but "made" in the human mind from Scripture. For the postmodernist, the authority of Scripture is not derived from the conviction that God spoke it. The authority comes from the fact that the church constructed a belief from what He spoke. The authority, then, lies in the commonly held church belief not in the written Word. For postmodernists, every thought that enters the mind is socially constructed by men. Men only believe what they believe because they have been socially programmed by their environment to do so. Such a mindset dismisses the inspiration of the Bible and, consequently, God's authority. It believes that there is no authority but human authority. The belief in relativism is ultimately a thorough-going humanism, at best only giving lip service to God.

One can understand, then, why postmodernists reject the truth claims of Jesus. When Jesus claims, "I am the way, and the truth, and the life; no one comes to the Father, but through Me" (John 14:6), He states that He is the true and only way to the Father. The postmodernist cannot tolerate the tyranny of a unique or single Savior. They may even challenge the idea of a need for any savior. In rejecting Christianity, they deny their steadfast conviction that truth must be diverse. They are unwilling to submit to any truth that they themselves must receive and cannot manufacture. No one view of truth can tyrannize and push out the other views. For postmodernists, Jesus cannot be the only way. They repudiate the dogmatism of such passages as Acts 4:12: "And there is salvation in no one else; for there is no other name under heaven that has been given among men, by which we must be saved."

To be dogmatic about anything is to be intolerant of the multitude of ideas present in today's society. For postmodernism, it is the greatest taboo to suggest that anyone who is different is wrong. Priding themselves in being most tolerant of any notion, postmodernists are oddly intolerant of dogmatism. A person who believes in absolute truth is considered dangerous by those who believe in relativism. A postmodernist will accept any view except one that excludes; here he becomes intolerant. He will not tolerate the intolerance of Christian conviction. It is all right for postmodernists to be intolerant of Christianity, but, oddly, it is not all right for anyone who believes in absolute truth to be intolerant. Postmodernists are unwilling to allow any view that excludes, because it "tyrannizes." If a dogmatic view is permissible, it may gain an advantage over competing views. The offense of dogmatism is that it upholds the old notion that there is absolute truth, and it rules out diversity. Christianity can be one religion among many, but it cannot be tolerated as the one and only religion. To remain in league with others, postmodernists demand that Christianity become open to doctrinal diversity. Some who are pushing for radical change are willing to make just such a compromise, but biblical Christianity cannot do that.

Postmodernists reject the exclusive nature of Christianity because they reject any exclusivism and are committed to inclusivism. Inclusivism means that they accept morally and theologically all the diverse beliefs of every culture; they do not want to think of anyone as "wrong." They are open to the humanly constructed beliefs of all people in all cultures, since they place them all on the same level. Everything is relative, and nothing is absolute – and they are absolutely certain this is so! What irony they practice the very thing they repudiate!

Justin Taylor, an apologist who works on college campuses, suggests that we might ask someone who denies absolute truth, "Well, are you sure that this is so?" He may answer yes.

"Are you absolutely sure?"

If he answers yes again, then he has essentially said, "There are no absolutes, excepting the absolute that there are no absolutes!"

Taylor's final question would be, "Due to the fact that you believe in one moral absolute, could it be possible for two to exist?" If his answer is no, then he has just given two absolutes!

Within Churches of Christ

Churches of Christ have not escaped the influence of postmodern inclusivism. For some people, dogmatic views can no longer be tolerated. The church, as a consequence, is engrossed in several disputes. In recent days many are shocked by the intensity to which these disputes are raging within individual congregations. It is with great sadness that divisions among us are occurring. The divisions are not occurring over small matters of opinion but over these fundamental questions: Can we know the truth? Who is in the family of God? What is scriptural baptism? How are we to understand the authority of the Scriptures? and What is the nature of the church?

It is not an accident that these questions should once again come to our attention in churches of Christ. The onset of postmodernism has created an environment where our most fundamental beliefs must be questioned. These foundations have been questioned before, and that should not frighten us. What is alarming is postmodernism seems to have such a casual dismissing of the evidence. Sometimes it is almost an elitist "so what?" response to long-held and proven beliefs. Some postmodernists in the church simply believe that they have a higher level of knowledge than the rest of us and wonder why we do not agree with them. The answer lies in our assumptions on foundational issues.

These foundational questions shake us because our identity and reason for existence is wrapped up in them. We need not fear the questioning of truth; it will stand on its own if given the opportunity. The problem today is not so much that truth is questioned as liberalism has done for more than a century. The problem is that traditional truth, in the form of "one Lord, one faith, one baptism," has been dismissed as too tyrannical. It has been dismissed as a threat to freedom on one hand and as trivial on the other. It has been replaced with a reconstructed belief system that is claimed to be more inclusive and less dogmatic.

The idea behind the present inclusivism is that since there are no absolutes, we cannot know the truth with finality. In the past we have spoken in terms that suggested there is one right way and there can be no other. We do not want to continue offending anybody with this kind of traditional arrogance. We really cannot be sure anymore that what we believe is the absolute truth, so we will not be dogmatic toward those with whom we once disagreed. We can then be like everyone else; we can open our arms to everyone.

This reconstructed belief system is really disbelief. It is incapable of confidence, for it must take back what it affirms in the presence of those who disagree. Can you imagine Peter saying, "Repent, unless you do not think it is necessary?" Can you imagine Paul affirming one gospel but saying it is no problem to distort that gospel?

The postmodern mindset mocks what we have been, whether it presents an alternative or not. For two decades it has become fashionable to make fun of the traditional churches of Christ. Such mockery is not done in the spirit of a "lover's quarrel" but with sarcasm and condescension. It is mostly a repudiation of what some have just ceased to be. These doubts are designed to devas-

tate and deconstruct the traditional positions held by churches of
Christ. For example:

- We are not sure that there is just one church, so we will
  fellowship other churches.
- We are not sure that baptism is only immersion, so we
  will fellowship non-immersionists.
- We are not sure that baptism must be for the remission
  of sins, so we will fellowship those who believe they
  are saved before baptism.
- We are now a denomination,[4] so we do not have to be
  sectarian anymore.
- We are not sure that women today are to be silent, so
  we will have women leading our worship.
- We are not sure that we cannot have instrumental music in worship, so we will fellowship those who worship with the instrument.

This postmodern mindset is in great conflict with the teachings
of Scripture. The Scriptures claim that they were written so as to be
understood.[5] Furthermore, the Scriptures present a gospel that would
go out into all the world and was to be preached to every person in
every culture and in every time period until the end of the world
(Matthew 28:18-20; Mark 16:15-16).

The fact that there is but one gospel implies that men were to understand that gospel and to distinguish it from any other presenta-
tion. Indeed, Paul condemns with an anathema anyone who would
preach any other gospel (Galatians 1:8-9).[6] Such a view demands
that the gospel be the same for all people of all cultures from the
cross until the end of the world.

The biblical teaching that there is only one gospel will not permit the kind of diversity some are eager to adopt. There cannot be
one gospel and many gospels at the same time and with the same
blessing of God; otherwise the word "one" is meaningless. It is contradictory and absurd to think that "one" and "many" can both be
true at the same time. Has God contradicted Himself? If we regard
God as having spoken with such little meaning to His words about

the gospel itself, how can we have any assurance with regard to anything He has spoken? If God cannot be plain and consistent, one might as well ask if God knows what He is talking about on any subject. The problem is not – nor has it ever been – with God; the problem is with us.

Here again, logic's law of noncontradiction comes into play. The law of noncontradiction says that "no two contradictory statements can both be true at the same time and in the same sense."[7] God's words have meaning. That God expects us to understand and to comply with His meaning is evident. Jesus said, "He who rejects Me, and does not receive My sayings, has one who judges him; the word I spoke is what will judge him at the last day" (John 12:48). What kind of God presents such an uncertain criteria of our eternal judgment? What kind of God makes promises and gives commands with words that change their meaning? How can we give our loyalty and allegiance to a God whom we cannot understand and who speaks but does not mean what He says? How can we know what the criteria of our judgment is if it keeps changing? How could God judge us fairly if His standards keep changing? Believing that God's truths are relative speaks against the character of God and turns Him into a confusing, irrational Being unworthy of our devotion.

One of the current heated discussions among us deals with the necessity of baptism to salvation. Up until now, churches of Christ were in overwhelming agreement that baptism is for the forgiveness of sins (Acts 2:38). Some inclusivists are questioning our ability to know whether that is true or not. They say, on one hand, that they believe in baptism for the remission of sins; but, on the other hand, they take it back when asked whether an unbaptized believer is saved. If truth is relative and not absolute, one can understand why they hold these contradictory positions. Their reasoning behind this confusion is that we are merely creatures of our socially constructed theology; we believe what we believe because we were taught that. They reason that if our understanding of baptism had been different, we would have acted differently.

When they say this, they ignore the fact that the Bible has only taught one gospel and one baptism. They also ignore the fact that our restorationist forefathers bucked the socially prevalent view of their day that baptism followed salvation. Early restorationists rebelled against the denominational leaders and beliefs of the day. They examined the traditions of the day with the Scriptures and rejected popular, human notions. They were a minority group going against the culture of the day. They sought a unity based on the rejection of humanly devised beliefs and practices in favor of that which can be found only in Scripture.

Brethren who are embracing the postmodern mindset have unwittingly bought into the idea that our belief that baptism saves is a socially constructed tradition. In their minds there is no need to say that the Bible teaches that baptism saves. Such beliefs are socially constructed, and churches of Christ came up with that from a rationalistic, Lockean way of thinking. Baptists, for instance, who have grown up believing that their sins were forgiven when they said the "sinner's prayer," went to the baptistery to declare the salvation that had already happened in their lives. That is socially constructed Baptist theology. To postmodernists, the belief that salvation comes after baptism is a socially constructed doctrine of the "church-of-Christ" denomination. The reasoning is, however, that since both were done with honorable hearts to obey God and because we cannot be absolutely sure of the truth, both views of baptism are acceptable and approved of God. It is an amazing assumption to think that if these views are acceptable to us, then they will be acceptable to God.

Are both baptisms really the same? If one is baptized so that one's sins might be forgiven or washed away, one is not saved before baptism. Otherwise, what sins does he have to wash away? It cannot be both that one is saved before baptism and baptized to be saved. The law of noncontradiction means that the beginning of salvation cannot come both before and after baptism.

The teaching of Jesus on the matter should settle the question. The postmodern mindset is so sold on pluralism that it does not even see a problem. It might ask, "What's the big deal?" It suggests that it does not matter what the belief or when the person was baptized as long as he was immersed in water. The problem with that kind of carelessness is that it does not consider God. It leaves God's will out of the quest for the truth. It ignores what God desires in order to appease people and justify human traditions.

We may like to trust in our opinions, but our opinions are not equivalent to the teaching of the Lord. We cannot pronounce people saved if they are lost nor can we declare people lost if they are indeed saved. Only the Lord can do that. In our country where we treasure our freedoms and democracy, we must be careful not to liken the church to our society. The church is not a democracy but a kingdom, and Jesus is the only King and Lord. His truth and His law are not determined by opinion polls or popular vote. Jesus did not first consult us when He taught on this matter. Our task is not to sit in judgment of others but to accept the judgments He has already made. How has He judged? That is the real issue. Whether you or I think it is a big deal is not as important as whether He thinks it is a big deal.

Jesus said, "Truly, truly, I say to you, unless one is born of water and the Spirit, he cannot enter into the kingdom of God" (John 3:5). This statement is His Word, the word that will judge us on the last day. There is an authority in this statement about the new birth that will affect our eternity. Whether we agree with it or not, whether we think it fair or not, whether we like some other view or not, Jesus will judge us on the basis of what He said and what He meant. If Jesus is Lord, then we must all listen to Him and Him alone. Our confusion does not come from listening to Him but from interrupting Him with our own opinions and ideas of what we think He should have said.

God is expected to approve whatever postmodernists think He should, and to them this would include a variety of contradictory positions. If postmodernism be the truth, one must wonder at times why God ever bothered with inspiring a Bible. The postmodernist says that the Bible itself is not the authority; the authority comes from how various cultural groups interpret the Bible. There can be no authority in any inspired writing if men may take it and make out of it whatever they wish. So why would God compose and inspire a book that could be twisted and manipulated to say whatever men wanted it to say? Postmodernism reduces the Bible to an utterly confusing book, permitting any view of any thing to be as valid as any other view. In the end, postmodernists make the Bible nonsense, incapable of communicating any serious and binding truth about anything. Of course, that is what they want.

Reading the Bible for itself, however, presents a different view of reality. This view of reality came long before the Age of Enlightenment or John Locke. It predates the scientific method and inductive logic. It is a view that truth can be in a settled form, understood, taught cross-culturally, and handled correctly. In contrast to postmodern pluralism, the Bible speaks of but one gospel and demands that all men everywhere adhere to it (Galatians 1:6-9). Peter speaks about some people who twist the Scriptures to their own destruction (2 Peter 3:16); but if postmodernism is true, there cannot be any such thing as a twisting of the Scriptures – merely a new approach to the truth.

If the religiously correct have their way, one wonders how Paul could have insisted that the badly divided members of the church at Corinth all agree and be of the same mind and judgment (1 Corinthians 1:10). Why didn't he congratulate them for their diversity and demand they accept every view as equally valid? Why did he worry about the man living with his father's wife? After all, what constitutes immorality is changing all the time. How could there be one faith (Ephesians 4:5)? How could Paul expect Timothy to handle the Word of truth correctly (2 Timothy 2:15)? How could Peter imagine there are destructive heresies (2 Peter 2:1-2)? The language of the Bible itself argues convincingly against the postmodern mindset and argues that truth is not relative to time and culture.

The question, then, comes down to what we are going to trust with our souls. Are we to trust in God and His inspired, inerrant Word, or are we to trust the shifting sands of cultural beliefs? Are we to recognize the revealed truths settled in heaven, or are we to be "children tossed to and fro by every wind of doctrine"? We are not now playing children's games with no consequences; we have entered the most serious matter of our lives. How we answer these questions will affect us for an eternity. This is why Paul tells Timothy, "Pay close attention to yourself and to your teaching; persevere in these things; for as you do this you will insure salvation both for yourself and for those who hear you" (1 Timothy 4:16). Paul wanted Timothy to believe the right things and to teach the right things because they matter.

One of the battle lines in all of this discussion among churches of Christ is that of what is now being called "precision obedience." The baptism issue we already discussed is a good example of what we mean. Does God expect us to obey Him with any degree of precision, or will His grace permit us the freedom to vary from His instructions? How do we deal with the silence of the Scriptures? Are we to regard God's silence as permissive as long as we approach each issue with prayer? Or is God's silence a statement of His prohibition?

That the old covenant expects precise obedience from the nation of Israel is beyond dispute. The book of Deuteronomy provides in detail the kind of response that God expects of His people. He wants them to obey lovingly, carefully, completely, fearfully and accurately what He has commanded them to do.[8] Notice these sample verses from Deuteronomy that describe the kind of obedience God desires:

- You shall not add to the word which I am commanding you, nor take away from it, that you may keep the commandments of the LORD your God which I command you (4:2).
- So you shall observe to do just as the LORD your God has commanded you; you shall not turn aside to the right or to the left (5:32).
- And it will be righteousness for us if we are careful to observe all this commandment before the LORD our God, just as He commanded us (6:25).

- And now, Israel, what does the LORD your God require from you, but to fear the LORD your God, to walk in all His ways and love Him, and to serve the LORD your God with all your heart and with all your soul, and to keep the LORD's commandments and His statutes which I am commanding you today for your good? (10:12-13).
- You shall therefore keep every commandment which I am commanding you today, so that you may be strong and go in and possess the land into which you are about to cross to possess it (11:8).
- Whatever I command you, you shall be careful to do; you shall not add to nor take away from it (12:32).
- You shall follow the LORD your God and fear Him; and you shall keep His commandments, listen to His voice, serve Him, and cling to Him (13:4).
- According to the terms of the law which they teach you, and according to the verdict which they tell you, you shall do; you shall not turn aside from the word which they declare to you, to the right or the left (17:11).
- Now it shall be, if you will diligently obey the LORD your God, being careful to do all His commandments which I command you today, the LORD your God will set you high above all the nations of the earth (28:1).
- And the LORD shall make you the head and not the tail, and you only shall be above, and you shall not be underneath, if you will listen to the commandments of the LORD your God, which I charge you today, to observe them carefully, and do not turn aside from any of the words which I command you today, to the right or to the left, to go after other gods to serve them (28:13-14).
- He said to them, "Take to your heart all the words with which I am warning you today, which you shall command your sons to observe carefully, even all the words of this law. For it is not an idle word for you; indeed

it is your life. And by this word you shall prolong your days in the land, which you are about to cross the Jordan to possess" (32:46-47).

These and many other verses teach us clearly that under the old covenant God expected His people to obey His laws scrupulously and with precision. They were neither to add to them nor take away from them. God was interested in their loving and careful obedience as a sign of their faithful devotion to Him.

In the same way, Jesus provides an example of faithful, precise and loving obedience. In John 14:31 Jesus said with a view to the cross, "but the world must learn that I love the Father and that I do exactly what my Father has commanded me." That's how Jesus did things.[9] Other passages in John go into more detail:

- Jesus therefore answered and was saying to them, "Truly, truly, I say to you, the Son can do nothing of Himself, unless it is something He sees the Father doing; for whatever the Father does, these things the Son also does in like manner" (5:19).
- I can do nothing on My own initiative. As I hear, I judge; and My judgment is just, because I do not seek My own will, but the will of Him who sent Me (5:30).
- For I have come down from heaven, not to do My own will, but the will of Him who sent Me (6:38).
- Jesus therefore said, "When you lift up the Son of Man, then you will know that I am He, and I do nothing on My own initiative, but I speak these things as the Father taught Me. And He who sent Me is with Me; He has not left Me alone, for I always do the things that are pleasing to Him" (8:28-29).
- He who rejects Me, and does not receive My sayings, has one who judges him; the word I spoke is what will judge him at the last day. For I did not speak on My own initiative, but the Father Himself who sent Me has given Me commandment, what to say, and what to

> speak. And I know that His commandment is eternal
> life; therefore the things I speak, I speak just as the Fa-
> ther has told Me (12:48-50).

Even the Holy Spirit was never so presumptuous as to venture beyond the revealed will of God so as to teach things that He had not
heard from the Father. In John 16:12-13, Jesus explains,

> I have many more things to say to you, but you cannot
> bear them now. But when He, the Spirit of truth, comes,
> He will guide you into all the truth; for He will not speak
> on His own initiative, but whatever He hears, He will
> speak; and He will disclose to you what is to come.

The precision with which Jesus and the Holy Spirit act in response
to the revealed will of God ought to say something to us today. If
both Jesus and the Holy Spirit were unwilling to go beyond what is
revealed but remained within what they heard, then so must we.

It is for this reason that perverting the gospel brings an accursing
(Galatians 1:6-9). Those who will not remain within the teaching
of Christ but go beyond it lose their relationship with Jesus Christ
(2 John 9).[10] Jesus made it clear, "If you abide in My word, then you
are truly disciples of Mine; and you shall know the truth, and the
truth shall make you free" (John 8:31-32). One mark of true discipleship is the determination to stay within the teaching. It is only
by doing this that men can know the truth and so be set free. Perhaps one of the reasons why there is so much confusion and religious blindness is that many modern and postmodern people are unwilling to buy the truth by staying with the Word of God. The privatization of truth and individualism of our times has unleashed us
from the moral ties that held this country together. What has happened morally is also happening theologically. The more we throw
off the foundations, the further we drift away from God. There are
consequences to our demand for theological freedom.

Discussion Questions

1. What are the characteristics of the Bible that make its teachings absolute?

2. Upon what basis do people today reject absolute truth?

3. What is the difference between manufacturing truth and discovering truth?

4. Name some traditional teachings among churches of Christ of which some Christians are now unsure.

5. What is a socially constructed tradition?

6. What is "precision obedience" and does God expect it of Christians?

CHAPTER 5

Reclaiming Our Rudder
WE DO MAKE JUDGMENTS

R aymond Kelcy, serving as head of the Bible department at Oklahoma Christian University, used to quip that the best known verses of the Bible were 1 Timothy 5:23 and Matthew 7:1. He said you could take the worst reprobate in society, a person who never went to church, and he would know these verses: "Drink a little wine for your stomach's sake" and "Judge ye not, that ye be not judged." Of course, people using these verses to justify their questionable lifestyles have not taken time to find out what else the Bible says. Their understanding of truth suffers greatly from their ignorance. Our world especially likes to quote the gist of Matthew 7:1 and make an absolute prohibition against judging. They are so opposed to judging they will judge against anyone who judges. Of course, in their judgments they exempt themselves. The people of our time want no judgments; they want tolerance.

The problem of tolerating sin goes even beyond this point. The world has made it a very bitter experience to expose any sin or error. Anyone who decides to speak against sin or error must be willing to pay the price of wrath. One of the great ironies of our time is that some who demand tolerance for themselves are the most intolerant people of all. This, frankly, has been one of the great weaknesses of those among us who call themselves progressive inclusivists. They want to gain freedom by going beyond the traditions of "church-of-Christ" theology and include into our fellowship all who claim to be Christian. They want respect and approval from traditionalists but are unwilling to tolerate those who disagree with them about making judgments. For them, the only acceptable course is to adopt a mindset of nonjudgmentalism.

Postmodern America has suspended the idea of making moral judgments. Former Miss America and Florida Orange Juice spokesperson Anita Bryant in the 1980s led a campaign in Florida against special rights for homosexuals. Speaking frankly against the homosexual agenda ended her career as an entertainer and won for her the status of being one of the most hated women in America for her alleged bigotry. Her offense was pointing to Christian principles that teach homosexuality is a sin and a perversion. Rather than seeing her as a moral hero and champion of godliness, many in America castigated her as arrogant, self-righteous and judgmental. From the days of Sen. Joseph McCarthy in the 1950s, Americans have loathed finger pointing. It has become a greater taboo to point out someone's sin than to commit a sin. No one likes a snitch.

The social climate of our time follows along political correctness mandates that we accept the morality and ethical practices of other cultures. In chapter 2, I mentioned Robert L. Simon's observation that his students no longer made moral judgments against the Nazis' extermination of the Jews in the Holocaust. He explained that the students did not want to "draw a line in the sand." To them, people who make moral judgments are "absolutists," and, "of course, we all know there are no absolutes." Those who assert absolutes – for instance, "God said stealing is wrong, and therefore it is wrong" – are considered dogmatic and intolerant. Simon's students believed that making moral judgments meant that they were closed to further discussion – that they would be taking an inflexible stand that they would have to maintain come what may.

To Simon, moral relativism comes from intellectual laziness: "Crude relativism is an easy and undemanding position to hold. Rather than think through a problem to a reasoned conclusion, students can throw up their hands and ask, 'Well, who's to say, anyway?' "[1] Such a view conveniently permits them to ignore moral issues. No one is more right than anyone else, and no one has to make a judgment on anything.

The problem with nonjudgmentalism is that no one can consistently practice it. The decision to be nonjudgmental is itself a judgment. The contradiction of withdrawing into a nonjudgmental mindset shows itself when one becomes the victim. People downplay the sins they commit but have a very different perspective when they have been sinned against. *My* harmless talk about you is no big deal, but *your* cruel gossip about me is unforgivable. Drugs are a victimless crime until *my* loved one overdoses. I may support the sexual revolution until someone sleeps with *my* spouse. People's attitudes change greatly when they become the offended rather than the excuse-making offender. Reality wakes us up. Those who have adopted "moral correctness" often have not considered the implications of their new value system. Simon argues,

> [D]eep down they are not true moral relativists or skeptics. Rather, they actually hold to a disguised morality that emphasizes tolerance and respect for diversity. However, by denying themselves the moral authority to condemn such great evils of human history as the Holocaust, slavery, and racial oppression, these students lose the basis for morally condemning wrongdoing anywhere, and so must ultimately abandon the very values that led them to advocate tolerance and respect for diversity in the first place.[2]

This is why political correctness, when applied to morality and faith, destroys the foundations of morality and decency. Being nonjudgmental does not make us morally better; it makes us morally impotent. We may be more tolerant for being morally correct, but it is a tolerance that robs us of the authority to correct the immoral. When society becomes impotent in correcting its wrongs, evil will flourish.

Pluralism

Pluralism takes the fact of the world's cultural diversity and makes an idol out of it. It goes beyond extolling the virtue of understanding and appreciating cultural differences. Pluralism holds that distinct cultural beliefs are true for that particular culture but not for cultures that operate out of different paradigms or constructs. What is true for one society may not be true for another. Pluralists explain that truth is a social construction, created through social consensus and tradition. They reject the notion that truth is discovered in a reality that exists independently of our beliefs. For them, God is not the source of truth; rather, different cultures manufacture their own truths and beliefs. Truth is subjective interpretation (what the culture thinks and says it is) not objective reality (what actually is).

America is a blended society; some are determined never to allow any one socially constructed truth to dominate any other. They are especially determined to see that Christianity ceases to have its special advantage over other religions. They do not want the Christian worldview to dominate in such a way that it is truer than other worldviews. The Native American view of religion, in their mind, is just as valid as Christianity. Christianity for them is just one religious choice among many and cannot be regarded as truer than other religions.

We live in a time of syncretism for many people. Syncretism is the reconciliation or union of conflicting beliefs. People choose what elements of various religions they believe and blend them together. In syncretism a naive dismissal of conflicts says all religions believe the same things anyway. Of course, all religions do not believe the same things. The first-century proponents of emperor worship persecuted and slaughtered Christians because Christians would not accept Caesar as Lord. The people who populated Samaria after the fall of the northern 10 tribes blended together their belief. They "feared God but served other gods" (2 Kings 17:24-41). In many ways Americans give lip service to Jesus Christ but serve their own gods of pleasure and things. It has become politically correct to consider each religion as equally valid and true. This tolerance for all religion directly conflicts with the teachings of Jesus Christ, but the modern American feels free to choose what he likes and to dismiss what he does not like.

Some members of churches of Christ reject broad-based syncretism only to embrace a syncretism within Christendom. They realize that Buddhism is not right, but they are not so sure about many in denominational churches. Many are not willing to embrace denominationalism, but they are not willing to condemn it either. They dismiss any judgment of right and wrong concerning anyone's beliefs. Not willing to make firm choices between conflicting Christian views, they blend together truth with error.

Others decide simply to keep their mouths shut about any error. They are willing to be Christians and to say, "Yes, I believe in the gospel of Jesus Christ. I believe in immersion for the remission of sins. I believe we are saved by grace through faith." These preachers and leaders are willing to say this in their discussions of theology. What they are not willing to do is speak out against an opposite view. To put it another way, they are willing to affirm, but they are not as willing to deny. They are willing to be positive, but they are not willing to say anything negative. They are unwilling to apply the law of noncontradiction so as to say that what is false truly is false. Such silence and unwillingness to condemn error is a compromise of the truth.

The world around us gladly tolerates a nondoctrinal Christianity, allowing for a gospel emptied of theological content and meaning. But why would the church want a gospel like that? Such a gospel would be devoid of the biblical emphasis on sin, judgment and forgiveness of sin. No doubt such a gospel would be welcomed by many who now stand aloof from the church. This would not be because the world has embraced the church but because the church has merged into the world. Few phenomena in the theological world are more striking than the impatience exhibited on every hand with the effort to define truth and to state with precision the doctrinal presuppositions and contents of Christianity. Why make much over what appear to be minor points of difference among those who serve the one Christ? Because a pure gospel is worth preserving. A mutilated gospel produces mutilated Christianity.

Christians Must Make Judgments

Life is filled with so many important choices, and they are found in every aspect of life. A lady visits the grocery store and must make many judgments regarding the quality and the price of the items she buys. It is not enough to call an item a bargain; she must consider the wholesomeness of the food.

A man enters of car dealership with a desire to buy a vehicle, but he must make judgments about the car he plans to buy. "Can I afford it?" "Is it safe and dependable?" "Does it meet my needs?" He does not merely buy the first car he sees; rather, he wants to spend his money wisely.

Major investments require lots of thinking, reasoning, assessing and weighing out every detail so that you get the most for your money. When a family buys a house, a husband and wife look at the quality of construction, the mortgage payment and interest, the location, and their access to schools and businesses.

The high school graduate thinking about further education must choose between scores of universities and colleges. His choice matters because he is entering not only a school but an environment. The judgments one makes often have much larger implications than one may realize. One cannot live his life and not make decisions and judgments based on quality and value.

We make ethical choices in determining our physical safety. Will we wear a seat belt? How will we drive our cars? Will we smoke, drink or take drugs? Will we watch television, go to movies, or read pornography? On the other hand, will we attend church, and how involved will we become in our faith? It is absurd to think that we should make decisions about everything under the sun except religious matters. Yet our postmodern society is suggesting this very thing.

Abusive Judging

Do not judge lest you be judged. For in the way you judge, you will be judged; and by your standard of measure, it will be measured to you. And why do you look at the speck that is in your brother's eye, but do not notice the log that is in your own eye? Or how can you say to your brother, "Let me take the speck out of your eye," and behold, the log is in your own eye? You hypocrite, first take the log out of your own eye, and then you will see clearly to take the speck out of your brother's eye (Matthew 7:1-5).

Jesus said these words at a time when judging others over man-made traditions was a habit. The judging here was not taking place over biblical matters but over the imposed laws made by men. The Jews were famous for hanging a mountain by a thread – that is, building an entire set of traditional laws and rules out of a single reference. Many of these laws had nothing to do with the context of the passage. For instance, Exodus 23:19 says, "You are not to boil a kid in the milk of its mother."[3] The Jews developed an entire system of what was and was not "kosher" from this passage and determined never to mix any meat and dairy products. The original law came because idolatrous Canaanites were boiling kids in their mothers' milk. The Israelites of Moses's time knew what it meant, but later generations out of misguided zeal took it to an extreme. They went far beyond the original intent of the Law and "hung a mountain on a thread." The Pharisees who held to the oral traditions began to judge people, not on the basis of God's Law, but on their man-made applications of the Law. They bullied and condemned others on the basis of their traditions. Jesus was not arguing against making any judgments at all but against making abusive judgments on the basis of human traditions.

First-century Pharisees practiced a lot of silly piety derived from the teachings of rabbis in previous generations. They took God's Law and mixed it with their traditions to the point of absurdity. They regarded their traditions as an "oral Torah," an oral Law, having an authority equal to or even higher than the written Law. They considered it a sin to break the "traditions of the elders" and accused Jesus and his disciples of sinning when they did not wash their hands according to the rituals set down in their traditions (Matthew 15:2; Mark 7:1-4). Pharisees refused to save a woman from drowning for fear of touching a female, assuming that she was in her menstrual cycle and

was consequently unclean. Pharisees would wait to take off their phy-
lacteries before pulling a child out of the water. Pharisees did not wear
sandals with iron nails on the Sabbath, since the iron weighted down
the sandals, causing the Pharisees to work on the Sabbath. Pharisees
took down their mirrors on the Sabbath lest their women should pass
by, see an unwanted hair, pluck it out, and work on the Sabbath. If a
Pharisee gave alms to the poor on the Sabbath, he would not stick his
hand outside the door to give the money but would expect the beggar
to stick his hand inside the door. Pharisees would not eat an egg laid
on the Sabbath day but would sell it to a Gentile.

One can readily see just how far the Pharisees would go to keep
the Law scrupulously. Unfortunately they went far beyond the written Word to their own system of law-keeping. They sought to develop a system of self-righteousness (Romans 10:1-2) and self-jus-
tification (Luke 18:9-14), and in their zeal the Pharisees became
judgmental of anyone who did not live up to their high standards.
They classed themselves as clean and worthy "neighbors" and other Jews as "people of the land" – common and unclean. At times
Pharisees would take up stones to keep anyone they considered unclean from getting too close. The Pharisees went into the business
of judging their neighbors and their eternal salvation on the basis
of keeping these oral traditions. In Matthew 7:1-5 Jesus declares all
such judging as wrong.

Paul dealt with a similar type of abusive judging in Romans 14.
Some weaker brothers, whose consciences were tender but untaught,
were judging others who felt the freedom to eat meat sacrificed to
idols. Those who were eating felt contempt for those who would
not eat. Paul instructs both to stop judging the other. "Who are you
to judge the servant of another? To his own master he stands or falls;
and stand he will, for the Lord is able to make him stand" (Romans
14:4). Christians must be careful not to judge in such matters of
opinion. Paul notes that whether one eats meat or whether one regards one day above another, one does what he does "for the Lord"
(vv. 5-6). Both groups act with thanksgiving to God, and both groups
are accepted by God. As a result, Paul asks, "But you, why do you

judge your brother? Or you again, why do you regard your brother with contempt? For we shall all stand before the judgment seat of God" (v. 10). Christians must realize they are the judged, not the judges. "Therefore let us not judge one another anymore, but rather determine this – not to put an obstacle or a stumbling block in a brother's way" (v. 13).

At this point Paul reveals an important principle: "I know and am convinced in the Lord Jesus that nothing is unclean in itself; but to him who thinks anything to be unclean, to him it is unclean" (Romans 14:14). Paul knew it was not wrong to eat meat sacrificed to idols, but not everybody thought that way. Some who had abandoned idolatry and had lovingly embraced the Lord simply could not in good conscience return to any activity associated with that idolatry. Although there is no such thing as "gods" – there is no God but one (1 Corinthians 8:4) – not everybody understood this (v. 7). Weak in conscience, they thought that they were sinning and being disloyal by eating meat sacrificed to idols. Paul made it clear that when a person went against his conscience, he sinned. Paul said, "But he who doubts is condemned if he eats, because his eating is not from faith; and whatever is not from faith is sin" (Romans 14:23). The weaker brother needed to learn God's teaching more accurately so that he would not wound his conscience by eating. The stronger brother needed to be careful not to allow his liberty (in conscience) to allow him to behave in such a way as to present a stumbling block to the weaker brother. In the meantime, both brothers were to live by the law of love, neither judging nor presenting a stumbling block to the other.

There are many differences of opinion as to which of these principles clearly ought to apply. Christians may choose whether they want to celebrate a family holiday at Christmastime or not, but neither has a right to judge the other. In matters of expediency, whether to practice a thing a certain way or not should not be a cause for judging others. Those who cause church splits over things like the order of worship, whether to have Bible classes, how many containers are on the Lord's table, and other such things ought to remember that there is but one Lord who judges. We recall Diotrephes

(3 John 9-10) not for his goodness but for his domineering and caustic ways. He made judgments where he had no right. Some today who bully and judge others unfairly over matters of opinion will one day face the great Judge and give an account of themselves (Romans 14:12).

Nevertheless, some go to another extreme with Romans 14 and wish to apply its principles to every doctrinal difference. Citing Romans 14, they push for nearly total nonjudgmentalism, applying the passage far beyond what the Holy Spirit intended. Romans 14 was not written to permit men to believe or practice error. The individual who believes Jesus established a multitude of churches, however tender and sincere in conscience, holds to error. The Judaizing Christians of Galatians, however zealous and sincere, were teaching an error that severed them from Christ and led to their anathema (Galatians 1:6-9; 5:4). Those who went beyond the teaching of Christ no longer possessed God (2 John 9). Romans 14 does not provide a license to add to or take away from the teachings of Jesus Christ. Once the covenant terms have been set, no one can change them (Galatians 3:19).

In particular, some have used Romans 14 to justify the use of instruments of music in New Testament worship. Deciding the use of an instrument is a matter of opinion, some called for those who oppose its use to stop judging others for using it. By declaring the use of instruments as opinion, its proponents seem to ignore the basis for its rejection. Those who oppose the instrument do so because the Scriptures do not authorize it. While the Scriptures do authorize the eating of meat and observing of days, it does not authorize instruments of music. The opposition comes from the explicitly taught principle that no one has a right to add to God's instructions.[5] This is not an optional principle or one permitting differences of opinion. Romans 14 clearly does not apply. Consequently, we must be careful not to apply this chapter beyond its limits.

Is It Ever Right to Judge?

We began this study with a reading of Matthew 7:1-5, but these passages need to be understood in the light of a larger context. For instance, consider the next verse: "Do not give what is holy to dogs, and do not throw your pearls before swine, lest they trample them under their feet, and turn and tear you to pieces" (v. 6). Who are the dogs and the swine? Doesn't this passage call for using our wisdom to distinguish between dogs and non-dogs, and between swine and non-swine? Jesus further teaches us that we should watch out for evil, and that we ought to know it when we see it. "Beware of the false prophets, who come to you in sheep's clothing, but inwardly are ravenous wolves. You will know them by their fruits" (vv. 15-16). Life demands making judgments; we cannot escape them. Hebrews 5:14 reminds us that mature Christians "because of practice have their senses trained to discern good and evil." Any parent struggling to rear his children knows the daily judgments he must make for the sake of the children. He knows, too, that his task is to train the children to make right decisions. Making judgments is a large part of growing up.

Isaiah said, "Woe to those who call evil good, and good evil; Who substitute darkness for light and light for darkness; Who substitute bitter for sweet, and sweet for bitter! Woe to those who are wise in their own eyes, And clever in their own sight!" (5:20-21). God grieves over those who are unwilling to make judgments about good and bad because they promote a permissiveness that infects the young and the weak with diseased values. The nonjudgmentalism so rampant in our culture has destroyed our nation's moral strength. The rise in crime, illegitimate births, abortions, runaways, addictions and divorces comes from our unwillingness to condemn anyone. William J. Bennett, in *The De-Valuing of America*, points out the severe changes for the worse in "The Index of Leading Cultural Indicators." Bennett declares,

> The empirical evidence is clear: during the last three decades, American society has experienced substantial social regression. And this has exacted an enormous cost in terms of wasted, shattered, and lost lives. This is the inevitable result of divorcing social policy from moral precepts. The enervation of strong religious beliefs, in

both our private lives and our public conversations, has led to a "de-moralized society," in historian Gertrude Himmelfarb's phrase. Modern society is relearning a lesson as old as the republic itself: we ignore religion and the lessons it teaches at our peril.[6]

The problem with the Pharisees was not judging but abusive judging. Jesus describes how we are to judge: "Do not judge according to appearance, but judge with righteous judgment" (John 7:24). Jesus knew that appearances could deceive, so he cautioned people to make righteous judgments based on the Scriptures and on the facts. The Scriptures are the basis for what is right and wrong, and facts tell us whether or not God's laws are transgressed. Jesus announced a judgment on Judas, calling him the son of perdition (John 17:12) and stating that it would have been better for him not to have been born (Mark 14:21). Jesus did not do this with a mean spirit, for, in spite of it all, he loved Judas. Jesus judged him on the basis of the facts. Judas was a thief (John 12:6), and for 30 pieces of silver he gave a betrayal kiss to his Master. I am convinced that Jesus would have even forgiven Judas, had Judas returned in penitence. The record, however, shows that while Judas regretted his sin, he never repented. Unfortunately, unlike Jesus, some jump too quickly to mistaken judgments. They judge unfairly or unrighteously before the Scriptures are examined or the facts are known. Nevertheless, when the Scriptures are clear and the facts are known, we must judge.

Paul led the way in judging the man who had his father's wife. He rebuked the church at Corinth for being unwilling to take the steps necessary to deal with the wicked man. He said, "[Y]ou have become arrogant, and have not mourned instead, in order that the one who had done this deed might be removed from your midst" (1 Corinthians 5:2). He made it clear: "I ... have already judged him who has so committed this, as though I were present" (v. 3). When the church was assembled, Paul commanded them "to deliver such a one to Satan." He knew that if he allowed this man's sin to go unpunished that a "little leaven leavens the whole lump of dough" (v. 6). His counsel was, "Remove the wicked man from among yourselves" (v. 13). Judging is necessary when the sin threatens the purity of the church. We sometimes must ask what Paul did: "Do you not judge those who are within the church?" (v. 12).

Paul told the church at Thessalonica, "But examine everything carefully; hold fast to that which is good; abstain from every form of evil" (1 Thessalonians 5:21-22). Church members needed knowledge of the Scriptures and discretion to discern between good and evil. Knowing the difference was not enough; knowledge was to make an impact on their behavior. When a brother or sister failed to behave the way he or she should, Paul told Timothy, "Those who continue in sin, rebuke in the presence of all, so that the rest also will be fearful of sinning" (1 Timothy 5:20). This may very well be the most ignored command in Scripture today. We do not want to censure anyone nor do we wish to hear anyone censured. As a result, by negligence we allow sin to continue unchecked and souls to be lost.

One must wonder at the difference in our churches if we were to publicly rebuke sin. Paul urges Titus to deal with some sins severely. He remarked, "One of themselves, a prophet of their own, said, 'Cretans are always liars, evil beasts, lazy gluttons.' This testimony is true. For this cause reprove them severely that they may be sound in the faith" (Titus 1:12-13). The Greek term "reprove" in this passage is far more than a mere rebuke. Richard Trench explains: "[I]t is so to rebuke another, with such effectual wielding of the victorious arms of the truth, as to bring him, if not always to a confession, yet at least to a conviction, of his sin (Job 5:17; Proverbs 19:25)."[7] Such a severe reproval in today's church is so politically incorrect as to be nearly nonexistent. This is not to suggest that church leaders become mean-spirited or vindictive, but neither must they turn a blind eye to continuing sin. There is a time for severe reproving.

Churches cannot allow men to go on teaching false doctrines. They must take the time to know what is being taught and to act appropriately. John said, "Beloved, believe not every spirit, but test the spirits, to see whether they are from God" (1 John 4:1). It is only right that those who shepherd the flock know what their preachers and teachers are saying. In a day of uncertainty, church leaders ought to ask many questions of those whom they hire. Preachers and teachers should not resent congregations who ask them to fill out questionnaires upon their application to serve. Sound teachers have nothing to hide, but false teachers do not usually reveal themselves until they have done their damage. Jesus commended Ephesus because "you cannot endure evil men, and you put to the test those who call themselves apostles, and they are not, and you found them to be false" (Revelation 2:2). Jesus appreciated their conscientious devotion to the truth; and though Ephesus had a love problem in other matters, Ephesus stood approved in this matter. Churches simply cannot permit the ruin that comes with false teaching.

John made it clear that churches must judge the teaching of those who come to them. He said,

> Anyone who goes too far and does not abide in the teaching of Christ, does not have God; the one who abides in the teaching, he has both the Father and the Son. If anyone comes to you and does not bring this teaching, do not receive him into your house, and do not give him a greeting; for the one who gives him a greeting participates in his evil deeds (2 John 9-11).

Apparently there were some "antichrists" who were traveling around denying Jesus had come in the flesh (1 John 4:2-6). These arrogant men had gone beyond the teaching and in doing so had lost their relationship with God. It is always wrong to go beyond the teaching of the Bible, whether about the deity of Jesus or any other doctrine. The sin of these false teachers arose from their refusal to abide in the truth; their progress beyond truth made them false. Going beyond the teaching is "evil," and Christians must not support any teacher who does so. False teachers have no relationship with God, and one must abide in the teaching of Christ to maintain fellowship with the Father and the Son. Are we to judge such men? Of course, we must.

Many church members have chosen nonjudgmentalism as their path. When good men remain silent, evil has free reign to do as it pleases. When we blind our eyes to the falsehoods around us, we provide little protection to the weak, the naive and to the young. We need shepherds who will protect the sheep from wolves and watchmen who will guard the walls from the encroaching enemy. We cannot afford silence. We cannot tolerate any longer those who would destroy our churches with their unbelief and postmodern mindset. Is it ever right to judge? Yes, it is right; and more than that, it is mandatory.

Recognizing the Judgments God Has Made

We must also recognize the judgments God has already made. In some cases God has already pronounced a judgment on certain beliefs and behaviors. Jesus said, "He who believes in Him is not judged; he who does not believe has been judged already, because he has not believed in the name of the only begotten Son of God" (John 3:18). Again, "He who believes in the Son has eternal life; but he who does not obey the Son shall not see life, but the wrath of God abides on him" (v. 36). Knowing these things, we have an obligation to warn those who are not obedient to God's will. We evangelize the lost because Jesus said that unbelievers will be condemned (Mark 16:15-16). Our urgency in persuading people to obey the gospel is grounded in our fear of the Lord (2 Corinthians 5:11). One reason liberal churches are declining is that they frankly do not see the need for evangelizing. When there is no such thing as heresy and no one is really lost, few people see the need to reach out with the gospel.

It is not enough for people merely to believe something. God expects His people to believe the right things. Concerning His being the Messiah, Jesus told the Jews, "I said therefore to you, that you shall die in your sins; for unless you believe that I am He, you shall die in your sins" (John 8:24). Whether a person believes that Jesus is the Christ (Messiah) or not is a salvation issue. To speak of belief but have no reference to what one believes is nonsensical. We must live above the giddy Marilyn Monroe who, being asked what she believed, replied, "I believe everything." G.K. Chesterton said, "The trouble when people stop believing in God is not that they thereafter believe in nothing; it is that they thereafter believe in anything." Belief in any and everything is not really belief at all. The postmodern mindset leads people to have so few restraints that they believe everything, but they believe nothing with conviction.

Jesus also drew a line at repentance. Asked about the Galileans whose blood Pilate mingled with their sacrifices, Jesus said, "Do you suppose that these Galileans were greater sinners than all other Galileans, because they suffered this fate? I tell you, no, but unless you repent, you will all likewise perish" (Luke 13:2-3). Repentance is not optional, and those who fail to repent will perish. The Corinthians became arrogant over the man who had his father's wife. They refused to do anything about him. Though they knew he was acting wickedly, they were unwilling to say or do anything about it. They were unwilling to accept God's judgment of the man. Their unwillingness to act imperiled the sinful man and their own souls as well.

We too must accept that baptism is necessary to our salvation. Jesus made it clear: "Truly, truly, I say to you, unless one is born of water and the Spirit, he cannot enter into the kingdom of God" (John 3:5). Some among us have so compromised the faith that they are unwilling to accept what Jesus has ruled in this matter. In arrogance and rebellion they have overruled the Lord by telling people that they are saved at prayer and without baptism. Such dangerous preachers pervert the gospel and give those they deceive a false sense of security with God. Here the blind are leading the blind, and both will fall into the pit. We must believe God enough to accept what He says is true and to reject everything else. Paul warned,

> But even though we, or an angel from heaven, should preach to you a gospel contrary to that which we have preached to you, let him be accursed. As we have said before, so I say again now, if any man is preaching to you a gospel contrary to that which you received, let him be accursed (Galatians 1:8-9).

Perverting the gospel is a salvation issue for those who teach and for those who listen to their false teaching.

The judgments of God are not my judgments or yours; they are God's. God is God, and we are not. If we desire to serve Him, we ought to honor His judgments. Jesus said, "And why do you call

Me, 'Lord, Lord,' and do not do what I say?" (Luke 6:46). We need to believe that God will judge righteously and fairly, but we must also commit ourselves to Him strongly enough to accept that what He has said is the right judgment. We do not regard God very highly if we feel that we must correct His judgments to suit our thinking. Let us join David who said,

> The fear of the Lord is clean, enduring forever; The judgments of the Lord are true; they are righteous altogether. They are more desirable than gold, yes, than much fine gold; Sweeter also than honey and the drippings of the honeycomb. Moreover, by them Thy servant is warned; In keeping them there is great reward. Who can discern his errors? Acquit me of hidden faults (Psalm 19:9-12).

Discussion Questions

1. How does "theological correctness" compare to "political correctness?"

2. What are the dangers of being unwilling to speak out against error?

3. Cite some biblical examples of abusive judging.

4. What are the responsibilities of the stronger brother and the weaker brother in Romans 14 and 1 Corinthians 8?

5. What are some judgments Christians must make?

6. How important is what we believe?

CHAPTER 6

Resetting
Our Anchor
WE MUST HOLD ON!

The postmodern mindset is not interested in finding truths revealed in centuries past; it is more interested in developing its own faith and in allowing others to do the same. It does not wish to restore but to reinvent. Truth to the postmodernist is manufactured not discovered. Consequently, there is little to commend the idea of restoration to the postmodernist. He may have a curiosity in what went before him, but he will selectively choose what he pleases to incorporate in his own stylized faith. Far from wanting a pure religion, the postmodernist wants his very own religion.

In recent years some among churches of Christ have rejected the Restoration ideal and plea, claiming that it is too narrow and divisive. This position was articulated as early as 1972:

> The problem with a restoration theology is that it rests on the premise that the mission of the church is to set up a "true church" in which all the details of church life are exactly like they were in the first century world. It functions on the assumption that there is a blueprint or pattern in the New Testament that the church is to reduplicate in each succeeding generation. Such a theology makes the church's mission egocentric and past-oriented rather than outward looking and future-oriented.[1]

Such statements show the break-away mindset that began a generation ago and is still advanced today:

There is neither a set of doctrines nor a series of activities that can guarantee the existence of the church. No sequence of rituals or election of a governing body distinguishes it with certainty. All these features are to the identity of the church what marble and printer's ink are to the identities of David and Abraham Lincoln. They are marks, shadows, and expressive representations of certain features of the church. But the church is something distinct still.[2]

If these authors are speaking of the doctrines of men, such may be true; but if they are speaking of the Word of God, they have erred greatly. God can teach us what He wishes for us to know about His church. Men can sufficiently know the will of God and can repent of error to the extent that they can know that they are pleasing to Him. The Bible itself gives a much higher view of the teaching of Scripture than the above authors indicate in their statements. The Word of God, the seed of the kingdom (Luke 8:11), can still reproduce New Testament Christians and the New Testament church. The doctrines of Jesus, when obeyed lovingly, give life (John 6:63). They are a measuring stick of righteousness and the approval of God (Matthew 7:21-17). If the teachings of Jesus are the means by which we are to be judged one day, then there realistically can be no other means by which we can measure whether we are a church meeting the approval of God.

What Is Restoration?

It is said that the purest water is always found at its source. With time and movement, even the purest things can be polluted or corrupted. As a result, there is a need to go back to the source where the pure water is found. This is restoration. A man buys a car that he really loves, but as the years go by his car begins to deteriorate. The tires are worn, the belts and hoses begin to crack, there are tears in the seats, the paint is wearing thin, and the engine does not run as smoothly as it once did. Because he wants to recapture the car he had in the beginning, he buys the original stock parts and restores his car to its original and pristine state. To restore is to bring back to a former or normal condition. There are some assumptions that go with the idea of restoration: (1) that whatever is to be restored was good and right in the first place, (2) that something has happened to cause it to break down or lose its proper condition, and (3) that it ought to be returned to its former condition and be functional again.

In spiritual matters restoration is the return to the ideal state that Christ desires of His church. Of course, this assumes that there is an ideal state, that there has been a movement away from that ideal into error, and that there is a mandate to return to that ideal. The need for restoration becomes necessary because repentance from error is necessary. The notion that one may acceptably remain in error indefinitely is never considered in the New Testament.

The American Restoration Movement sought to return to the ancient order of things. The Restorationists believed that Christians ought to "speak where the Bible speaks" and to "be silent where the Bible is silent." They wanted to cast aside all human names, creeds and practices and go back to the Bible. They wanted to do Bible things in Bible ways. They believed that the movement away from the Bible brought error and division, that it was a curse upon Christianity, and that it ought to be abandoned. As a result, they began an intensive study of the Scriptures to see what God desired from the early church. They believed that if they went back to the forms and patterns found in the New Testament church, that they would please God and stand in His favor.

Alexander Campbell wrote in the *Christian Baptist* in 1825:

> A restoration of the ancient order of things is all that is necessary to the happiness and usefulness of [C]hristians. No attempt "to reform the doctrine, discipline and government of the church" (a phrase too long in use,) can promise a better result than those which have been attempted and languished to death. We are glad to see, in the above extract, that the thing proposed, is to bring the [C]hristianity and the church of the present day up to the standard of the New Testament. This is in substance,

though in other terms, what we contend for. To bring the
societies of [C]hristians up to the New Testament, is just
to bring the disciples individually and collectively, to
walk in the faith, and in the commandments of the Lord
and Savior, as presented in that blessed volume; and this
is to restore the ancient order of things.[3]

Campbell knew that to accomplish this, individuals and congregations must "discard from their faith and their practice every thing that is not found written in the New Testament of the Lord and Savior, and to believe and practice whatever is there enjoined."[4]

God has always expected His people to come out of error, whether moral or doctrinal, whenever they learn the truth. This, very simply, is what repentance is all about. When the church at Pergamum held to the teachings of Balaam and the Nicolaitans, Jesus sternly warned them to "repent therefore or else I am coming to you quickly" (Revelation 2:14-16). Jesus further warns Thyatira not to "tolerate" Jezebel and her teachings. Again He demands repentance from them as to their deeds and their teachings (vv. 20-23). While Ephesus had other problems, Jesus commends them for not enduring false apostles but putting them to the test (v. 2). That Jesus Himself will not "tolerate" evil teachings that lead people away from God is evident. God expects people to do better once they find out what the truth is. While the grace and patience of God gives men time to repent, there comes a time when His patience is exhausted.

James made it clear that what one believes matters; straying from the truth can lead a soul to death. He said, "My brethren, if any among you strays from the truth, and one turns him back, let him know that he who turns a sinner from the error of his way will save his soul from death, and will cover a multitude of sins" (James 5:19-20). The work of restoration, then, is actually soul-winning, since it leads a lost soul out of sin and back into life. If this be true of an individual, how much more true it is of a group of individuals or a church. Jesus anticipated the disciplining of whole congregations in Revelation 2 and 3. If a whole congregation remains in apostasy, the Lord will remove its candlestick; it will cease to be in His grace. Jesus warned of false teachers, "Leave them alone, they are blind guides of the blind. And if a blind man guides a blind man, both will fall into a pit" (Matthew 15:14). The deceived will share the same fate as the deceiver. The answer to the apostasy of a congregation is repentance and restoration. If apostasy (falling away from the faith) can lead people out of grace, repentance can bring them back.

The Biblical Basis for Restoration

The Scriptures reveal men who repented of their error in the desire to restore the will of God in their lives. King Hezekiah was such a man who led Israel to turn from idolatry and to follow the way of God. Hezekiah, the son of the weak and unprincipled Ahaz, inherited a kingdom filled with sin and idolatry. The writer of the book of Kings described Israel and Judah in the days of Hezekiah's youth as a people who "followed vanity and became vain; they went after the nations which surrounded them" (2 Kings 17:13-15). Despite his father and the times in which he lived, Hezekiah had a heart set on serving the Lord. Second Kings 18 tells the story of the restoration:

> And he did right in the sight of the LORD, according to all that his father David had done. He removed the high places and broke down the sacred pillars and cut down the Asherah. He also broke in pieces the bronze serpent that Moses had made, for until those days the sons of Israel burned incense to it; and it was called Nehushtan. He trusted in the LORD, the God of Israel; so that after him there was none like him among all the kings of Judah, nor among those who were before him. For he clung to the LORD; he did not depart from following Him, but kept His commandments, which the LORD had commanded Moses. And the LORD was with him; wherever he went he prospered (2 Kings 18:3-7).

Hezekiah made sweeping changes in Judah, based on his trust and devotion to God. The idolatrous religions were removed from the nation and the Lord's will was exalted before the people. This passage not only tells of Hezekiah's clinging to the Lord but also how that relationship was manifested. Hezekiah did not depart from following the Lord "but kept His commandments." Even in the Old Testament a relationship with God was determined by both the devotion of the heart and the overt acts that demonstrated that devotion. Right attitudes and sincerity were not enough. Restoration meant a convicted heart that acted to right the wrongs and to remain devoted to that right direction. The writer of Kings makes it clear that Hezekiah's trust could be clearly seen in his keeping the commandments of the Lord. Trust and obedience always go hand in hand. Hezekiah stood out among the kings of Judah in his devotion to the Lord first, last and always. He wanted to do things right. He determined to keep the Law. The result was that the Lord went with him and prospered him wherever he went. Hezekiah stood in the grace or favor of God. The Chronicler observed this of Hezekiah: "and he did what was good, right, and true before the LORD his God. And every work which he began in the service of the house of God in law and in commandment, seeking his God, he did with all his heart and prospered" (2 Chronicles 31:20-21).

We too need to learn that the approval of God follows those who are willing to keep their hearts and their actions firmly focused on serving Him. This is significant because it helps us to understand how God looks at people and particularly at us. The writer of Chronicles observed, "For the eyes of the LORD move to and fro throughout the earth that He may strongly support those whose heart is completely His" (16:9). People stray from the truth when they take their hearts off of God and begin flirting with the world. Oddly enough, many people who flirt with the mindset of our culture and the world have no idea that their hearts are drifting away from the God of heaven. Like the people of James' day, they suppose that they can hold onto the Lord with one hand and the world with the other. Becoming a friend to the world and its thinking makes one an enemy of God (James 4:4).

The devil works overtime and is constantly tempting and testing each of us. The restoration of Hezekiah lasted in his time, but later kings of Judah returned to idolatrous practices and wicked ways. Manasseh became king at 12 years old and reigned 55 years. He seduced Judah to do more evil than even the nations whom the Lord destroyed before the sons of Israel (2 Kings 21:9). The writer of Kings tells us:

> And he made his son pass through the fire, practiced witchcraft and used divination, and dealt with mediums and spiritists. He did much evil in the sight of the LORD provoking Him to anger (v. 6).

Manasseh filled Jerusalem with innocent blood from one end of Jerusalem to the other (v. 16). Manasseh's son Amon reigned but two years, but he was like his father in his wickedness (vv. 19-21). When he died, Josiah at age 8 became king. But Josiah's heart was not like his father's or his grandfather's. "He did right in the sight of the LORD and walked in all the way of his father David, nor did he turn aside to the right or to the left" (22:2).

It was during the reign of Josiah, when the temple was being repaired, that Hilkiah the priest found the "book of the Law in the house of the Lord" (v. 8). When Shaphan the scribe read the words of that book to Josiah, it made such an impact that he tore his clothes in repentance. Josiah immediately acted to find out the truth. He told Hilkiah:

> Go, inquire of the LORD for me and the people and all Judah concerning the words of this book that has been found, for great is the wrath of the LORD that burns against us, because our fathers have not listened to the words of this book, to do according to all that is written concerning us (v. 13).

For Josiah restoration started with a desire to know the will of God exactly. He realized that the wrath of God was upon Judah because they had not done "according to all that is written concerning us." Going back to the written revelation in the book of the Law was the means by which Josiah could determine how to stand once again in God's favor and to avoid His wrath. As things stood, God had every right to be angry with Judah. Huldah, the prophetess who lived in Jerusalem, confirmed the anger of the Lord against the evil Jerusalem. She spoke of how His wrath burned against that place and of how it would not be quenched (v. 17). Despite that, God revealed to her a different attitude He had toward Josiah who wept and tore his clothes, because his heart was tender and humble toward "the words which you have heard" (21:18-19). The Lord's words are important to men of God, because the Lord is important. We listen to God when we love Him; what He has to say matters. Restoration begins by listening with love.

Josiah called all of Judah together, great and small. He read the book of the Law in their hearing and made a covenant before the Lord "to walk after the LORD, and to keep His commandments and His testimonies and His statutes with all his heart and all his soul, to carry out the words of this covenant that were written in this book. And all the people entered into the covenant" (23:3). Restoration requires a heart humbled and penitent, but it cannot do its job without direction. The words of the covenant written in the book were the means by which this humbled heart could return to God. His relationship with God could not be changed without a change also in his commitment to keep the commandments. So devoted was Josiah that he did not want to vary at all from the commandments, "to the right or to the left." His repentance meant that whatever wrong he had been doing would cease and that whatever right thing God wanted he would start doing. His covenant with God was no temporary desire; covenants are lifelong oaths. Once taken, they could not be changed. Once taken they bear curses on the individual who breaks them. Josiah meant serious business.

His determination to do right was more than talk. He removed the idolatrous vessels from the temple, he did away with the idolatrous priests, he removed the Asherah from the temple, he broke down the houses of the male cult prostitutes, he defiled Topheth and ended the child sacrifice to Molech, he smashed the idolatrous altars of Ahaz and Manasseh, he broke down the idolatrous pillars Solomon and Jereboam had built, and he removed the mediums and the spiritists.

Not content merely to do away with the evil practices, Josiah proclaimed Passover was to be celebrated. The people were to do it "as it is written in this book of the covenant" (v. 21). Doing things carefully and accurately was important to Josiah. He did what he did so that he might "confirm the words of the law which were written in the book" (v. 24). So was his covenant with the Lord, and so he did. "Throughout his lifetime they did not turn from following the Lord God of their fathers" (2 Chronicles 34:33). The result was that "before him there was no king like him who turned to the LORD with all his heart and with all his soul and with all his might, according to all the law of Moses; nor did any like him arise after him" (2 Kings 23:25).

We must learn to take the advice of Jeremiah the prophet, who said, "Thus says the LORD, Stand by the ways and see and ask for the ancient paths, Where the good way is, and walk in it; And you shall find rest for your souls" (Jeremiah 6:16). We must go back to the Bible. Our covenant, unlike that of Israel and Judah, can only be found in the teachings of Jesus Christ and is ratified by His blood. If we today are to walk in old paths, it must be with a devotion to the words of Christ. We must abide within His Word, if we are to be true disciples (John 8:31). Only then can we know the truth and the truth make us free.

The Eternal Nature of Christ's Teaching

The restoration idea is built upon the conviction that God has given us an eternal message to which He expects us to hold. Herb Alsup wrote about the days when he was an 11-year-old boy in Murfreesboro, Tenn. Willard Collins, preaching in a gospel meeting, said, "If God can take a little acorn and make a mighty oak, think what He can do with you through Jesus." That statement prompted Herb to obey the gospel. Some years later when Herb entered David Lipscomb College, he had Brother Collins for his freshman Bible class and took many class notes. Still later, Herb heard Brother Collins make the same statement in Dothan, Ala. Filled with pride, Herb said, "Brother Collins, your lesson tonight was Class Note 57!" What Herb heard from Brother Collins next would stay with him for decades. He said, "Herb, it's the same Bible, isn't it."

The same Bible? Indeed it is the same Bible! There's only one, and it has not changed. When the New Testament, the covenant of Jesus Christ, was given, it was given for all time. Jude reminds us that we are to contend for a "faith which was once for all delivered to the saints" (Jude 3). The faith for which we are to contend was a "delivered" faith, a handed-down faith, a faith that had its source in Jesus Christ. This faith is not a subjective faith of what I think, feel or believe; but it is the message passed from Jesus through the Holy Spirit to the apostles. This "delivered" faith was given "once for all," i.e., once for all time. The Greek word here is *hapax* and is the same term used in Hebrews 9:26 of Jesus' once for all sacrifice upon the cross. It is used also in verse 27 to refer to our one-time appointment with death. In the same way "all truth" was given through the Spirit to the apostles only once (John 16:12-13; Jude 3). It is an error to look for some other delivering, some new revelation that takes us away from the first-century teaching.

Jesus said of His delivered teachings, "He who rejects Me, and does not receive My sayings, has one who judges him; the word I spoke is what will judge him at the last day" (John 12:48). Jesus fully explained that His same teaching would be around on the judgment day to judge those who rejected it. He said on another occasion, "Heaven and earth will pass away, but My words shall not pass away" (Matthew 24:35). In His giving of the Great Commission, Jesus said, "teaching them to observe all that I commanded you; and lo, I am with you always, even to the end of the age" (Matthew 28:20). There is no suggestion here that the gospel would change or that it needed revising. Peter makes this observation of the gospel:

> [F]or you have been born again not of seed which is perishable but imperishable, that is, through the living and abiding word of God. For, "ALL FLESH IS LIKE GRASS, AND ALL ITS GLORY LIKE THE FLOWER OF GRASS. THE GRASS WITHERS, AND THE FLOWER FALLS OFF, BUT THE WORD OF THE LORD ABIDES FOREVER." And this is the word which was preached to you (1 Peter 1:23-25).

Such passages make it very clear that Jesus expected His teaching to be carried forward till the end of time. The changing of the millennium will not change the Word of God; it will remain the same. If the world should stand through the 21st century, the Word will say just what it has always said. The same truths will be true in the 31st or the 41st century, if the world should stand so long! God's Word is as authoritative as He is, and it is as eternal as He is.

It is for just this reason, that the getting away from the Word of God is so serious. To leave the Word of God is to leave the eternal message of God. Such behavior in this life leads to eternal consequences in the next one. The Word is the key to maintaining our relationship with God because it tells us how we are to love God. Devotion to God manifests itself in our devotion to His Word. Returning to God with a heart humbled and penitent means that we love God enough to listen to Him and to do things His way and not our own. I cannot be devoted to the faith of Christ Jesus and at the same time practice the privatization which characterizes our time. Restoration means Jesus is my Lord; privatization means I make myself Lord. Privatization is a deceptive idolatry, putting one's self on the throne in defiance of God. Privatization denies that there is an eternal message for all people everywhere and suggests that one can customize his own religious belief system to his own liking. This is why restorationism has come upon hard times in the culture in which we live. Postmodern people do not want God to reveal to them the eternal truth; they want to manufacture their own truths.

Biblical Injunctions to Stand Firm and Hold On

God knew the weakness of men. He knew how easily they could be persuaded to stray from His teachings and lapse into false religions. The history of Israel is one of constant struggle to stay faithful to the covenant made at Sinai. The book of Judges presents an interesting set of cycles wherein the people of Israel alternated from abandoning God to embracing Him in penitence. As one reads through the histories in Kings and Chronicles, one observes the constant influence of the false religions in the nations around Israel and Judah. The inspired writer says in 2 Kings 17:6-8 that:

> Hoshea, the king of Assyria captured Samaria and car-
> ried Israel away into exile to Assyria ... because the sons
> of Israel had sinned against the LORD their God ... and
> they had feared other gods and walked in the customs of
> the nations whom the LORD had driven out before the
> sons of Israel, and in the customs of the kings of Israel
> which they had introduced.

God punished Israel and cut the 10 tribes off because of their idolatry. Those who prove unfaithful to God eventually lose their
covenantal relationship with Him. Forsaking the covenant, they lose
the promises and the blessings of that covenant.

In the same way, Christians who prove unfaithful to the covenant
of Christ by leaving the truth ruin their relationship with the Lord.
John observed that those who go beyond the teaching of Christ "do
not have God" (2 John 9), i.e., lose the blessing of a continued communion with God. Jesus identified His true disciples as those who
"abide in [continue in, remain in, hold onto] My word." Love is not
the only identity mark of a disciple – so is abiding in the Word.

This is why there are the repeated admonitions in Scripture for
Christians to hold on to the things that they have been taught from
God. The early church in Jerusalem was "continually devoting themselves to the apostles' teaching" (Acts 2:42). Paul congratulated
Corinth in 1 Corinthians 11:2, "Now I praise you because you ...
hold firmly to the traditions, just as I delivered them to you." He told
them that they would be saved by the gospel, "if you hold fast the
word which I preached to you, unless you believed in vain" (15:2).

Paul told the Colossians that they would stand holy and blameless
before God, "indeed you continue in the faith firmly established and
steadfast, and not moved away from the hope of the gospel that you
have heard" (Colossians 1:22-23). The inspired apostle admonished
the Thessalonians, "But examine everything carefully; hold fast to
that which is good; abstain from every form of evil" (1 Thessalonians 5:21-22). He gets more specific later saying, "So then, brethren,
stand firm and hold to the traditions which you were taught, whether
by word of mouth or by letter from us" (2 Thessalonians 2:15).

Paul commands Timothy, "Retain the standard of sound words which you have heard from me, in the faith and love which are in Christ Jesus ... continue in the things you have learned and become convinced of" (2 Timothy 1:13; 3:14).

Paul in giving the qualifications of elders to Titus says that they are to be "holding fast the faithful word which is in accordance with the teaching, that he may be able both to exhort in sound doctrine and to refute those who contradict" (Titus 1:9). Not only are elders to hold onto the Word, but they are also to refute anyone contradicting that Word. That Word was clear enough to be understood and embraced. Should anyone come along teaching something different, elders have the mandate to put a stop to the false teaching. There is a standard to be maintained at all costs.

What can be done, what should be done, when Christians and churches get away from that standard by leaving the truth? They must come back! They further must repent of the sin of having left the Way in the first place. Repentance means that they regard their straying into error as wrong and that they now oppose that error.

Let's say that a friend has come to that point in his life where he realizes that theological pluralism or denominationalism is wrong. By his study of the Scriptures, he has come to believe that the Lord only intended that there be one church. Repentance means that he not only comes to be a part of that one church but also opposes the pluralism or denominationalism he left. Believing that there is only one divine church means that one must also oppose the concept that there are many, man-made churches that have the approval of God.

The drunkard who repents not only quits his drunkenness, he also regards drunkenness as sinful. The sprinkled person who comes to know the truth not only embraces immersion, he also rejects sprinkling as baptism. If one does not regard what he has left as wrong, one has not really left it. Repentance is both turning to Jesus and turning away from Satan. Our problem today is not that we are unwilling to embrace Jesus; it is that we are not willing to say that man-made religion is of Satan.

Jesus did not redefine baptism into multiple-choice modes, i.e., immersion, sprinkling or pouring. Our Master did not redefine His one body, the church, with the theological pluralism of denominationalism. The Messiah did not introduce instruments into our musical worship. Jesus did not change His mind on the role of women in the leadership of His church. He did not make any announcements that once a person is saved, that person is always saved. The Lord did not replace Himself with a pope, a council, a president or a synod. All these things, and many others, were introduced by men long after the New Testament was given. They are not from the Lord.

Ultimately Satan dreamed up these counterfeits to lead the elect astray. The fact that so many people have accepted these counterfeits is a testimony to Satan's effectiveness. The big lie is to suggest that there are no counterfeits, that every choice is acceptable. The devil delights in persuading us that it is all right to stray from what is right. After all, "we won't really die if we eat" the forbidden fruit. Satan tells us that God is not so mean as to condemn anyone for a mistake in judgment. Or is He? The Judaizers taught many truths of the gospel, but they added their Law. When they added the Law they perverted the gospel and were consequently accursed (Galatians 1:6-9; 5:1-4). Any change away from truth is perversion and stands condemned. Paul noted that their pressing for the Law meant they were severed from Christ; they were "fallen from grace." Grace does not excuse a perversion; it does not sanctify error. It matters what one believes!

When men did not hold firm to the delivered teachings but strayed into error, they also fell from the grace of Christ. They no longer had communion with God. Those who blindly followed the counterfeits of Satan thought they had a relationship with God. Satan wanted them to think that. As long as they remained blind to the truth, they would see no need to change. Josiah was content until he read the book of the Law that Hilkiah found in the temple. That book opened his eyes, and reading the Bible will open eyes today. When people start reading and listening to the Bible, they will learn what God's will is and how they need to change.

106

The Restoration Plea says, "Let us go back to the teaching of the New Testament, to Christ and the apostles." It points to that generation because Jesus promised the apostles that they would be guided into all truth (John 16:12-13). It points to that generation, because the faith was once for all time delivered to the saints in their time (Jude 3). It points to that generation, because it was then that Jesus inaugurated the new covenant with His blood. Once the terms of a covenant are set, those terms can never be annulled or changed (Galatians 3:15; Matthew 26:28). True restoration is not a plea to return to the standards set in the days of Campbell and Stone or to later decades. Raymond Kelcy observed in 1954 at the Abilene Christian College Lectures:

> Loyalty to the restoration principle does not necessarily involve being loyal to the teachings of Stone, the Campbells, Walter Scott, John Smith or to any other man or group of men who have lived since their day. It involves only being loyal to the New Testament.[5]

Occasionally one hears such statements as this, "Which New Testament church do you want to go back to? Do you want to restore the doubting, immature and immoral church at Corinth? Do you want to restore the Judaizing churches of Galatia? Do you want to restore the lukewarm church at Laodicea?" Such quibbles miss the point miserably.

The desire is not to reproduce some particular congregation but to reproduce the will of God in churches today. As always, it is the will of God in the Word that is the means of our restoration, not the examples of fallible, individual congregations. Restoration begins with lovingly and humbly asking, "What does God desire?" It is accomplished when Christians listen and lovingly obey. If doing the will of God is what it takes to enter the kingdom of heaven (Matthew 7:21), then it should be the priority. If doing the will of God is what it takes to maintain a relationship with the Lord, then it should be the continuing priority. It is the Word that tells us what to do to repent, what to avoid, and what to embrace. There can never be restoration without a serious heeding of the Word of God.

107

The need of our day is a Josiah, who will give his heart and soul to obedience to the Word. Josiah was not a legalist; he was a devoted servant who was willing to live by the covenant. As Christians we have a covenant with God. God has promised to bless and forgive us; and we have promised to love, to trust and to obey. The terms of God's new covenant, made with the blood of Jesus our Savior, have been set and cannot be changed. Our promise of submission to God's will means that we live within the terms of that eternal covenant. Should anyone get away from those terms and break that covenant, he loses the favor of God. The only way to restore that favor is to restore in our lives a willingness to meet those terms. In short, we must repent. We need bold preachers who will call us to repentance, to turn back to the one gospel with one baptism into one body. That is the message of hope and reconciliation; it will bring men out of darkness into light. It will bring about changes for the better in the church. It is a positive message of redemption and unity, not of confusion and compromise.

In our time, some would keep us adrift in uncertainty, suggesting that we really cannot know anything for sure. Such a thought never occurred to Josiah. When he heard the reading just once, Josiah knew what he needed to do. He repented and restored Israel to the will of God. It is Satan who majors in doubt and confusion; he loves nothing better than to keep men undecided. We must resist Satan and reset our anchors in the one true hope of life, Jesus Christ. It is only by holding onto His teaching that we can survive the storm that is brewing around us. As the world becomes more antagonistic toward revealed religion and resists more firmly the directive we have to evangelize, we must hold on to those things we have heard and learned. The teachings are sure because they are inextricably tied to God. Our anchor holds because God holds it.

Although some have readily jettisoned the restoration ideal as outmoded, we do not. We embrace it because there are still things we need today to restore. Every generation has its own blindness and temptations, and every generation must come to grips with its own sin. Restoration is the process by which each generation reads once again the timeless truth of the new covenant and brings their own convictions and practices into line with that truth. The restoration of the past does not mean that we have no work to do. Kelcy observed that we "never arrive at a time when it is entirely done so that no more thought need be given it. There is a likelihood that each generation will have its own abuses, peculiarities, corruptions, and innovations."[6] We have the complete revelation, but our human weaknesses ought to keep us humble. We have not become perfect. We must continue to have an honest, searching mind and an obedient, submissive heart. We must with open eyes look into our own lives to see if there be any faults we have hidden from ourselves. But to suggest that the process of repentance and restoration is unnecessary because we are imperfect is unthinkable. Repentance is our way back to God. To lose that anchor of hope is to be hopelessly lost.

Discussion Questions

1. Why is the concept of "restoration" not appealing to the postmodernist?

2. What part does "repentance" play in restoration?

3. What characteristics did Hezekiah and Josiah illustrate in their lives and which led them to prosper?

4. How have counterfeit beliefs affected members of the church of Christ?

5. How loyal should restorationists be to the teachings of Stone and Campbell?

CHAPTER 7

Reclaiming Our Identity
WE KNOW WHOSE WE ARE!

"For whoever is ashamed of Me and My words, of him will the Son of Man be ashamed when He comes in His glory, and the glory of the Father and of the holy angels" (Luke 9:26).

The world can be an intimidating place. It must have been intimidating to those in the first century who endured persecution for the name of Jesus Christ. Peter remarked, "If you are reviled for the name of Christ, you are blessed, because the Spirit of glory and of God rests upon you. By no means let any of you suffer as a murderer, or thief, or evildoer, or a troublesome meddler; but if anyone suffers as a Christian, let him not feel ashamed, but in that name let him glorify God" (1 Peter 4:14-16). The name of Christ is so close to the heart of any devoted Christian that he will be unwilling ever to deny or shame it. Polycarp, who was martyred in the early second century, had to decide whether he would deny Christ and embrace Caesar or maintain his faith and lose his life. Polycarp held his ground.

> And as he was brought forward, the tumult became great when they heard that Polycarp was taken. And when he came near, the proconsul asked him whether he was Polycarp. On his confessing that he was, the proconsul sought to persuade him to deny Christ, saying, "Have respect to thy old age," and other similar things, according to their

custom, such as, "Swear by the fortune of Caesar; repent, and say, Away with the Atheists." But Polycarp, gazing with a stern countenance on all the multitude of the wicked heathen then in the stadium, and waving his hand towards them, while with groans he looked up to heaven, said, "Away with the Atheists." Then, the proconsul urging him, and saying, "Swear, and I will set thee at liberty, reproach Christ;" Polycarp declared, "Eighty and six years have I served Him, and He never did me any injury: how then can I blaspheme my King and my Savior?"[1]

Polycarp died that day for the name of Jesus Christ. He died because he said, "I am a Christian." He knew who he was and was not ashamed of it.

For some years many people within churches of Christ have been going through an identity crisis. Some people have reacted negatively to what they perceived to be undesirable and have sought to create a new image for the church. They did not want to be identified with the church or the beliefs of the church. In some cases they were right to desire a change in our attitudes and our behavior. Some were arrogant in their overzealous attempts to bring people to the truth. Some, frankly, have portrayed a "better-than-thou" attitude toward those with whom they disagreed. Some, like the Pharisees, took on a view that only their brothers were their neighbors. Others were out of balance in their hellfire and brimstone preaching and lacked an understanding of grace. Some were too quick to condemn others over opinions and man-made laws. These attitude problems, pride and selfish ambition, led to petty divisions and broken congregations.

It became fashionable, however, to blame so many of our weaknesses on our hermeneutic and theology. Critics were sure that it was our beliefs that made us divide so badly, so they attacked our beliefs in precision obedience and pattern theology. They accused us of widespread Phariseeism and narrow-mindedness.

Young preachers began to mock and laugh at those who came before us and anything that smacked of tradition. Quoting Scripture was replaced with a "pop-psychology" theology, and meeting "felt" needs became more important than a "thus saith the Lord." Our sermons changed from declaring first principles to essays on self-esteem and stress.

We were not happy with who we were, so it became necessary – at least in the minds of some – to reinvent ourselves to be more appealing to the world. We did not want to be embarrassed any longer in front of our denominational friends. We began experimenting with our worship, looking for emotional experiences. We began thinking that a new name would allow us to create a new image for our communities. We began loosening up with a more inclusive posture, unwilling to make judgments on the pious unimmersed or those who played the instruments. We relegated the controversial to opinion, taking the view that we could not be certain of Bible teachings. We did not want to be seen as people who made narrow judgments.

Ultimately, we decided that we were not going to make hard and fast decisions on who is and who is not a Christian. We knew spiritual people among other groups, and we did not want to condemn them or be embarrassed in front of them. We wanted to join them in order to have the unity that Jesus prayed for. We were not afraid to admit that we too were a denomination. We became ashamed of what we were and became like the spiritual nations around us. We became ashamed not of our abuses but of our strengths. We shed the things that were most valuable to our identity as children of God in order to accommodate a likeness to the world.

Ashamed of the Name "Church of Christ"

Among churches of Christ, the name "church of Christ" has come upon hard times. Some today are now rejecting the use of that name, claiming that it is sectarian. Others are rejecting the name because they do not want to be associated with the undesirable behavior that some members of the "church of Christ" have manifested. The old statement that "those people believe you have to be a member of the church of Christ to be saved" has led some to be ashamed of anything that uses the phrase, "church of Christ." Consequently, a new generation of churches of Christ has adopted some alternative names. Some now go by "Community Church," putting the phrase "a church of Christ" on the sign in small letters. A minister favoring the change recently gave this explanation:

> The truth is that the name "Church of Christ" carries the baggage of an exclusivistic mentality to many people in our culture. "Oh, yeah," somebody says, "those are the people who think they're the only ones going to heaven." One lady said that she never would have come into our building if she had known we are a "Church of Christ." Once she came in and experienced the presence of God in this body, however, she is not about to leave! She and her children – from a very different denominational background – are reveling in the experience of Christ in this community of faith.[2]

Such statements show that some are embarrassed and ashamed of the phrase "church of Christ." Will these same people one day be ashamed of the phrase "family of God" when they suppose that there is too much offensive baggage associated with that name? Would they change their personal name if some member of the family should disgrace it? Many of the postmodernists who are so quick to embrace the unconditional love and grace of God are slow to forgive what embarrasses them.

It is no accident that this generation has adopted some new names nor is it surprising that these new names suggest a change in attitude and may say more about the nature of the new congregations than is at first intended. A nearby denominational group subnames itself, "The People's Church." What does that say? I suppose that the members of the congregation want the community to know that they are a church "of the people," i.e., that the common people of the city are part of the congregation. Perhaps they want to play up their large size and their appeal. Perhaps they want the community to know how "in tune" they are to common opinions and beliefs.

My thought is this: if the church belongs to the people, how can it belong to Jesus Christ? If the desires of people are its driving force, how can Jesus be its Lord? Something of this same idea might also be said of the "community" church. Perhaps the idea is that the church is to be identified with the community. This has a fine marketing appeal, but where is the Lord glorified? Does a community church belong to Jesus or to the community? One must also ask how the designations "community church" or "family of God" are less sectarian than other names. Sometimes those who are ready to trash a tradition merely begin a new one. Perhaps they should consider the consequences of their new tradition a generation or two from now.

The words "church of Christ" are not a formal name so much as they are a description of who we are. The Scriptures do not give any title to the church, but no one should doubt that the church uniquely belongs to Jesus. Jesus is the builder of the church (Matthew 16:18); He is the One who purchased it with His blood (Acts 20:28); He is the one and only foundation of the church (1 Corinthians 3:11); He is the head of the church (Ephesians 1:22-23); and He is the one and only Savior of the body (5:23). When Jesus spoke of the church, He called it "my church" (Matthew 16:18); and when Paul describes the congregations, he calls them "churches of Christ" (Romans 16:16). There is much to be said for associating the church to the name of Jesus Christ.

It must be further pointed out that we as Christians do whatever we do in His name. When we were baptized, it was in the name of Jesus Christ (Acts 2:38). When we pray, we pray in His name (John 14:13-14). We give a cup of cold water in His name (Mark 9:41); we gather in His name (Matthew 18:20); and we suffer persecution for His name's sake (1 Peter 4:14-16). Repentance and remission of sins are preached in His name (Luke 24:47); we believe in His name (John 1:12); and we have life in His name (John 20:31). Peter reminds us that there is "salvation in no one else; for there is no other name under heaven that has been given among men, by which we must be saved" (Acts 4:12). Indeed the apostles taught in His name (5:41), Philip preached His name (8:12), and Paul bore His name before the Gentiles (9:15). It is His name that is to be magnified (19:17); His name that we are to call upon when we are baptized (22:16); and His name that washes, sanctifies and justifies us (1 Corinthians 6:11).

Saints are those who call upon His name (1:2). It was in the name of Jesus Christ that Paul both exhorted the Corinthians and turned the wicked man over to Satan (v.10; 5:4-5). Paul describes the name of Jesus as that which is above every name (Ephesians 1:21); and it is the name at which every knee will bow and every tongue will confess to the glory of the Father (Philippians 2:9-10). Whatever we do in word or deed, we are to do in the name of the Lord Jesus (Colossians 3:17); and His name is to be glorified in us (2 Thessalonians 1:12). Even slaves are to live worthy of the name of Jesus Christ (1 Timothy 6:1). Consequently, those who name the name of Jesus ought to abstain from wickedness (2:19). The name we name is more excellent than the name of the angels (Hebrews 1:4). To His name we offer a sacrifice of praise, the fruit of our lips (13:15). When we minister to saints, we show love to His name (6:10). The name of Jesus Christ, by which we are called, is a fair name (James 2:7); it is the name in which we are to glorify God (1 Peter 4:14-16). We must hold fast to that name (Revelation 2:13), fear His name (11:18), and never deny His name (3:8). With all these emphases on the name of Jesus Christ, it is unthinkable that any Christian would abandon it.

Should the church wear the name of Jesus Christ? Yes. Should the church denominate that name? No. The phrase "church of Christ" ought always to be a description of who we are and whose we are. Those who are critical of our use of that name, saying we have somehow denominated it ought to be careful that they are not guilty of the same error with other descriptions.

Ashamed of the Teaching

Jesus not only acknowledged that some would be ashamed of Him, He also knew that some would be ashamed of His teachings. It is surprising indeed that some want to be recognized as Christians but are unwilling to be constrained by His teachings. It is as if they think they ought to be more righteous than Jesus, or they need to update His teachings so that they will be more in tune with the times. To be ashamed of Jesus' teachings is to be ashamed of Him. One cannot separate the message from the person of Christ. Indeed the message of Jesus is a part of His very identity as the Son of God.

The drive to grow churches has led some to a point of view that they are willing to do whatever it takes to enlarge their numbers. The desire to grow is noble; any faithful Christian wants the Lord's body to increase and will work tirelessly to see that it does. Growth, however, is not the same thing as making disciples. Swelling numbers is not a guarantee of growing disciples. It takes more than filling a pew to be a disciple. Some have suggested that the only healthy churches are the ones that are growing numerically. They further imply that if a church is not growing, it needs to change. This may or may not be the case.

In Revelation, John remarkably never mentions numerical growth when he assesses the spirituality of the seven churches of Asia. He says much, however, about their spiritual growth, their works, their love, and their faithfulness to the Lord and the truth. The healthy churches were those who remained faithful during times of persecution, those who remained free from idolatry and immorality, those who avoided the libertine temptation, and those whose love remained strong. Jesus spoke through John about those who "overcome." We may ask the question, what was it they had to overcome? The answer for them is the same for us – the devil.

Having the largest congregation in the world is of little good if the devil runs it; and he will try! One of the ways he enters churches is by the promise of numbers. The devil tempted Jesus with quick growth if Jesus would jump off the pinnacle of the temple. Jesus declined and pointed to a deeper spiritual truth. The devil tempted Jesus with the world at His feet if Jesus would merely bow down to him. Jesus declined and pointed to the one true God. We must be careful to assess the cost of church growth that is too quick and too easy. The cost may be higher than we imagined.

The Bible does not mandate "church growth"; it mandates gospel preaching and making disciples. The real disciples of Jesus are those who abide in the word of God (John 8:31), who bear fruit (10:8), who love others as Christ does (13:35), and who remain faithful to Him (6:63-66). It is better to make one true disciple than to add 100 to a congregation run by the devil. This is not to approve laziness and a lack of evangelistic fervor; it is to point out that numbers are not necessarily the proof of God's blessing. Jeremiah preached 40 years with little success. God did not honor him for his numerical success but for his faithfulness. We might be numerically successful with a watered-down gospel, but a watered-down gospel does not make disciples who will die for the faith. If we compromise our message to get large numbers, we will have to compromise even more to keep those numbers. In the end our faith will become worldly, insipid, irrelevant and ineffectual. Indeed, for nominal Christians it is already all of these things.

Jesus did not compromise or waver on the things that mattered. He held firm to the hard line. The Lord meant what He taught. He did not take back what He said when the tide of public opinion turned against Him. Our Savior said, "If anyone comes to Me, and does not hate his own father and mother and wife and children and brothers and sisters, yes, and even his own life, he cannot be My disciple. Whoever does not carry his own cross and come after Me cannot be My disciple" (Luke 14:26-27). The One who went to the cross to have His hands and feet pierced was a man of conviction and devotion to the message He came to deliver. It is a mockery of the Cross to suggest that He did not really mean what He said.

At one point Jesus taught His disciples a very difficult thing. They asked, "[W]ho can listen to it?" (John 6:61) Jesus was conscious of their grumbling and asked them, "Does this cause you to stumble? What then if you should behold the Son of Man ascending where He was before?" Jesus knew that some of the people there simply did not believe Him. But Jesus placed an extremely high premium on His teachings. He said, "It is the Spirit who gives life; the flesh profits nothing; the words that I have spoken to you are spirit and are life" (John 6:64). This is why it is wrong to be ashamed of His teachings; they are the source of life. To be ashamed of what Jesus teaches is to cut yourself off from hope of life. The story continues:

> And He was saying, "For this reason I have said to you, that no one can come to Me, unless it has been granted him from the Father." As a result of this many of His dis-

ciples withdrew, and were not walking with Him anymore. Jesus said therefore to the twelve, "You do not
want to go away also, do you?" Simon Peter answered
Him, "Lord, to whom shall we go? You have words of
eternal life. And we have believed and have come to know
that You are the Holy One of God" (vv. 66-69).

There simply is no substitute for the gospel message; only it has
the words of eternal life. To be ashamed of the words of Jesus is to
cut oneself off from the blessings of the Lord.

When the people left, Jesus did not trip all over Himself trying to
get them to come back. He did not take back His message in order
to get or keep the numbers. He did not apologize. He did not reduce
His standards in order to give more people an opportunity. He did
not complain to the Father that His way was too narrow and exclusive. He let them go. The temptation here is to think that Jesus' behavior is not very compassionate. Does He not love them? Is He not
the Good Shepherd who leaves the 99 to recover the one lost sheep?
Yes, He is all these things. Why did He not react?

Jesus stayed silent with these fair-weather followers because He
knew the stubbornness and the weakness of their hearts. He had giv-
en a demanding challenge to them that they were unwilling to accept. If there had been any other discussion, it would have meant that
Jesus would have had to compromise. He was unwilling to do that
and really had nothing else to say to them. If He had given in on this
point to keep them, what else would He have had to do to keep them?
God's standards cannot be bought at the price of popularity. The cost
of discipleship is a cross. William Barclay makes this observation:

Some shirked the challenge of Jesus. Fundamentally their
point of view was that they had come to Jesus to get
something from him; when it came to suffering for him
and giving to him they quit. No one can give so much as
Jesus, but if we come to him solely to get and never to
give we will certainly turn back. The man who would
follow Jesus must remember that in following him there
is always a Cross.[3]

Many religious groups who have gone the way of entertainment to get a crowd have the constant headache of what to do to top last week's performance. Their eyes are not turned toward the Cross but toward the demands of the populace. Having gone the way of Pontius Pilate, they have sacrificed a commitment to Jesus in order to please the people. One compromise calls for another, and in the end there is no resemblance to Christianity. The worship (if one can call it worship) has become a religious performance judged on its artistic qualities rather than spiritual qualities. Hired singers who may or may not believe what they sing come center stage. The question becomes whether everyone had a good time rather than if God was pleased.

Further, the question of women's role in the church now comes into play. One of the prime reasons that some have sought a more active role for women in the church is that if churches of Christ do not, they will "lose women, especially young women."[4] Some have believed that the change was necessary to use these women's talents. Such thinking prompted a rethinking of the role of women, and traditional understandings of the biblical teachings were abandoned in order to accommodate the desire to allow women to use their talents. One might wonder how God could have been so narrow for so long! One might wonder why God allowed women to waste their talents for so many centuries! One might glory in the enlightened people of today who are able to see opportunities for women that had been covered up for centuries ! How fortunate we are that people can be trained in "how to read and study the Bible rather than using the old-style literalist approach!" Will we be more righteous than Jesus and run after the women who are rapidly leaving us to fulfill opportunities to use their talents?

If we do, where will it end? Are we to rewrite the Bible each and every time someone feels cheated and threatens to leave? We are already seeing some willing to tear down the boundaries of gospel obedience to be more inclusive. Are we to weaken our message because fair-weather disciples find it difficult to accept? Are we to pad the cross with exceptions and accommodations? Are we to mock Christ with our new and improved form of Christianity? Are we to presume that we can correct Him and improve on His time-tested ways because they may seem offensive in our postmodern world? The real issue is this: are we willing to be obedient believers with traditional, biblical understandings or will we allow our desires and fears to move us into a culturally manufactured understanding? When Solomon urged us to buy the truth, it was because he knew that truth costs something. The truth can cost us relationships with those who are unwilling to yield to it. As much as God loves everyone and wants all people to be saved, we do not find evidence that He is willing to change His covenant to accommodate fair-weather disciples. Perhaps we should remember that He is God, and we are not. He makes the rules, and we do not. We cannot hold God at bay with emotional blackmail. He will not apologize and change His mind. Our task is to obey Him – not expect Him to accommodate our desires.

Ashamed of Confronting

The Christian faith is in and of itself confrontational. It demands repentance and conformity to the image of Christ. The primary message of John, Jesus, His apostles, and the 70 was "repent, for the kingdom of Heaven is at hand" (Matthew 3:2; 4:17; 10:7; Luke 10:9, 13). Peter was so bold at Pentecost that he pointed the finger directly at the Jews who crucified Jesus and called them to repentance (Acts 2:36-38). Paul at Mars' Hill called the pagan philosophers of Athens to repent, because God had fixed a day in which He would judge the world (Acts 17:31).

Paul charged Timothy to preach the Word, to be ready in season and out of season, to reprove, to rebuke, and to exhort with great patience and instruction (2 Timothy 4:1-2). To reprove is to "censure, as for a fault"; in reproving one expresses disapproval of an act or a belief. Some synonyms for the verb "reprove" are admonish, chasten, chide, reproach, and scold. To rebuke is to reprimand sharply or to express a strong disapproval. Paul demands that those who continue in sin are to be rebuked "in the presence of all, so that the rest also may be fearful of sinning" (1 Timothy 5:20). One could not imagine going to a church and hearing someone rebuked for continual sin today. This may be the most neglected command among us.

Our society has changed so much and so rapidly that it is often difficult to grasp what has happened to us. One of the major changes has been to move away from dealing with sin and use an approach that deals with self-esteem. We are told that we must be sensitive to the felt needs of the culture in which we live. Self-esteem has become the primary focus of our times; we are told that growth and success can only come about when people have good self-esteem.

Robert Schuller argues that all the "problems facing the church will find healing answers if we start with and do not get distracted at any time from meeting every person's deepest need – his hunger for self-esteem, self-worth, and personal dignity." He calls human dignity the "ultimate human value."[5] For him and others, the call is for an unconditional love that is nonjudgmental. They believe that it is an "unchristian, uncouth strategy to attempt to make people aware of their lost condition."[6] We must rise above a Jesus that makes people feel any kind of guilt. Jesus is to be seen as a friend who makes us feel good about ourselves and who helps us make it through the day; but we must not present Jesus as the Savior who died for our sins.

Schuller tells us that if we wish to fill our churches, our preaching must only be positive. We must not preach "sermons" but deliver inspirational messages. In fact, preachers should drop the word "preacher" because it carries a negative connotation. Even the word "sermon" has a negative ring to it these days. For Schuller, man's problem is not sin but "low self-esteem." The person in the pew is not asking, "Was God glorified?" but "Was my ego renewed?" Schuller argues, "We are saved by the blood," not "by the Book." Schuller believes that the variety of interpretations has badly divided Christendom, so we must turn to a direct control of Christ through the Holy Spirit.[7] It never occurs to Schuller that the religious groups looking to the direct leading of the Holy Spirit are as badly divided among themselves as any. The only clear means by which we can exalt the Lordship of Jesus Christ is to do what He says (Luke 6:46). The only way we can be sure that we are doing what He says is through a conscientious study of the Bible. We must further recognize that the written Word is the means by which God gives His saving message (Romans 1:16; 1 Corinthians 15:1-3; James 1:21; 1 Peter 1:23-25).

In recent years we have heard a great deal within churches of Christ about "non-threatening" Christianity. The idea was that Christians present classes, seminars and group meetings in which no one would feel uncomfortable with what was being taught. Once a potential disciple got comfortable with talking about the Bible, then some brother or sister could pull him aside and talk straight about the gospel. There would be no public confrontation, only a private one so as not to embarrass or "run off" anyone. As time has passed the fear of offending has caused many to reject the need for any confrontation whatsoever. Some churches warned their preachers not to preach negative sermons, and some preachers were fired because they dared to confront their congregations with the truth. Some want every aspect of Christianity to be "non-threatening," non-embarrassing, and non-confrontational. What they actually want is a Christianity without having to bear a cross. The problem is: how does one do this and yet remain true to the commands calling for repentance and rebuking error? One cannot.

The real issue here is what kind of God we serve. I fear that some have Him pictured as a kindly, old grandfather who smiles and blesses everyone in every aspect of life. He is quick to hear every prayer, deeply understanding, and compassionate. He naively and gently laughs off our indiscretions, saying, "boys will be boys." He is too good to condemn anyone, and His patience with us has absolutely no end. He is one who warns and threatens but never sees His threat through. He is too good to send anyone to hell. He may or may not see what we do, but our sins really do not matter much to Him. In the end He pats us on the back no matter how we have behaved and ushers us into heaven.

No one wants to diminish the inexhaustible love and grace of the God of heaven, but the above picture of a god is not the God of the Bible. It is the picture many want, but it is incomplete and full of errors. The God of heaven is a just God, who recompenses every man according to His deeds (2 Corinthians 5:10). He indeed does have a cross for us to bear and holds us accountable if we do not bear it. Jesus said, "Whoever does not carry his own cross and come after Me cannot be My disciple" (Luke 14:27). It all comes back to the real issue of whether we wish to accept the God revealed in the Bible or wish to manufacture one of our own.

The God of heaven by His own initiative sent His Son to die for our sins. He did this while mankind was full of sinners and helpless people (Romans 5:6-8). He acted out of love for us. We were not morally worthy of such love, but God thought that having an eternal relationship was worth the sacrifice of His Son. God did not wait until man became perfect but took the initiative in order to demonstrate His love for us and to prompt us to be drawn to Him (John 12:32). The act was unconditional on God's part; it was His plan to redeem man. Some have assumed because of this that God's love and blessings are unconditional in every aspect. Nothing could be farther from the truth. Even John 3:16 shows that "whosoever believeth" is a part of God's plan. The mercy and salvation of God are dependent upon a conditional response, which is also a part of God's plan.

On another occasion Jesus declared twice that those who do not repent will perish (Luke 13:3, 5). On still another occasion Jesus said that we must be born again and that unless a man is born of water and the Spirit, he cannot enter into the kingdom of God (John 3:3-7). Not everyone will believe, not everyone will repent, and not everyone will be baptized. Jesus also said that the one who does not believe is condemned already, because he has not believed in the name of the only begotten Son of God (John 3:18). Salvation is dependent upon the response of the one hearing the gospel. It is in this framework that Peter urges the people, "Save yourselves from this perverse generation" (Acts 2:40).

No one is suggesting here that man earns his salvation. What we are saying is that the cross upon which Jesus died has a means of distinguishing those who accept it from those who reject its saving power. Paul noted in Romans 3:21-26:

> But now apart from the Law the righteousness of God
> has been manifested, being witnessed by the Law and

the Prophets, even the righteousness of God through faith in Jesus Christ for all those who believe; for there is no distinction; for all have sinned and fall short of the glory of God, being justified as a gift by His grace through the redemption which is in Christ Jesus; whom God displayed publicly as a propitiation in His blood through faith. This was to demonstrate His righteousness, because in the forbearance of God He passed over the sins previously committed; for the demonstration, I say, of His righteousness at the present time, that He might be just and the justifier of the one who has faith in Jesus.

God is entirely just in condemning those who reject Him, and yet His whole-hearted desire and intention for man is to be the justifier of those who believe in Him. Obedient faith is the demarcation between those who are made righteous by the blood of Christ and those who are not. The goal of Paul's preaching was the obedience of faith (Romans 1:5; 16:25-27), i.e., to bring about an obedience derived from believing. It was never enough in his mind for one merely to agree that Jesus was the Christ; a convert has to make Jesus his Lord by his obedience. To do that requires confrontation. Conversion itself requires submission to a cross. Jesus reminds us that if the world hated Him, it will also hate us (John 15:18,19). Perhaps the greatest failure of our time is the deafening silence from people afraid of the hatred of the world.

Wanting a King

Among some in churches of Christ, there is a desire to be like the worldly religious groups around us. We are much like the children of Israel in the days of Samuel. They wanted a king so that they could be like all the nations (1 Samuel 8:20). In spite of the Lord's warning and all the difficulties that would arise from having a king, the people demanded one. Samuel became depressed and opposed them having a king, thinking that such a choice was a rejection of him personally. God, however, told Samuel that such a choice was not a rejection of him but of the One who spoke through him. God was rejected, so Israel could be like "all the nations." When the desires of men grow strong, God and His will become disposable. Sometimes, people just have to have their way.

Many in churches of Christ, having rejected God's plan for one church, have been pushing for the church to become like all the religious groups around us – to become a "denomination." Being a denomination means that we could abandon our "exclusivist" mindset. It means we could acknowledge others outside our present fellowship as brothers and sisters. It means that we could embrace a religious pluralism, admitting that there is no certain truth. It means that we could join in the chorus of voices saying that all the churches are headed in the same direction regardless of what they believe. It means that we would not have to be so different from the worldly churches surrounding us. We would no longer be embarrassed at being backward. We could finally get over that awful, elite tag saying churches of Christ think they are the only ones going to heaven. In all of this, they, like Israel, are rejecting the will of God in order to fit in.

For some, there is nothing better than a "fashionable" Christianity. Wanting to be at the cutting edge of whatever is happening in the culture around us, they are not content to embrace a faith once for all time delivered to the saints. They feel cheated if they are kept from embracing the latest theories and the latest interpretations. They somehow feel they are more scholarly and elite if they are familiar with the latest developments, never considering if they are in line with the whole counsel of God. They are not content with an "old rugged cross, so despised by the world," an "emblem of suff'ring and shame." They prefer a comfortable cross, contoured to the culture of this present world. They crave a cross that does not ask for repentance but demands change from the outmoded ideas of the past. They want a church that meets all needs but asks nothing that demands real sacrifice.

What these churches of Christ who want so badly to adapt to the postmodern culture are actually doing is becoming worldly. They have ceased to be transformed and are demanding to be conformed to the world. They want a king but not the King. They want a church but not the church Jesus died for. They want a cross but not the Cross of Jesus Christ. They want their way no matter what. Satan has sold them a counterfeit, promising them success in church growth and popularity. And they bought it. They will be like the churches around them. As with all of Satan's sales, the cost is higher than they really want to pay. Jesus said,

> For whoever wishes to save his life shall lose it; but whoever loses his life for My sake shall find it. For what will a man be profited, if he gains the whole world, and forfeits his soul? Or what will a man give in exchange for his soul (Matthew 16:25-26).

Discussion Questions

1. What is precision obedience and pattern theology, and is there a biblical basis for them?

2. How should Christians regard the name of Christ?

3. Discuss the differences between "church growth" and "making disciples."

4. How should the church deal with fair-weather disciples?

5. It is said "we should not go through the windows, because denominationalists go through the doors." In what ways can we be like the denominational churches, and in what ways must we differ?

CHAPTER 8

Finding the Map
WE KNOW WHERE WE ARE!

nclusivists desire to accept everyone regardless of their religious
views of the truth. Not wishing to judge or speak ill of anyone,
they dismiss the concept of absolute truth in order to accept conflicting and contradictory doctrines. Inclusivists willingly sacrifice
the truth to retain friendly relations with those who differ with them
religiously. Deciding that absolute certainty concerning truth is un-
attainable, they become unwilling to say that anything may be untrue or immoral. Rather than accept the plain statements of Scripture as binding truth, inclusivists focus on exceptions and the silence of the Scripture to provide a basis for their alternatives.

Christian inclusivists fall into two categories: those who accept
pious people outside of Jesus Christ as saved and those who accept
within Christianity those who hold conflicting and contradictory
doctrines and practices. In the first category might be groups such
as the Disciples of Christ who in their 1989 convention in Indianapolis were unwilling to pass a resolution stating that Jesus is the
only way to heaven. Not willing to judge anyone or to accept the
judgments of Jesus in Scripture, they decided to remain silent. After all, they did not want to hurt their interfaith discussions with
their non-believing friends.[1]

The first kind of inclusivism reveals a fundamental unwillingness
to confess there is truly "one Lord" (Ephesians 4:4-6). It certainly
stands in stark contrast with the preaching of Paul in the Areopagus

(Acts 17:22-31) where Paul denounced any humanly devised god. It denies Peter's affirmation that "there is salvation in no one else; for there is no other name under heaven that has been given among men, by which we must be saved" (Acts 4:12). It mocks the blood of Jesus by suggesting there is another way to be cleansed from sin and go to heaven.

The second kind of Christian inclusivism promotes a tolerance and acceptance of those who call themselves Christians but hold to unscriptural and antiscriptural beliefs and practices. It embraces those who confess Christ but have not obeyed the gospel according to the teachings of the Lord. It sidesteps the authority of the New Testament to fellowship those who "go beyond" the teaching. It makes Christianity a confusion of conflicting, alternative theologies. Inclusivists are undeniably pluralists who must overlook the heresy of those they embrace. Whatever doctrine inclusivists believe, it is nullified when they accept a doctrine, supposedly from God, that conflicts with what they believe. No matter how firmly they hold to immersion, they must take back their conviction in order to fellowship a sprinkler. No matter how convicted they are that baptism is for the penitent believer, they must compromise in order to embrace a pious baptism of precious infants. They dismiss the truth to get along with "sweet-spirited people who love God."

For more than a century and a half, churches of Christ and Christian Churches have debated how to deal with the "pious unimmersed," i.e., people who display a Christian spirit but have only been sprinkled for baptism. Some considered sprinkled people as brethren while others only recognized the immersed. This dispute became the basis for the division between Christian Churches and the Disciples of Christ, a division beginning in 1929 and culminating in 1962. While the Disciples openly fellowship the sprinkled, the independent Christian Churches demanded an immersion for fellowship. The question centers around the openness of fellowship. Can or should Christians accept as a brother someone who has not obeyed the gospel according to the teachings of the Scriptures?

Restoration leaders first began to dispute this issue in September 1837 when Alexander Campbell, in response to a letter from a lady in Lunenburg, Va., said in the *Millennial Harbinger*:

> Should I find a Pedobaptist more intelligent in the Christian Scriptures, more spiritually-minded and more devoted to the Lord than a Baptist, or one immersed on a profession of the ancient faith, I could not hesitate a moment in giving the preference of my heart to him that loveth most. Did I act otherwise, I would be a pure sectarian, a Pharisee among Christians. Still I will be asked, How do I know that any one loves my Master but by his obedience to his commandments? I answer, In no other way. But mark, I do not substitute obedience to one commandment, for universal or even for general obedience. And should I see a sectarian Baptist or a Pedobaptist more spiritually-minded, more generally conformed to the requisitions of the Messiah, than one who precisely acquiesces with me in the theory or practice of immersion as I teach, doubtless the former rather than the latter, would have my cordial approbation and love as a Christian. So I judge, and so I feel. It is the image of Christ the Christian looks for and loves; and this does not consist in being exact in a few items, but in general devotion to the whole truth as far as known.[2]

Campbell created further confusion when he argued in the November issue:

> I cannot be a perfect Christian without a right understanding and a cordial reception of immersion in its true and scriptural meaning and design. But he that thence infers that none are Christians but the immersed, as greatly errs as he that affirms that none are alive but those of clear and full vision.[3]

The thrust of Campbell's argument was that one's "general obedience" overruled his specific obedience in the matter of immersion. The temperament of one's heart, one's devotion to the truth that one knows, or one's love for Christ is a more clear indication to Campbell that one is a Christian than if one has been buried with Christ for the remission of his sins. No one standard is sufficient for excluding one from the name "Christian."

There are some distinct problems with this view:

1. What right has Campbell or any other man to overlook a command of God simply because other commands have been met? Campbell said, "But mark, I do not substitute obedience to one commandment, for universal or even for general obedience." The question, then, is whether or not that one commandment is really necessary. Is baptism essential to salvation? Could one leave it out and still please God? Does one commandment really make that much difference? Does a right heart make baptism optional? Does "general obedience" set aside the command to be baptized?

One might ask: Would it be right to ignore the need to confess if one were to believe, repent and be baptized? If, dear reader, you should answer yes, could you set aside belief itself? How about repentance? If you can set aside one command, why can you not set aside two or three? If "general obedience" permits failure to do right in one area, then is it still sin to fail to do what is right? How many commandments can be overlooked and a person still be considered as having entered into a saving relationship with Christ Jesus? The Scriptures teach that one believes, or he will die in his sins (John 8:24). Jesus taught that one must repent or perish (Luke 13:3). In the same way, Jesus taught that one must be born again of water and the Spirit, or he cannot enter God's kingdom (John 3:5). Such categorical statements make it clear that each one of the three is just as essential as the other two.

Jesus wanted those He commissioned to preach the gospel to teach every one "to observe all things whatsoever I have commanded you" (Matthew 28:18-20). Jesus believed that every one of His commands was significant. When Jesus criticized the Pharisees for not keeping the weightier matters of the Law, He did not excuse them from keeping the smaller matters (vv. 23-24). Jesus Himself noted that in His relationship with the Father, "I always do the things that are pleasing to Him" (John 8:29). Paul wanted the Colossians to please God in all respects (Colossians 1:10). James 2:10-12 says:

> For whoever keeps the whole law and yet stumbles in one point, he has become guilty of all. For He who said, "Do not commit adultery," also said, "Do not commit murder." Now if you do not commit adultery, but do commit murder, you have become a transgressor of the law. So speak and so act, as those who are to be judged by the law of liberty.

Far from dismissing any command, the New Testament asks for a commitment to keep the whole law of Christ. This is how one who is to be judged by the law of liberty is supposed to speak and act. No one has the right to edit God's laws or commands or to decide selectively which are necessary and which are not. Such a notion is presumptuous.

When Campbell suggests that the more "spiritually-minded" Baptist or Pedobaptist (infant baptizer) is more generally conformed to the requisitions of the Messiah than one who precisely acquiesces with me in the theory or practice of immersion as I teach, he concludes that the former rather than the latter "would have my cordial approbation and love as a Christian. So I judge, and so I feel." Whether one ought to trust Campbell's judgments and feelings, the reader must decide for himself. It ought to be unnecessary to remind ourselves that Campbell's judgments are not the basis of the Judgment on the last day, but the words of Jesus Christ will be!

Campbell suggests, "With me mistakes of the understanding and errors of the affections are not to be confounded. They are as distant as the poles." One might ask why it is that the affections somehow have greater weight than one's understanding of the truth. The current thought is today circulating that what one believes does not matter "as long as one loves the Lord." The idea is that one is judged not on the basis of what the text says but on the basis of whether or not one obeys what one understands the text to say. In effect, he is saying that affectionate misunderstanding is a little matter but understanding without affection is a graver sin. The fact is that both are inadequate to please the Lord. Our Father desires both the heart and the head; one without the other is not sufficient to please Him. The greatest commandment is to love God with all our hearts, and all our souls, and all our minds (Matthew 22:37). God wants the total person wholeheartedly to understand and to obey out of love. Nothing less will do.

2. What right has Campbell or any other man to set aside what Christ the Lord has legislated? Jesus made it clear about the necessity of baptism to one's salvation in His categorical statement to Nicodemus: "Truly, truly, I say to you, unless one is born again, he cannot see the kingdom of God" (John 3:3). When Nicodemus questions Jesus about how this takes place, Jesus explains in the strongest terms:

> Truly, truly, I say to you, unless one is born of water and the Spirit, he cannot enter into the kingdom of God. That which is born of the flesh is flesh, and that which is born of the Spirit is spirit. Do not marvel that I said to you, 'You must be born again' (John 3:5-7).

The words "truly, truly" in the original language are "amen, amen." Jesus wanted to make it doubly clear in "amen" truths that He meant what He said. He further emphasizes the essentiality of baptism by using the word "must"; it was morally necessary if one were to enter the kingdom to be born again. Exceptions are not considered. "Unless" one is born of water and the Spirit, he "cannot" enter the kingdom. The word "cannot" (ου δυναται) points to an utter inability to enter the kingdom of God. How can anyone set aside what Jesus clearly is demanding? The unimmersed cannot claim the same promise as the immersed. A sprinkled baby has not undergone the new birth of baptism, because sprinkling is not immersion. People may not like to recognize this difference, but they will not be the judge. Only God will be the judge, and those who devote themselves to Him make a conscious decision to follow His will explicitly.

When Campbell says, "There is no occasion, then, for making immersion, on a profession of faith, absolutely essential to a Christian,"[4] he contradicts the Lord. Campbell may say that immersion is not an absolute "must" to be a Christian; but if the Lord says it is a "must," then let the Lord be true. Jesus is never wrong, even if Campbell may be.

Is God Ever Exclusive?

That God is exclusive ought to be clear to every student of the Bible. From the beginning of time to the present, God has made distinction between those who serve Him and those who do not. When Adam and Eve sinned, God pronounced that Adam would return to the dust of the earth and "sent him out from the garden of Eden" (Genesis 3:19, 23). God had regard for Abel's faithful offering but did not regard Cain's offering, because it was not by faith. Some years later

> the LORD saw that the wickedness of man was great on the earth, and that every intent of the thoughts of his heart was only evil continually. And the LORD was sorry that He had made man on the earth, and He was grieved in His heart. And the LORD said, "I will blot out man whom I have created from the face of the land, from man to animals to creeping things and to birds of the sky; for I am sorry that I have made them (Genesis 6:5-7).

Fortunately, Noah was a righteous man and found favor in the eyes of God. The LORD said to Noah, "Enter the ark, you and all your household; for you alone I have seen to be righteous before Me in this time." God made a way for those who loved him by the building of that ark. "And those who entered, male and female of all flesh, entered as God had commanded him; and the LORD closed [the door] behind him" (Genesis 7:16). One can only imagine the horror in the hearts of the wicked people of that day when the rains began. How they must have wanted to be on that ark! But the door was closed. God excluded them. It might surprise many today to realize God excludes those who disobey.

Another example of God's exclusiveness comes at the time when the 12 spies went up to look over the Promised Land. Ten of the spies came and gave a very bad report. Deciding that the sons of

135

Anak were unconquerable, they came back defeatists. All night long the children of Israel wept and worried over the matter. Because of their lack of faith in God and their grumbling rebellion, God said,

> Surely all the men who have seen My glory and My signs, which I performed in Egypt and in the wilderness, yet have put Me to the test these ten times and have not listened to My voice, shall by no means see the land which I swore to their fathers, nor shall any of those who spurned Me see it. But My servant Caleb, because he has had a different spirit and has followed Me fully, I will bring into the land which he entered, and his descendants shall take possession of it. "Say to them, 'As I live,' says the LORD, 'just as you have spoken in My hearing, so I will surely do to you; your corpses shall fall in this wilderness, even all your numbered men, according to your complete number from twenty years old and upward, who have grumbled against Me. Surely you shall not come into the land in which I swore to settle you, except Caleb the son of Jephunneh and Joshua the son of Nun (Numbers 14:22-28).

Of all the hundreds of thousands of Israelites who could have entered the Promised Land, only two actually did.[5] God excluded the rest of the people.

In the parable of the five wise and five foolish virgins, those who prepared their lamps entered the wedding feast with the bridegroom. The unprepared, foolish virgins were not so blessed. Matthew 25:10 says, "And while they were going away to make the purchase, the bridegroom came, and those who were ready went in with him to the wedding feast; and the door was shut." They were not allowed into the feast. They cried, "Lord, Lord, open up for us." But he answered and said, "Truly I say to you, I do not know you" (vv. 11-12). Many people think they have a relationship with the Lord by virtue of their former association, but He says He does not know them. He is not in a relationship with them because they are unprepared for His coming. Jesus excludes them. This parable demonstrates that God does not accept everybody and does reject people on the basis of their behavior.

Jesus urges those who would follow Him in Luke 13:24, "Strive to enter by the narrow door; for many, I tell you, will seek to enter and will not be able." God expects those who want to follow Him to make a serious effort. Those who are unwilling to pay the price will not be able to enter. The word "strive" in the original Greek is αγωνιζεσθε, the word from which we get our word "agonize." This word pictures an athletic contest in which competitors are struggling to win. They will strain every muscle and make every effort to achieve their goal. This is what Jesus asks of us as we strive to enter the narrow door. Some will zealously seek to enter but will not be able because they were not willing to pay the price.

Are you saying that God is a respecter of persons? Absolutely not. What I am saying is what Peter said, "I most certainly understand now that God is not one to show partiality, but in every nation the man who fears Him and does what is right, is welcome to Him" (Acts 10:34-35). God does not make distinctions on the basis of skin color, intelligence, appearance or nationality.

God distinguishes the one who is welcome to Him on the basis of whether or not that person fears Him and does what is right. The one who does not fear Him or fails to do right will not be acceptable to Him. He will exclude that person. God loves everyone, but we must choose whether or not we are willing to submit to the will of God. Paul said,

> Do you not know that when you present yourselves to someone as slaves for obedience, you are slaves of the one whom you obey, either of sin resulting in death, or of obedience resulting in righteousness? But thanks be to God that though you were slaves of sin, you became obedient from the heart to that form of teaching to which you were committed, and having been freed from sin, you became slaves of righteousness (Romans 6:16-18).

Man's free will allows him to choose whether to be a slave of sin or a slave of righteousness. Despite the fact that one may have first chosen sin, he has the opportunity to become obedient from the heart to a form of teaching and thereby become a slave of righteousness, freed from sin. God in His grace gives man this opportunity to repent and change his life. The idea that man ought to be given blessings whether he does right or not mocks the grace of God. He teaches us to deny ungodliness and worldly desires and to live sensibly, righteously and godly in this present world (Titus 2:12).

Only God Has the Right to Exclude or Include

The real distinction between whether or not a person is acceptable to God is whether or not that person has been forgiven of his sins. God has added those who are saved or forgiven to the church (Acts 2:38, 41, 47). Those who are saved have been washed, sanctified and justified in the name of the Lord Jesus (1 Corinthians 6:11). Regardless of what one has been before, the blood of Jesus is able to loose one from His sins (Revelation 1:5). It is at this point that one comes to be in the kingdom of God and outside of the rule of Satan. Paul said of the church in Colossae, "For He delivered us from the domain of darkness, and transferred us to the kingdom of His beloved Son, in whom we have redemption, the forgiveness of sins" (Colossians 1:13-14). It is God who transfers us, not we who transfer ourselves. It is God who adds us to the kingdom; He does this at His will and does not consult us for our advice.

Forgiveness is an act of the heart and spirit; forgiveness from God takes place in His heart. Whether I think I am forgiven or not, the crucial thing is what God thinks. I may feel sure in my heart that I am saved, but it is God who does the saving. One of the most curious teachings of the Bible is that some who think they are saved are not. Some who think that they know God, i.e., have a relationship with God, are people who will one day find out that God does not know them. The consequence is that man is not the decision maker; man is not the judge of salvation. Only God can do that! When the scribes and Pharisees complained at Jesus' forgiving the paralyzed man they said, "Who is this man who speaks blasphemies? Who can forgive sins, but God alone?" (Luke 5:21) Even they realized that Jesus' claim to forgive sins meant that He was God; no one else could forgive our sins.

The Nature of Obedience

Perhaps at this point it is necessary to ask what it means to obey. Some have suggested that anyone who is being baptized "to obey the Lord" is baptized correctly. If we were to ask those who are being sprinkled for baptism about their reasons, we would likely hear that they were doing so to obey the Lord. They misunderstand much about baptism but suppose they are being obedient. No one doubts their motives, but their action differs from the scriptural instructions. Those who believe baptism is for those who are already forgiven nevertheless go to the baptistery in their minds to obey the Lord. They misunderstand much about baptism but suppose they are obedient. Have sprinkled people obeyed the Lord in baptism? Have people who are immersed as a public confession of their past salvation[6] obeyed the Lord in an appropriate baptism? Some say yes, and others say no. How much does one have to understand in order to be truly obedient? This question makes it important to know just what gospel obedience is.

Before we begin this study, we must realize that there is such a thing as spiritual blindness. Solomon said, "There is a way that seems right to a man, but its end is the way of death" (Proverbs 14:12). People can for any number of reasons be misled in what they believe. In such cases they obey what they believe is the truth, though in reality it may not be right. The Pharisees were certainly people in this category; Jesus in fact speaks of their blindness toward Him and toward the Word of God. He said, "Let them alone; they are blind guides of the blind. And if a blind man guides a blind man, both will fall into a pit" (Matthew 15:14). On another occasion, Jesus warned His disciples of the "leaven (or teaching) of the Pharisees" (16:6-12). Jesus taught His disciples that they needed to beware of a false teaching which could cost them their souls.

A physically blinded person is simply unable to see what is around him. A spiritually blinded person may be able to see physically, but something is keeping him from correctly seeing things spiritually. The devil is an expert at blinding people to keep them from obeying Christ. Paul said,

And even if our gospel is veiled, it is veiled to those who are perishing, in whose case the god of this world has blinded the minds of the unbelieving, that they might not see the light of the gospel of the glory of Christ, who is the image of God (2 Corinthians 4:3-4).

The god of this world blinds minds by lies and falsehoods. He would, for instance, deny the reality of God, the inspiration of the Bible, the deity of Jesus, or the necessity of baptism for the remission of sins. But we must also understand that the devil is exceptionally subtle and cunning. Satan particularly likes to make counterfeits. Paul explains, "But I am afraid, lest as the serpent deceived Eve by his craftiness, your minds should be led astray from the simplicity and purity of devotion to Christ" (11:3). It is at this point that Paul warns the Corinthians of the false apostles who were teaching "another Jesus" and a "different gospel." These "false apostles, deceitful workers," were "disguising themselves as apostles of Christ. And no wonder, for even Satan disguises himself as an angel of light" (vv. 4, 13-14). Sometimes, what appears closest to the truth is the most deceptive. It appears genuine but is phony; it looks real but will deceive. When one obeys a counterfeit, one is obeying in blindness.

This counterfeiting of the gospel is a perversion. While some elements look genuine, there are others that are changed. The Judaizers of Galatia were perverting the gospel by demanding Gentile Christians to "keep the whole law" in addition to their obedience to Christ (Galatians 5:3). If we were to talk to these men, we would learn they believed many things correctly. Their perversion came from adding requirements God did not command (Galatians 1:6). Paul by inspiration condemned anyone who participates in this or any perversion of the gospel (1:8-9). Even small perversions can be deadly. Rat poison is 98 percent corn meal and only two percent poison. If it were otherwise, the rats might not eat it. Counterfeit gospels look appetizing, but they are deadly.

What, then, does it mean to obey? The answer to this question comes in looking at how Jesus obeyed His Father and what example He left for us.

Jesus obeyed the Father by first humbling His heart. Obedience is first a submission of the will. Like Jesus our hearts need to pray, "Your will be done, on earth as it is in heaven" (Matthew 6:10). This was not lip service for Jesus, for on another occasion He said, "My food is to do the will of Him who sent Me, and to accomplish His work" (John 4:34). Obedience was Jesus' life and passion. Jesus intertwines obedience with love, when He says, "If you love me, you will keep My commandments" (John 14:15). Loving, submissive obedience to Jesus was the means of maintaining a relationship to the Father. Jesus said, "If anyone loves Me, he will keep My word; and My Father will love him, and We will come to him, and make Our abode [home] with him" (v. 23). It is not an accident that Jesus in His confession of love to His Father connects His love to obedience: "but the world must learn that I love the Father and that I do exactly what my Father has commanded Me" (v. 31 NIV). Jesus humbled himself and took the form of a servant; and it was this mindset or attitude that made it possible in the Garden of Gethsemane for him to become obedient to the point of death, even death on a cross (Philippians 2:5-8). Obedience starts with an inward conquering of our wills, so that we too might say, "not My will, but Yours be done" (Luke 22:42).

Jesus obeyed the Father by listening to Him. The word "obey" comes from the Greek term, *hupakouō*, which literally means to "hear under." Wayne Detzler observed about the word that

> [in] secular Greek the word spoke of one standing at a door, listening intently, almost eavesdropping. Such was the reference in the writings of Plato to describe a doorkeeper. Later on the word came to mean obedience, for after one hears and understands a command or request, he should obey it.[7]

Inherent within the idea of hearing is one understanding what he has heard. Jesus put great importance on listening as a guide to His actions. In John 5:30 Jesus said, "I can do nothing on My own initiative. As I hear, I judge; and My judgment is just, because I do not seek My own will, but the will of Him who sent Me."[8] Jesus refused to be an innovator beyond the revealed will of His Father. His judgments were just because He accurately heard and did His Father's will – not His own. Jesus gave us the admonition at the close of the parable of the soils, "He who has ears to hear, let him hear" (Mark 4:9).

Listening – really listening – may be one of the hardest tasks of life. Our postmodern culture urges the manufacturing of our own truths, while New Testament Christianity urges us to listen to Jesus. It is the downfall of man that he is talking when he ought to be listening. Jesus said, "He who rejects Me, and does not receive My sayings, has one who judges him; the word I spoke is what will judge him at the last day" (John 12:48). Jesus makes our listening crucial to our judgment on the last day. Men need to make sure they have not only heard but have heard correctly. Blending our own desires and beliefs with the Word of Christ will cause us to pervert the message. Jesus was unwilling to do that with His Father, and Christians should be unwilling to do that as well. Half listening will bring about half obedience, and perverted listening will bring about perverted obedience. One cannot hear wrong and obey right.

Jesus cautions us to take heed how we hear and what we hear (Mark 4:24). The children of Israel listened to the bad report of the 10 spies and spent the next 38 years wandering in the wilderness. Rehoboam listened to the advice of the young men rather than to the wiser, older men and divided the kingdom of Israel. On the other hand, many Jews in the Jesus' day grew dull of hearing and hardened their hearts. They could not obey, because they would not obey. They simply did not want to hear what the Lord of Glory had to say. How we hear and what we hear will influence us to act accordingly. People believe false doctrines, because they have been listening to false doctrines. They were listening to the wrong source of information. There will always be someone saying what we would like to hear. In a society where market-driven churches are making decisions on the basis of appeal, one must be cautious that he is hearing the truth. False teaching outside the Word of God does not make true disciples (John 8:31). Misleading teaching makes misled people.

Jesus obeyed by doing exactly what He was told. On the night before His death, Jesus said, "the world must learn that I love the Father and that I do exactly what my Father has commanded Me" (14:31 NIV). In the Sermon on the Mount, Jesus contrasted the wise man and the foolish man in His concluding illustration. The wise man's house survived, but the other's did not. The wise man "hears these words of Mine, and acts upon them" (Matthew 7:24), but the foolish man "hears these words of Mine, and does not act upon them" (v. 26). It is not merely that the wise man acts; the wise man acts "upon" these words of Mine. The foolish man may or may not act, he may do what he wants, or he may act on another's advice. One thing is sure: he did not do what the words of Jesus told Him to do. He did nothing or did something else. Satan's counterfeiting provides something else to do which appears to be correct but is deadly. The two houses in the parable were probably very much alike. The difference between the foundations, however, was crucial. All through the Sermon on the Mount Jesus provided the contrast between a false religion and true devotion to the Lord. The warning Jesus gives of false prophets immediately before these verses must not be overlooked. The sermon is not dealing with failure to do anything but with doing the wrong things.

Jesus obeyed the Father by doing all the Father commanded. When Jesus died upon the cross, He could say, "It is finished" (John 19:30). The Scriptures make it clear that Jesus fully obeyed His Father. In His own baptism, Jesus sought to "fulfill all righteousness" (Matthew 3:15). He was not content to leave anything undone or unfinished in the work His Father had given Him. Jesus could pray before His Father, "I glorified You on the earth, having accomplished the work which You have given Me to do" (John 17:4). Jesus did all His Father asked of Him, and much of it was neither simple nor easy. Because He set His heart to seek first the Father's will, He accomplished the Father's work. He did it lovingly and did not complain. He did not ask the Father to change the rules or make exceptions. He lovingly, submissively, and devotedly heard His Father at every point.

In the same way, Jesus expects His apostles to teach His people "to observe all that I commanded you" (Matthew 28:20). Christianity is not a "smorgasbord" religion, in which its disciples may pick what they will and ignore the rest. To challenge any commandment of God is to challenge God Himself. To challenge God on the smallest point is still a small rebellion. If men only obey the commandments they like, they really have not obeyed God at all. What they have obeyed is their likes or choices. Postmodernism makes it easy to fool ourselves into thinking we may short God in our obedience but still expect His grace. Jesus calls that foolishness.

Obeying the Gospel

Some among churches of Christ say an immersed, penitent believer, even if somewhat misled in the purpose of baptism, is a true brother in Christ. They claim that if a person has been baptized for "a" right reason (although believing some wrong reasons), this baptism is as good as being baptized for all the right reasons. Specifically speaking, they believe one who has been baptized to obey God (even though they believe their sins were forgiven during a prior sinner's prayer), has obeyed the gospel as surely as a brother who believes his sins are forgiven at the time of his baptism. They maintain that while this person is misled, he has nonetheless obeyed the Lord.

What does the Bible say? The Bible clearly teaches baptism precedes salvation. While in times past there might have been some confusion over the meaning of the phrase, "for the forgiveness of your sins," in Acts 2:38, the message is much clearer today. In fact, in recent years several versions have translated Acts 2:28 so clearly there can be no misunderstanding. While some have alleged the phrase "for the remission of sins" means "because of," the consensus of the more recent versions argue convincingly against this view. We are not baptized because our sins have already been forgiven but so that our sins might be forgiven. Notice these versions' renderings of the phrase in Acts 2:38:

> Phillips: "so that you may have your sins forgiven."
> Today's English Version: "so that your sins will be forgiven."

Amplified New Testament: "for the forgiveness of and release from your sins."

Goodspeed: "in order to have your sins forgiven."

God's Word to the Nations: "so that your sins will be forgiven."

Contemporary English Version: "so that your sins will be forgiven."

Easy-to-Read Version: "Then God will forgive your sins."

McCord's: "so that your sins might be forgiven."

New International Version (1974): "so that your sins may be forgiven."

William Barclay: "so that your sins may be forgiven."

New Revised Standard Version: "so that your sins will be forgiven."

The Message: "so your sins are forgiven."

In addition to several versions, two prominent Greek lexicons support the view one is baptized to receive the forgiveness of his sins.[9] Commenting on the view of the early church, Everett Ferguson, one of the most highly regarded patristic scholars in America, said,

Quite impressive is the way all second-century authors speak of the meaning and benefits of baptism. Among the blessings ascribed to baptism in these writers are the following: remission of sins, salvation, illumination, eternal life, regeneration, and the gift of the Holy Spirit. ... The unanimity and vigor of the early second-century statements about baptism are presumptive of a direct relationship between baptism and forgiveness of sins from the early days of the church. The consistency with which second-century authors make the statements which they do would have been impossible if this had not been the common Christian understanding earlier. It is inconceivable that the whole Christian world reversed its understanding of the meaning of its central rite of conversion within fifty years of the lifetime of the apostles.[10]

Evidence suggesting salvation comes at the time of faith and a sinner's prayer but before baptism is just not encountered in second-century Christian writings. While an argument from early church history is not conclusive in and of itself, this one does confirm the teaching of the Scripture that baptism is when God forgives our sins.

The question comes back, "but must a person know that baptism is when his sins are forgiven in order for him to have a valid baptism?" From the time of Pentecost , the apostles taught people that forgiveness of sins follows baptism. Saul of Tarsus knew it (Acts 22:16); the Romans knew it (Romans 6:3-7); and the Colossians knew it (Colossians 2:12-13). Peter taught baptism saves (1 Peter 3:21). Jesus himself demanded one be born of water and the Spirit to enter the kingdom of God (John 3:3-7). Paul noted this "washing of regeneration" was the time when God saved and lavished His Spirit upon us (Titus 3:3-7). They all knew what Jesus desired in our obedience.

Not until the time of Huldrich Zwingli and John Calvin did men begin claiming baptism was a good work. Since good works cannot save, baptism does not save. This 16th-century teaching dominated Reformed theology, which greatly influenced the beliefs of English and American Evangelicals. This notion, however, found great resistance from Martin Luther, who in his *Large Catechism* grew alarmed that anyone would think baptism did not come of grace.[11] The continued wide circulation of the Reformed view has led many to accept it without question. The fact that large numbers hold this belief, however, does not make it right or true. Satan has successfully led large numbers of sincere and good people into deception quite often. He is a noteworthy counterfeiter to the masses.

The Roman Catholics believed baptism (which means immersion) was "for the forgiveness of sins; but Satan convinced them they could and should sprinkle unbelieving babies. The Anabaptists of the Reformed movement abandoned the sprinkling of babies and returned to immersing adults; but Satan led them to think baptism was not essential to salvation. One might ask: how can Baptists require Catholics to know baptism is immersion to be properly baptized, when Baptists are not required to know baptism is "for the re-mission of sins" to be properly baptized.

We are asking the question, "how much must one know about baptism for one's baptism to be valid?" If we require a person to know how he is to be baptized scripturally, ought we also to require him to know why he is being baptized scripturally? If a person is immersed "because his sins are already forgiven," he unwittingly is contradicting the Scriptures.

Obedience demands that one's heart be right, that one listen to the gospel, that one do the right thing, and that one fully obey. If this be true, how can the false, evangelical teaching on baptism fulfill the requirements of gospel obedience? The Scriptures nowhere speak of a "sinner's prayer" saving anyone; they nowhere speak of baptism as "an outward sign of an inward grace"; and they nowhere speak of salvation coming prior to baptism. Wrong information does not lead to right obedience. Distorted half-truths do not lead to obedience. When teachers mislead people, telling them to be baptized to make a declaration of their accomplished salvation, they are perverting the gospel. They may speak about obedience, but what are they obeying? Are they obeying Christ or obeying what they have been taught? A religious message which omits the essentiality of baptism is not the gospel of the New Testament. Satan has offered a counterfeit.

We now hear the question: "Should we baptize again someone who was mistaken about the purpose of baptism?"

If we were talking to a person who had been sprinkled for baptism, would we tell this person he has not been baptized scripturally? Of course, we would. Actually, to speak of baptizing him "again" is a mistake, since he has not been baptized scripturally. A sprinkled person may be baptized in the eyes of some, but he has not met Christ's gospel requirements. When we immerse him, we are now baptizing him as God desires. In the same way, a person who is immersed but misled as to purpose may think he has been baptized; but when he proclaims his salvation prior to baptism, he is not obeying the gospel of Christ. He has intended to do something other than, and contra-dicting, what God requires in His word. He is not acting so that his sins may be forgiven; he is declaring that God has already forgiven him. That may be an immersion, but it differs significantly from the baptism of the New Testament. How can anyone say he is obeying God, when he by his baptism is affirming something that is opposed to God's teachings. We are not then re-baptizing such a person because he has not yet been biblically baptized.

Let us include everyone and exclude no one who has scripturally obeyed the gospel. We should find those who previously have been misled into a supposed obedience of a counterfeit gospel and kindly and lovingly show them the way of the Lord more perfectly.

Discussion Questions

1. Describe the two kinds of inclusivism and how they the deal with biblical teaching.

2. What does Campbell mean by "general obedience?"

3. Upon what basis does God ever reject or exclude people?

4. What is forgiveness, and what distinguishes the forgiven from the unforgiven?

5. How did Jesus obey the commandments of His Father? What implications does His obedience have for the church today?

CHAPTER 9

Seeing the Big Picture
WE KNOW WHOM WE SERVE!

The question of how churches worshiped in song in the first century and how churches should worship in song today is important for anyone who seeks to do the will of God in every respect. While churches of Christ have generally agreed that vocal music is authorized and that instrumental music is sinful in worship, they are now questioning the roles people play in worship. They are asking if the Scriptures warrant solos or "special" singing by groups during the worship services. They are asking if humming, clapping, and unintelligible vocal sounds are scriptural in worship. They are wondering if the boundaries of Christian worship apply to hymns used in entertainment settings. Is it authorized to use small groups who sing hymns to entertain gatherings of Christians? If it is all right to have groups sing hymns after a banquet, why can they not be used in worship services? How do entertainment and worship differ? Can worship be entertaining? Can entertainment also be worship? What is edification and how does it relate to entertainment? Are small changes in our worship today opening doors for greater changes in the years to come? Are churches of Christ losing their distinctiveness by imitating denominational methods of worship? Are "worship teams" actually choirs in disguise?

Another source of confusion in the church today is the existence of so many professional performers among the many religious TV programs outside of the churches of Christ. Many members of the church watch such programs and wonder why worship services in churches of Christ cannot be more like the denominational churches. Many who watch these programs are convinced that the simple, traditional worship in churches of Christ cannot possibly compete with the slick, theatrical performances of others. It may be that some of the changes we are seeing in churches is to appeal to an audience that does not understand New Testament Christianity.

These questions disturb and confuse many. They are leading to a great deal of controversy and could divide the church. It is for this reason that we must reexamine the Scriptures in coordination with an honest look at our own practices. The Christian's goal is not only to remain biblical but also to please God in every way (Colossians 1:10). Jesus said, "I always do what pleases" the Father (John 8:29).

Some Basic Definitions

Worship: "to adore or pay divine honors to as a deity; to reverence with supreme respect and veneration."[1]

Entertain: "to engage the attention of, with anything that causes the time to pass pleasantly, as conversation, music or the like; to divert; to please; to amuse." Entertainment: "something that entertains; an interesting, diverting, or amusing thing, as a show or performance."[2] Entertainment in and of itself is by no means sinful. It has its place in the Christian life.

Perform: "to give a performance of; to render or enact, as a piece of music, dramatic role, etc." Performance: "a formal exhibition of skill or talent, as a play, musical program, etc.; a show."[3]

"Special" singing is often used to describe songs sung by solos or small groups.

Difference in Worship and Entertainment

God intends the worship of His church in song to be both vertical (speaking to God above) and horizontal (speaking to those around us). First, Scripture instructs Christians to "sing and make music in your heart to the Lord, always giving thanks to God the Father for everything, in the name of our Lord Jesus Christ" (Ephesians 5:19-20).

They are to "sing psalms, hymns and spiritual songs with gratitude in your hearts to God" (Colossians 3:16). The Hebrew writer urges, "Through Jesus, therefore, let us continually offer to God a sacrifice of praise – the fruit of lips that confess his name" (13:15). This vertical dimension must be present for any song to be regarded as worship. God is first and foremost the audience of our worship. Our first task is to adore and to please Him. Any act that takes the focus off God or acts to the glory of man rather than God can never be regarded as worship. Those who seek or accept praise for themselves rather than glorify God have in all times been responsible for grave error (Numbers 20:12; Psalm 19:13; Acts 12:20-23). Christians are to do all things to the glory of God (1 Corinthians 10:31).

Second, musical worship has a horizontal dimension. Paul exhorted the Ephesians to "Speak to one another with psalms, hymns and spiritual songs" (Ephesians 5:19). He instructed the Colossians: "Let the word of Christ dwell in you richly as you teach and counsel one another with all wisdom, and as you sing psalms, hymns and spiritual songs" (Colossians 3:16). One reason why Christians assembled together was to "encourage one another" (Hebrews 10:24-25). Paul instructed the church at Corinth that their psalms were to edify; "let all things be done for edification" (1 Corinthians 14:26). Worship directed toward God was also to "build up" brethren. All Christians have the responsibility of speaking, teaching and counseling one another.

The function of entertainment as a pastime must never be confused with the reverent and sacred act of worship.[4] One must wonder at the behavior of some of the contemporary singing groups who have blended their religious songs with an entertaining style. It has left many confused whether to call their activity entertainment or worship. One group described as leading the congregation in worship wore hats and sunglasses as they performed their concert. Such language about this event has a tendency to confuse and mislead. Did they worship or did they entertain? Are they ministers or performers? This confusion serves their purpose; for if they are criticized for their actions in worship, they say they are entertaining.

SEEING THE BIG PICTURE

And if they are accused of entertaining, they speak of their ministry, "leading the congregation in worship."

A further confusion related to worship and entertainment is the function of the heart. Some, not understanding the nature of worship, believe that the stirring of their hearts constitutes worship. Songs of all kinds have the ability to stir the heart. Dramatic, theatrical and love songs can be charged with great emotion and passion. Emotion does not make them songs of worship. Many songs that contain religious thoughts may be filled with fervor and passion but not be worship. For example, one might think of the hauntingly beautiful song that Mary Magdalene sings about Jesus in the Broadway play *Jesus Christ: Superstar*. Such lovely melodies may move us emotionally, but one could hardly recommend this song for worship (doctrinally or otherwise) because of the words. Singing to worship requires understanding (1 Corinthians 14:15); its purpose is to teach and admonish, to give thanks and to praise. Worship in song is the intentional act of the heart and lips to glorify God. One must remember that simply because the hearts of an audience are stirred, God's name may not have been glorified or His heart pleased by the aroma of the sacrifices.

Things that are holy are not to be cheapened by making them common. God's name is never to be taken or spoken in vain. To turn our worship into a performance or a show can never please God. It fails to give God the glory due His holy name. The worship of the tabernacle in the Old Testament was a serious matter to God, because He is a holy God. He insists on being treated holy. This theme is a major tenet of the books of Exodus through Deuteronomy. To treat worship as a common matter is a great offense to God, no matter how pleasing it may be to men. It is the same for the church today. Those who enter worship must never do anything that takes the focus off of the holy respect due to our God.

Realizing the importance of God-directed worship, Jimmy Jividen correctly observed: "God desires worship directed from the heart of man. All of the pomp of men, all of the orderliness of form, all of the beauty of art and all of the emotional stimulation evoked through drama and music cannot substitute for the simple devotion of an humble heart."[5]

The First-Century Church's Worship in Song

Knowing how the early church fulfilled the instructions of Ephesians 5:19 and Colossians 3:16 is important for discerning truth from error and for knowing how to apply these passages today. We really know very little about how the early church rendered its hymns in the earliest centuries.[6] The singing was more in the nature of what is called a chant than it was melodic. The more melodic compositions are attested only for the fourth century. Even then, the singing was homophonic (all singing on the same pitch), and not polyphonic as in modern harmonies.[7] The sacred music of the early church probably consisted of a few simple tunes which could easily be learned, and which, by frequent repetition, became familiar to all. According to Hilary, A.D. 355 (Comment. in Psa. xxv.), everyone participated, young and old, men and women, and had a part. John Chrysostom said, "It was the ancient custom, as it is still with us, for all to come together, and unitedly to join in singing. The young and old, rich and poor, male and female, bond and free, all join in one song. ... All worldly distinctions here cease, and the whole congregation forms one general chorus."[8]

It is possible that the early church fulfilled the directive to "sing," "speak," "teach and admonish one another" in a variety of ways:

Antiphonal Singing: when two groups would sing the lines or phrases of a psalm back and forth to each other. "Antiphonal singing in which the congregation was divided into two choirs and chanted alternately came in alongside the responsorial chant in the late fourth century."[9]

Responsorial Singing: when a leader would sing the lines or phrases of a song, and the congregation would respond in unison with the words of the chorus. Psalms 107 and 118 may have been sung in this manner. Pliny, in his letter to Trajan, spoke of Christian singing "in alternate verses a hymn to Christ, as to a god" (*Letters*, Book X.xcvi). Ferguson observes that the phrase, "alternate verses" "should not be understood as 'antiphonally.' What can be deducted from Jewish influence on Christian practice suggests congregational responses to what is recited by the leader."[10]

Some scholars argue that responsive singing was not generally practiced until early in the fourth century. They argue that since responsive singing was then common in the theatres and temples of the Gentiles, it may have been discarded by the primitive Christians for the first three centuries.[11]

Congregational Singing: when the congregation would sing a familiar psalm or hymn together in unison. In Romans 15:6 Paul wished that God would give the Romans a spirit of unity among themselves as they follow Christ Jesus, "so that with one heart and mouth you may glorify the God and Father of our Lord Jesus Christ." Ignatius about A.D. 110 wrote to Smyrna, "Therefore by your concord and harmonious love Jesus Christ is being sung. Now all of you together become a choir so that being harmoniously in concord and receiving the key not from God in unison you may sing with one voice through Jesus Christ to the Father (Ephesians 4)" (*Smyrneans* 7:2).

Solo Singing: when an individual sang a psalm for the edification of the church (1 Corinthians 14:26). These songs may have been inspired by the Holy Spirit. In context, the purpose was likely didactic (for teaching). The early church had no songbooks or overhead projectors, but the need for the congregation to sing a song remained. An individual had to teach the song verbally to others so that all might sing. We cannot imagine one singing a psalm in the early church in order to showcase one's artistic skills or presenting a concert (complete with tapes and T-shirts for sale).

What kind of singing is spoken of in Ephesians 5:19 and Colossians 3:16? The exhortation to "speak to one another" and to "teach and counsel one another" is an important help in understanding what kind of singing was practiced in the first century. According to Dana & Mantey's *A Manual Grammar of the Greek New Testament*, the phrase "one another" in both passages may be considered as "reciprocal pronouns." They define reciprocal action: "when a plural subject is represented as affected by an interchange of the action signified in the verb, it is called a reciprocal construction."[12] Others describe these as reflexive pronouns used reciprocally. A.T. Robertson says that this pronoun brings out the mutual relations involved. The idea is that a plurality of people are having an interchange of action with each other. All are participating and involved in both the giving and receiving of the action.[13] Neither passage speaks to individuals alone; both assume that a plurality of people is present. It is poor reasoning that argues these passages refer to the Christian life in general and has nothing to say to an assembly of saints. Both Ephesians and Colossians were cyclical epistles, designed to be read to churches while they were assembled. An epistle is not a personal letter between individuals but a formal, public letter from an authoritative person to a group. Everett Ferguson notes:

> The corporate life of the church is the theme throughout Ephesians and certainly chapters 4-6, the so-called practical section of the treatise. The corporate nature of what is described in Ephesians 5:19 is made explicit by the "one another" (cf. the same word in 4:32). Colossians adds that the "word of Christ" is to dwell "among you," "in your midst." Moreover, Ephesians is making a contrast between pagan religious practices, where drunkenness and immorality were often associated with the cult, and Christian worship (verse 18). Both Colossians and Ephesians are describing a setting where the word of the Lord is dispensed and song to God is engaged in.[14]

Objections to Small Group Singing, Solos and Choirs During Worship Services

Small group singing and solos may take the focus off God and put it on the performer(s). A recent advertisement for youth encouraged them to "showcase" their talents as part of a singing group that would "perform" before thousands of other young people. The purpose of worship is to glorify God. One must wonder at the wisdom of teaching our youth that worship is a time to "showcase" their talents! The emphasis here may be put on the beauty of the voice rather than on the greatness of God. Such a concept forgets that God Himself is the audience. Our worship is to be directed to Him so that we might offer to Him a sacrifice of praise. Worship was never intended to be showy. Such an idea could never reflect the respect and reverence due to our Creator and Savior. Singing hymns is a sacred act of the heart and lips; its sole purpose is to express love and gratitude for God. People can perform the right act but with the wrong motive. Jesus sharply condemned the Pharisees for their "showy" religion (Matthew 6:1-18). We too must be careful that we do not practice our acts of righteousness to be seen.

Small group singing and solos are exclusive rather than inclusive. By their very nature choruses ask for trained singers and melodic voices. One music ministry advertised for singers to audition to be a part of their chorus. One must wonder if there are qualifications as to which Christians may worship publicly. The Scriptures, after all, instruct every Christian to sing. Why should anyone be excluded from worshiping because he is a poor singer or tone deaf? If God does not care whether a brother or sister is tone deaf, why should we? When small groups perform, there will always be the question of who may be a part of it. Artistic concerns, then, become a standard of inclusion and exclusion. Such standards could never have been part of the first century church. Paul opposed at every turn the sectarianism, arrogance and jealousy that the immature church at Corinth had experienced with their spiritual gifts. Solos and small group singing will inevitably lead to conflicts among the immature. The problems of jealousy and ego based upon musical skill will abound. Most denominations have had enduring problems with choirs, for it grants the opportunity for the worst in personalities to come out.

One must ask why anyone would pursue unnecessarily a course of exclusiveness. In many cases those who support special singing are those who have good voices and want to "showcase their talents." One may rightfully ask if the good singers were excluded from a program, how would they feel? Would they still feel that the worship is pleasing? Would they be hurt by being excluded? Would they feel unneeded? If a church were assembling a choir, there are some Christians who would never be asked to join. The reason is because they are not good singers. In small group singing and solos, artistic concerns become more important than one's right to adore God. We must ask when has God ever considered musical skill as a criteria for his worshipers? Why should anyone who has that skill have the right to include or exclude anyone on the basis of that skill?

The quibble is brought up here about part singing. If some parts sing while the rest remain silent in part of a song, why can some parts not sing the whole song while others listen? Further, if one part can sing a whole song, why can it not sing the whole service? In response we ask: if only the sopranos or only the basses sang a whole service, how could the others fulfill their responsibility to sing? Every Christian has the responsibility to sing when he has gathered with his brothers and sisters. In part singing where one group sings part of a song alone (such as the females singing the verses in "Angry Words"), the men temporarily do not sing the verses but are not altogether excluded from singing. This is not unlike the action in antiphonal or responsorial singing, both of which do not exclude anyone from singing some of the song.

Choirs as a separate group from the congregation were not present among the earliest Christians. It was an innovation that led to special singers for the congregation. Because they sang more difficult songs, others ceased to sing. According to McClintock & Strong,

> The appointment of singers as a distinct class of officers in the Church for their part of religious worship, and the consequent introduction of profane music into the church, marks another alteration in the psalmody of the Church. These innovations were first made in the 4th century; and though the people continued for a century or more to enjoy their ancient privilege of all singing together, it is conceivable that it gradually was forced to die, as a promiscuous assembly could not well unite in theatrical music which required in its performers a degree of skill, altogether superior to that which all the members of a

congregation could be expected to possess. An artificial, theatrical style of music, having no affinity with the worship of God, soon began to take the place of those solemn airs which before had inspired the devotions of his people. The music of the theatre was transferred to the church, which accordingly became the scene of theatrical pomp and display rather than the house of prayer and praise, to inspire by its appropriate and solemn rites the spiritual worship of God (VI:758).

McClintock and Strong further observe that until the sixth or seventh century the people were not entirely excluded from participating in the singing. They were allowed to sing in the choruses and in the responses. But "it soon came about that the many, instead of uniting their hearts and their voices in the songs of Zion, could only sit coldly by as spectators" (Ibid.).

Solos and small group singing asks the members of a church to worship through others. If one silently listens to others sing, one has not fulfilled his responsibility to praise God with his lips, to speak, to teach or to admonish. Every Christian has the responsibility to sing, and no one else can fulfill that responsibility for him. Although one's heart has been stirred by another's singing, one has not sung if one has merely "sung in his heart." Singing is an act of both the heart and the lips. To sing and not make melody in one's heart is not worship. It mocks God! In the same way, to stir one's heart but not speak with one's lips, is to fail to do what God has asked.

May one please God simply by observing others partaking of communion? Although one's heart may be stirred greatly in the remembering, has one obeyed the directive if he has not eaten the bread or drunk the cup?

May one please God simply by observing others contributing to the Lord's church? Although one's heart may be stirred deeply with love and gratitude, has one obeyed the Lord's instructions?

Has one become a Christian who has observed another being baptized? Although in his heart he may have believed and genuinely repented, is he regarded as obedient if he is not baptized? Obedience must be heartfelt (Romans 6:17-18), but one is not free from sin until he has acted in obedience. The heart and the act are necessary.

No one can worship for another. Observing another person fulfill his responsibility is not the same as one worshiping the Lord for himself.

Some argue that a mute person is not able to speak and thus fulfill the command. Does God not accept his worship in his heart? Yes, God accepts what a man can give and does not expect from him what he cannot do (2 Corinthians 8:12). But this is far different from a man who can sing and does not except in his heart. May one who is capable of giving money to the Lord do so in his heart only? What has this brother really given?

Another complaint is only one person prays audibly, yet the whole congregation is praying. Actually churches did often pray corporately. In Acts 4:24 when Peter and John were released from prison, they went back to their own people and reported all that had happened. "When they heard this, they raised their voices together in prayer to God." The word for "together" in Greek is *homothumadon*, an adverb, meaning "with one mind or purpose or impulse; unanimously."[15] Ferguson notes that prayers "as well as the Psalms were performed responsively (bTaanith 16b)."[16] It was the custom for the whole congregation to say "Amen" at the conclusion of a prayer (1 Corinthians 14:16). No one was excluded from saying, "Amen," and thereby participating in an active way.

There is a difference between the nature of prayer and singing. Prayer is one-way communication from man to God. One may pray to God for others. It is vertical. Singing, on the other hand, is both vertical and horizontal. Singing is speaking to one another, teaching one another, and counseling one another. It is to be reciprocal. Each one has the responsibility of edifying his brother through his own singing.

What about "Worship Teams?"

A worship team is a group of singers who lead the congregation in singing. While there is a song leader of the team and congregation, the group of both men and women singers each lead the congregation in his or her voice part. While they may not stand in front of the congregation as a choir would, they might sit on the front row. Each of them usually has his or her own microphone to amplify the voice part he or she sings. The purpose of worship teams is to enhance the worship and to encourage others to sing.

There are some advantages to worship teams. Each voice part is amplified so that the altos, for instance, may hear and sing their part correctly. The teaching capability in this matter is certainly advantageous. The sound of all parts takes on a richer tone quality, so that it is quite pleasing to the ear. One might even suppose, because of the amplification, that there are more people present than the crowd appears to have. The amplified voices are much more harmonious than merely amplifying only the song leader.

On the other hand, like choirs there is the tendency with worship teams to sit and listen to the group sing rather than to sing along. The amplified voices occasionally drown out the congregation much the way a piano or organ stifles singing. Another stifling aspect of this approach is that the team often sings new songs unfamiliar to the congregation. During these times the congregation becomes little more than spectators. While it is beneficial for the congregation to learn new songs, a regular practice of singing unfamiliar songs could make the team appear to be an exclusive and elitist group. The problems of the past comes very much into play here. Will worship teams over time lead many in the church to quit fulfilling their obligation to edify one another in song? Are worship teams merely a step away from choirs? Already worship teams have moved from the front row to the stage in front of the groups. We must ask why gifted singers may have microphones to the exclusion of others and why their singing appears like a performance.

Colleges, Quartets and Banquets

Christian colleges are not churches. They have every right to have choruses to represent their schools. Christian colleges have done immeasurable good by training young men and women in vocal music. The singing in churches everywhere is better because of the training that thousands of students have received. Colleges choruses have provided programs for their lectureships and to churches around the world. Their positive influence for the Lord and for their respective schools is unquestionable. Many souls have been drawn to the Lord by their efforts.

Everyone enjoys hearing trained voices sing the spiritual songs they love most. It uplifts, encourages and edifies one to hear beautiful hymns either in person or on tape. Colleges and singing groups have provided a wonderful source of encouragement by recording the moments when they are praising God. Christians who buy such inspiring tapes have invested wisely.

Christians who gather informally for festive occasions often ask trained groups or quartets to sing religious songs and hymns. Usually this practice is considered entertainment, though it may have religious overtones. This practice should not be looked upon with suspicion. Entertainment that delights our hearts and causes us to think of the Lord and His love for us is positive and not negative. Such groups are not attempting to worship for others or replace worship with a performance. They do not seek to exclude others from worshiping, because that is not their aim. Their aim is to pass the time pleasantly by providing delightful songs with religious themes. Christian entertainment is not unjustified.

Entertainment settings should not be regarded as periods of worship. It would be better for some religious entertainment groups who are performing not to leave the impression that they are there to worship. Herein lies the confusion. Hats, sunglasses, cute remarks and jokes are appropriate for entertainment but not worship. There is no harm in clapping with appreciation for the entertainer, but clapping in worship seems to take the focus off of God and put it on the performer. To be caught up in the skill of a performer and to lose sight of God dilutes and cheapens worship. The rock star status accorded to some entertainers has little place next to the Cross. In worship the focus must be on praising God, not the skills of men. Worship put on for show is clearly condemned in Scripture (Matthew 6:1-18; 23:5-12). Such worshipers have already received their reward.

What is done in entertainment settings, though it be a gathering of Christians, should not be held as a pattern for what is to be done on the Lord's day. Distinguishing between such settings, as the church has done for many years, keeps the boundaries of entertainment and worship definitive. The recent blurrings of these distinctions, coupled with the exposure to so many denominational worship services on television, services which feature professional performers, has created the confusion.

Humming, Clapping and Unintelligible Sounds

In recent years some groups have tried to enhance their singing by making unintelligible, background sounds with their voices. These sounds imitated instruments of music and often functioned as an accompaniment. Some were so good that the casual listener might not be able to tell the difference between a drum, for instance, and the vocal sound. The reasoning behind such vocal accompaniment was that as long as the sound was vocal, it was approved.

The fact that a sound is vocal does not mean that it necessarily fulfills the instruction to speak, teach and admonish. Drums, for instance, cannot speak; why would one want to imitate them as an act of worship? They do not do what God asks. People imitate drums to make their music sound more like the music of those who use instruments.

Jimmy Jividen points out that understanding is an essential element in worship in song (1 Corinthians 14:14-16):

> The importance of "understanding" is shown by Paul in his correcting the abuse of spiritual gifts at Corinth. It would appear that those who possessed the miraculous gifts of speaking foreign languages were causing confusion in the assemblies of the church. In their enthusiasm to show off their spiritual gift, they would all speak at the same time in whatever language their gift allowed. Confusion was the result.

Paul tried to correct this situation by showing that one cannot worship God or edify others with words which are not understood. Speaking words in a prayer or a song which one does not understand is not worship. It is unfruitful to the one uttering the words. Speaking words in a prayer or a song which those in the assembly do not understand is not worship. It is confusion.[17]

If speaking a foreign language is not edifying, how much more so is making unintelligible, vocal sounds! The fact that it enhances the effect of the music does not make it biblical. It smacks of hypocrisy to claim all sounds are vocal (a cappella) yet make vocal sounds that sound as if they were instruments of music. The Hebrew writer urges, "Through Jesus, therefore, let us continually offer to God a sacrifice of praise – the fruit of lips that confess his name" (13:15). The worship of the church is not only vocal, it is in the form of intelligent words that "confess."

Clapping during worship has a long history. McClintock & Strong observed that Neander regretted that in his day the sacred music of both Eastern and Western churches had already assumed "an artificial and theatrical character, and was so far removed from its original simplicity that even in the fourth century the abbot Pambo of Egypt complained of heathen melodies being introduced into the worship of the church accompanied "as it seems with the action of the hands and feet."[18] Isidore of Pelusium also complained of the theatrical singing, especially of the women, which instead of inducing penitence for sin, tended much more to awaken sinful desires (in *Biblioth. Patr.* vii, 543). One must wonder at the wisdom of clapping. Would it not be more scriptural for brethren to say a hearty, "Amen!"?

Conclusion

Michael R. Weed stated a few years ago in the *Christian Chronicle,* "It is high time that Christians decide whether the church – and particularly Christian worship – is going to become a kind of religious Disneyland – entertainment and excitement for both young and old – or, if it is going to be something else."

Perhaps our problem is that we are far more concerned with the effects of worship on the worshiper than on the One we worship. Have we pleased God in our acts of adoration? Singing praises to the Father is a privilege as well as an obligation. We must not allow our feelings and tastes to keep us from the primary task of glorifying His name. Nor can we in any way exclude any brother or sister from participating in the joyful celebration of God in our songs of praise. Yes, we must strive for excellence in our singing, for God deserves our best. But God wants the best from everyone not merely the selected few who are trained.

Let us strive to make our worship more reverent and meaningful. Let's sing with our hearts and lips a message of love and thanksgiving to the Father, while we teach and counsel one another. Let's not be afraid to learn new songs or to sing old ones in a fresh, new way. May our hearts and minds focus upon the words that we may sincerely and with understanding praise our God. Let's also examine our songs that we may worship in truth and not promote any error.

During those periods when we relax with each other, we should not be afraid to laugh and enjoy ourselves with entertainment. Rejoice in the Lord, and again, I will say, rejoice! Let some sing spiritual melodies that uplift and encourage our hearts. There is no sin in Christian entertainment as long as we do not confuse our entertainment with worship.

Discussion Questions

1. Discuss the meanings of the two words "worship" and "entertainment." Can worship be entertaining, and can entertainment be worship?

2. What are the reasons for the "vertical" and "horizontal" uses of musical worship?

3. What are some of the ways the early church fulfilled the instruction to sing?

4. How may solos and small group singing be exclusive?

5. What role does the mind or understanding play in our worship?

CHAPTER 10

Charting the Strait Course
PLOTTING A STRATEGY FOR HEAVEN

We are more knowledgeable today than at any time in history, but this is not an indication that we are wiser. There is a current belief that somehow the great knowledge of our times creates for us a world that does not need the wisdom of God. We have led ourselves to believe that we have the answers in our own wisdom.

From the days of Freud, Christians have been somewhat intimidated that our truths did not measure up to the latest findings of psychology. Preachers and elders suddenly found themselves unable to counsel anyone, because all they knew was a little about life and the Scriptures. Consequently, the Bible lost its authority with many Christians because we came to believe that the "old-fashioned," naive Bible did not have as much to offer us as psychology.

In later days, we were to learn that sociological findings were the key to growing large churches. We figured that if we could get the right mix of popular appeal, we could get people through our doors. In time, methods and attractiveness became a greater influence in church activity than the gospel itself. Ear-tickling replaced sound teaching in the name of being able to reach out. Gaining people (not their souls) became more important than teaching the truth. Appearance became more important than substance. As a result, we found it expedient to experiment with our worship, our sermons, our buildings and our truths. No cow became too sacred that it could not be sacrificed to "win" more people. We did not ask what we were winning them to; we just had to get them through the doors.

Churches of Christ like others in our religious world discovered they could market the faith in a way that attracted people. They learned that "felt needs" was a way to connect. Unfortunately for some, connecting became the focus of their efforts. Meeting "felt needs" in the quest for numbers became sovereign in their strategy. John MacArthur lamented the direction of evangelical groups, when he said,

> No longer are pastors trained to declare to people what God demands of them. Instead, they are counseled to find out what the people's demands are, then do whatever is necessary to meet them. The audience is regarded as "sovereign," and the wise preacher will "shape his communications according to their needs in order to receive the response he seeks."

> The effect of such a philosophy is apparent; more and more people-pleasers fill the pulpits of our churches. Moreover, Scripture is overruled by the marketing plan as the authoritative guide for ministry. One textbook on church marketing includes this statement: "The marketing plan is the Bible of the marketing game; everything that happens in the life of the product occurs because the plan wills it." Applied to church ministry, that means a human strategy – not the Word of God – becomes the fountain of all church activity, and the standard by which ministry is measured.[1]

The primary task of the devoted Christian is to love God with all of his heart, all of his soul, all of his mind, and all of his strength (Mark 12:30). No matter how successful he has been in other matters, if he fails at this he has failed entirely. Jesus' question is entirely appropriate for the builder of a great church: "For what will a man be profited, if he gains the whole world, and forfeits his soul? Or what will a man give in exchange for his soul?" (Matthew 16:26).

Satan would like nothing better than to lure us into a false sense of security with great numbers and apparent success. The deceiver of this world is, after all, a master at appearances and deceit. The prince of the power of the air would love to replace our faith with the latest technology and science. He has been telling us since the beginning that we can become our own God, and now Satan has given us the tools. According to him, the Bible needed help to teach and train us to do the work of service. Satan has supplied that training with all the bells and whistles. All it costs is our souls. In our own subtle way, we have lost sight of the supremacy and the all-sufficiency of the Scriptures.

Going to heaven not only demands our obedience to the gospel but also hearts that are aflame in doing the whole will of God. Baptism does not the end our relationship with God but begins it. Jesus instructed His apostles to teach the baptized converts to "observe all that I commanded you; and lo, I am with you always, even to the end of the age" (28:20). God is not merely concerned with our knowledge of the truth; He wills that we should live it out in our lives. We cannot earn salvation by our own efforts, but we are to work out our salvation (Ephesians 2:8; Philippians 2:12). We are to bring every thought captive to the obedience of Christ (2 Corinthians 10:5). Paul admonished the Romans, and he admonishes us, "And do not be conformed to this world, but be transformed by the renewing of your mind, that you may prove what the will of God is, that which is good and acceptable and perfect" (Romans 12:2). The Scriptures are complete and are not in need of editing, improving or changing. We presume that we are wiser than God when we think we have a better plan than He does.

It is easy to lose sight of our primary task of serving God. We may easily fool ourselves, thinking our numbers and good times guarantee we are pleasing God. Like others around us we may be contenting ourselves with what appears to be religious but has little substance. We may follow our religious neighbors into popular piety that is religiously impotent. Concerning evangelicalism, D.A. Carson in *The Gagging of God*, noted:

American evangelicalism is in desperate need of intellectual and theological input. We have noted that not a little evangelical television is almost empty of content. It is mawkishly sentimental, naively optimistic, frighteningly ignorant, openly manipulative. Let me again insist: I am not arguing for dry intellectualism, for abstract disputation. But entertainment is not enough; emotional appeals based on tear-jerking stories do not change human behavior; subjective experiences cannot substitute for divine revelation; evangelical clichés can never make up for lack of thought. The mentality that thinks in terms of marketing Jesus inevitably moves toward progressive distortion of him; the pursuit of the next emotional round of experience easily degenerates into an intoxicating substitute for the spirituality of the Word. There is non-negotiable, biblical, intellectual content to be heralded with conviction and compassion; by all means ... try to think through how to cast this content in ways that engage the modern secularist. But when all the footnotes are in place, my point remains the same: the historic gospel is unavoidably cast as intellectual content that must be taught and proclaimed.[2]

What Carson suggested of evangelicalism rings true of some churches of Christ. We ought to be alarmed when congregations have speakers that one could listen to for many weeks and not know what to do to obey the gospel. Paul knew "the time will come when they will not endure sound doctrine; but wanting to have their ears tickled, they will accumulate for themselves teachers in accordance to their own desires; and will turn away their ears from the truth, and will turn aside to myths" (2 Timothy 4:3-4). Many people find it more enjoyable to hear heart-rending stories than to hear a call for repentance or doctrinal truths. Many people would rather hear some word of reassurance than hear the truth about one church or one baptism. People want to know what the church stands for not what the church stands against. They do not want to hear anything that "reproves" or "rebukes." The ban on condemning reigns strong in the hearts of those given to their own desires.

The power of God unto salvation lies in the Word itself. Knowing that man could not save Himself, God chose to save believers by the preached message (1 Corinthians 1:21). Only the gospel itself has the power to save (Romans 1:16). Only God gives the increase (1 Corinthians 3:7). God alone has the power to forgive; we must remember forgiveness is a spiritual matter which takes place in His heart. No matter how loudly one proclaims his forgiveness, God will do things His way. Only God has the right to set the terms of forgiveness, and He has but one gospel (Galatians 1:6-9). Nothing can substitute for the gospel.

Evangelists need to remember to let the Word do its work. A watered-down gospel does a watered-down job. A user-friendly gospel may attract many people, but it may not be effective in bringing about meaningful transformation. We cannot please God by believing "somewhat" or repenting "somewhat." Jesus did not "somewhat" bear the cross; He suffered and died on it. We have not been called to bear a padded cross that never offends us; we have been called to die to this world and live to Christ (Galatians 2:20; 6:14). Churches cannot build strong faith or strong morals by compromise with the world. Salt is not worth much if you cannot taste the salt (Matthew 5:13). Diluting the gospel brings about diluted lives and weak members who hardly make any impact on a lost world. They are neither good to God nor good for the world. Devotion to the Lord and His Word makes Christians savory and effective.

The current doubts so prevalent in postmodernism have not left the church unaffected. Some have openly expressed uncertainty as to the inspiration and inerrancy of Scripture. Believing Scripture contradicts itself, they see the authority of Scripture in an inner witness rather than through an entirely trustworthy text. Their convictions rise more from their own leap of faith than from confidence in God's Word as God-breathed. Such faith is self-centered not God-centered. They make their own faith rather than receive the revealed one. This may explain why some find it so easy to set aside the instructions of God for more palatable views. For them, women can now serve in leadership roles, baptism is no longer essential to salvation, instrumental music in worship is a matter of opinion, and the church is one denomination among many.

George Barna in *Evangelism That Works* expressed his fear of the bad theology being preached among evangelicals. "This is frightening because evangelizers pass along what they believe as if it were the truth. Consequently, we have a nation of well-meaning believers who are sharing the gospel with nonbelievers but who are also sharing heresy (i.e., incorrect theology and doctrine)."[3] Barna specifies these heresies:

- One-fourth do not believe that the Bible is accurate in all that it teaches.

- One-third contend that if people are generally good or do enough good things for others during their lives, they will earn a place in heaven, thus negating the necessity of God's grace.

- Four out of every 10 evangelizers believe it does not matter what religious faith a person follows because all faiths teach similar lessons about life.

- One-fourth acknowledge that Jesus made mistakes.

Churches of Christ must not ignore the compromised beliefs creeping in among us. It is not enough for us to ask if our teachers believe in the inspiration of the Scriptures, we must further ask what kind of inspiration they believe. Some frankly believe that Matthew was inspired about as much as Shakespeare. When you hear their teaching, you hear a human explanation for the existence of nearly every passage. It should not surprise us that some have bought into the beliefs of the Jesus Seminar. They dare to make judgments on whether Jesus actually said what the gospels say He said or whether early Christian communities selectively used His words to press their agendas. We are hearing more and more questions about the canon of the Scripture, as if men determined what books belong in the New Testament. The goal is to convince us today that the Scriptures were the product of the church rather than the product of the Holy Spirit. By this means they can press the cultural argument (whatever was said in the first century was the church's response to their problems in their time and not binding today).

If we cannot place our full confidence in the Scriptures as God's teaching for us today, then what hope do we have? Some have suggested that God's Word is accurate in some places but not in others. If we cannot rely on the Word of God to be sure in its history, geography or its instructions, then how can we be sure of its promises? Faith in God is not selective; it cannot choose to believe what it likes and reject what it does not like. We must understand that we know God Himself through His revealed Word (1 Corinthians 1:21). Since the very character of God can be found in His written Word, we question His trustworthiness when we question Scripture.

If we preach a faith filled with questions and doubts, we really have little to say to a lost and dying world. If we only suppose we have the truth and if we cannot lay our full confidence down in an authoritative and final Word from God, then our message is never much more than a confused hope. James pictures doubters vividly; they are "like the surf of the sea driven and tossed by the wind. For let not that man expect that he will receive anything from the Lord, being a double-minded man, unstable in all his ways" (James 1:6-8). We cannot preach an unstable and changing gospel effectively. Should we attempt to do so, we can never be certain that our gospel has not changed, and we did not know it. Our assurance comes from the fact that God has spoken finally and fully. We can have conviction about God and His word because He does not change. We can believe in one gospel, one church, one faith and one baptism because we believe what the one Lord said. If our message in the end is "we are not sure," then why should the world listen to us? If we must take back or continuously qualify what we have said, then why say it at all?

Surely the apostles did not preach the death, burial and resurrection of Jesus with such apprehension and uncertainty. With boldness and confidence they spoke openly and clearly what they knew. What they preached became a stumbling block to the Jews and foolishness to the Greeks, but they did back off. They did not allow the Sanhedrin's ban on their preaching or their consequent flogging to keep them from their proclamation. Their own persecution and blood testifies to their unshakable faith as eyewitnesses of His majesty. They bore their crosses and did not look back to see if the world agreed or approved. Their prime directive was to preach the once for all faith to every culture. Their conviction gave their souls and their message strength; a faith filled with doubts would never have survived.

The kind of men we choose as our leaders will determine the kind of people we will have filling our pews. If we have men of faith, we will see people of faith; but if we have men who compromise and spread uncertainty, we will have confused and questioning people. Remarkably, many who pose questions and doubts speak of their mature faith. It is almost as if doubting is superior to faith and questioning superior to confidence. They imply faith is naive and childish, while the mature person questions the text. Such statements remind me of the marketers of pornography who are always claiming that the sinful behavior is for "mature" audiences. Paul told Timothy to "flee youthful lusts" (2 Timothy 2:22). The fornication, sensuality, homosexuality and adultery promoted by pornography seems far more in line with "youthful" lusts than with the maturity of a biblical marriage. The devil, however, knows his schemes. He knows he must display his products in the best possible light. He promises appearance but has no intent to deliver the substance. Mature doubts appear far better than naive faith. The doubter appears knowledgeable, asking questions that the common believer would not think to ask.

In Ezekiel 34, the Lord laments the shepherds of Israel who were not fulfilling their duties of feeding and protecting the flocks. We can only marvel at elders who have lost sight of the truth and have caved in to selfish demands of their flocks. In some cases they themselves fulfilled Paul's warning about those who tickle ears. When churches hire preachers who fulfill their desires rather than preach God's Word faithfully, they have lost sight of what God has called them to do and to believe. Elders who seek for flashy but unsound preachers to fill their pulpits or to present their seminars say to their members that they will compromise in order to please everyone. If churches compromise their faith to gain numbers or prestige, they will have little to boast about on the Day of Judgment.

In many areas where churches of Christ are plentiful, church hopping and shopping has become the norm. Elders may be tempted to place such a priority on appearances and numbers that they lose sight of spirituality and soundness. The fear of losing some young families (which hurts the attendance and the budget) may lead some leaders to make hasty and unwise choices. Some groups of families who have an agenda have actually held their leaders hostage by threatening to leave (or to withhold contributions) if the elders do not respond to their requests. Such selfish rebellion shows little respect for God, for the Scriptures, or for God's leaders (Hebrews 13:7, 17). Further, elders who cave in to such demands often lose their ongoing ability to provide meaningful leadership to the congregation.

The thinking of the world does not lead men to heaven, nor does it help us to love the Lord God with all our hearts and souls. We must be careful not to trade the truth for a worldly pragmatism. Some of what passes for church growth has little to do with New Testament Christianity. Pleasing God and feeding the "felt" desires of the unchurched may have little in common. It will be little compensation on the day of judgment if a church meets the family needs, educational needs, financial counseling needs, emotional needs, physical exercise needs, and social needs of its members but fails to preach grace and repentance. What good will be accomplished if a church prays for a physically sick brother but perverts the gospel to its own destruction? Good works and piety do not cancel out or excuse doctrinal sin. While Jesus praised Pergamum for their faithfulness in some things, He condemned them for holding the teachings of Balaam and the Nicolaitans. Jesus demanded, "Repent therefore; or else I am coming to you quickly, and I will make war against them with the sword of My mouth" (Revelation 2:16). If we could get into the heads of the church members at Pergamum, we could likely hear their reasons for following the teachings of Balaam and the Nicolaitans. They probably saw some great advantage in their lives; they might even have suggested that these advances would help the church to grow. It pleased them to hold these teachings, but it did not please God. The Nicolaitans were an antinomian group, "which had accommodated itself to the religious and social requirements of the pagan society in which they lived."[4] To be antinomian is to be against the restraints of law; they simply were not willing to live by the standards of Jesus with regard to moral purity.

An adrift church does not desire the restraints of Christ's teachings. It prefers to be set free and do its own thing, but it wants to maintain its validation and acceptance. It wants the benefits of Christianity but not the restraints. It wants the "Savior" Jesus but not the "Lord" Christ. It wants the love and warmth of God as long as it is free to pursue its own way. Far from praying what Jesus prayed at Gethsemane, the adrift church demands its own will be done. In its self-preoccupation it forgets what Jesus did to bring it into existence and what its prime task is.

The adrift church has adopted a philosophy of pragmatism, i.e., "if it works, it must be good." Though churches of Christ used to ask the question of whether an activity were scriptural, the question now seems to be whether it works. Amazingly, when something does work, churches quickly find a rationale to justify it. They quickly point out that one cannot argue with success. Never mind that worldly success and spiritual success differ. Concerning this bankrupt philosophy among his own, John MacArthur said,

> Do you see how the new philosophy necessarily undermines sound doctrine? It discards Jesus' own methods –
> preaching and teaching – as the primary means of ministry. it replaces them with methodologies utterly devoid
> of substance. It exists independently of any creed or canon. In fact, it avoids dogma or strong convictions as
> divisive, unbecoming, or inappropriate. It dismisses doctrine as academic, abstract, sterile, threatening, or simply
> impractical. Rather than teaching error or denying truth, it does something far more subtle, but just as effective

174

from the enemy's point of view. It jettisons content altogether. Instead of attacking orthodoxy head on, it gives lip service to the truth while quietly undermining the foundations of doctrine. Instead of exalting God, it denigrates the things precious to Him. In that regard, pragmatism poses dangers more subtle than the liberalism that threatened the church in the first half of the century.[5]

The prophecy Paul made so many years ago has become reality before our very eyes. Paul said, "For the time will come when they will not endure sound doctrine; but wanting to have their ears tickled, they will accumulate for themselves teachers in accordance to their own desires; and will turn away their ears from the truth, and will turn aside to myths" (2 Timothy 4:3-4).

The charismatics on television have made a profound impact on the weak among members of the church. Religious entertainment with tear-jerking stories, star-studded music, and circus hype has prompted some to believe our worship in churches of Christ is dull and boring. Longing for more excitement and believing that we are lacking in spirituality, they have sought to substitute theatrics and performances for our plain ways. Simple, heartfelt worship is no longer enough. We must have glitzy stars with trained voices under theatre lights and wearing stage makeup.

Preachers must become story tellers of the love of God. Amusements must replace sound teaching, and we must use semantic gymnastics to avoid the difficult or harsh truths of Scripture. We are told that we should never call anyone a sinner. We are pointed to the unconditional love of God that is supposed never to be judgmental or negative.[6] We are told that if we mention sin or guilt, we are mean-spirited and unloving. If we speak of doctrinal right or wrongs, we are called irrelevant.

The greatest taboo is to speak of hell. A survey among evangelical seminary students revealed that 46 percent believed preaching about hell to unbelievers is in "poor taste."[7] One can only suspect that some among churches of Christ feel the same.

For many Christians, the concept of sin itself is outmoded. Recently, in an interview with Robert Schuller, Billy Graham stated,

> I think everybody who knows Christ, whether they're conscious of it or not, they're members of the Body of Christ ... God's purpose is to call out a people for His name, whether they come from the Muslim world, Buddhist world, the Christian world, or the non-believing world, they are members of the Body of Christ, because they've been called by God. They may not even know the name of Jesus ... and I think they are saved, and that they are going to be in heaven with us.

> Robert Schuller (overjoyed): What I hear you saying is that it's possible for Jesus Christ to come into human hearts and soul and life even if they've been born into darkness and never had exposure to the Bible. Is that a correct interpretation of what you are saying?

> Billy Graham: Yes it is, because I believe that. I've met people in various parts of the world ... that have never seen a Bible or heard about a Bible, and never heard of Jesus, but they've believed in their hearts that there was a God.[8]

Such statements shock us as we recall the Scriptures. Jesus says that He is the only way to God (John 14:6); there is none other name under heaven by which we must be saved (Acts 4:12). Jesus said clearly that unless one believed in Him as the Messiah, one would die in sin (John 8:24). Surely if one could be saved apart from the gospel, one might wonder why Graham or anyone else needs to preach it.

The times in which we live are not so very different from the days of Jeremiah. Spiritually decaying Judah was rushing headlong into captivity. Self-deceived prophets were speaking out the imagination of their own hearts (Jeremiah 23:16-41) and calling their messages an "oracle of the Lord." Without shame they practiced and taught things of their own devising and which God had never authorized. When every man's own thinking becomes equivalent to the revelation of God, then one can be sure that God's displeasure is imminent. They prophesied continued peace and the blessing of God, in spite of the people's idolatry and rebellion. Jeremiah cried out against them and their false sense of security, "Is not My word like fire?" declares the LORD, "and like a hammer which shatters a rock?" (23:29). God had told them of their impending disaster if they did not repent. They did not want to hear Jeremiah; the people preferred their prophets who were saying "peace, peace" (4:10; 6:14; 8:11). Nebuchadnezzar marched in and destroyed their peace with all Jerusalem.

Preachers must preach the whole counsel of God (Acts 20:27). A selective gospel, which includes the love of God but excludes the wrath of God, can never bring men to a full understanding of the will of God. Postmodern preaching, which lingers on the compassion of God but never explains to men what to do to be saved, hardly compares to the models found on the pages of the gospels or the book of Acts. Jesus did preach on hell and did demand men repent or perish. The postmodern preacher must decide if he is willing to walk in Jesus' steps by preaching a whole message. Today's preacher must decide whether he will walk the broad way or the narrow way. He must decide if he will be faithful to the task of teaching people to "observe all things" that Jesus commanded.

Every evangelist has the responsibility to present the message of God with courage regardless of whom it may offend. The apostles in the face of persecution prayed for boldness to speak the message as they ought to speak (Acts 4:23-31; Ephesians 6:19-20). Knowing the "fear of the Lord," they persuaded men to obey the Lord (2 Corinthians 5:11). There was no tiptoeing around the truth or compromising with error. They were on the King's business to take the King's message to those who needed it. They did not call for people to come to the back of the stage to be counseled about what to do to be saved, as if they had something to hide. They preached openly for men to repent and be baptized in the name of Jesus Christ for the forgiveness of their sins. Because of their love and commitment to God, they determined to obey God rather than men (Acts 5:29).

When Paul preached in the Areopagus, some sneered at his belief in the resurrection. Paul did not apologize or take back what he said; nor did he edit his later sermons with a user-friendly message. In fact, Paul strongly insisted on truthfulness in his preaching. He knew that men could be deluded by persuasive arguments (Colossians 2:1). He was concerned that those he taught come to maturity in Christ and not be "tossed here and there by waves, and carried about by every wind of doctrine, by the trickery of men, by craftiness in deceitful scheming" (Ephesians 4:14). He knew that by "cleverness of speech," the cross of Christ could be made void (1 Corinthians 1:17). He explained to the Corinthians:

> And when I came to you, brethren, I did not come with superiority of speech or of wisdom, proclaiming to you the testimony of God. For I determined to know nothing among you except Jesus Christ, and Him crucified. And I was with you in weakness and in fear and in much trembling. And my message and my preaching were not in persuasive words of wisdom, but in demonstration of the Spirit and of power, that your faith should not rest on the wisdom of men, but on the power of God (1 Corinthians 2:1-5).

If there are truth-in-advertising and truth-in-lending laws in the world, should not gospel preachers also avoid any appearance of trickery or deception? Do preachers really advance the cause of Christ and the truth when they selectively preach the counsel of God for the sake of user-friendliness? We need preachers who will tell churches what their real needs are whether they are felt or not. We must once again place our confidence in the gospel itself.

The call for relevance needs some examination. Obviously, meaningful preaching remains important in every generation. The preaching of the cross exemplifies the epitome of relevance in every culture of every age. Yet, some in their wisdom plea for the relevance of other matters. D. A. Carson in *The Gagging of God* noted:

> Study after study has shown that pursuing relevance may achieve a certain instant "success," but is frequently the advance warning to bitter declension. Liberal churches

thought they were being terribly relevant in the '30s, the '50s, the '60s – and virtually without exception they are in massive decline.[9]

We are seeing some of that among us. Some of our preachers have caught the new philosophies and have seen mushrooming churches. But what comes quickly with compromise often leaves the same way. Those who cling to the faddish spirit of the times soon find that another generation comes along, whose ideas and values greatly differ. A new king and a new generation came along who did not know Joseph (Exodus 1:8). If we build our lives on the immediately relevant, what will happen when the times change? We will find ourselves obnoxiously dated.

We do far better to continue in those eternal truths which remain relevant in every society and in every age. History reminds us that as generations pass, so do attitudes. Nevertheless, the Scriptures address the most important questions of life, matters that each person must face. Every age faces the problem of sin, and it is naive to think the concept is outmoded. As long as man has a conscience, sin and guilt will be relevant. Some have thought that hell is irrelevant; but as long as wicked men are carried to the cemetery, people will consider the justice of God. Love and trust are as relevant as vows at a wedding. As long as men look into their own eyes in the mirror, there will be a need for peace.

Paul knew the relevance of preaching Christ and him crucified to an idolatrous and immoral world. He learned some would not listen, but others did. He knew that his task was to be faithful to that one gospel regardless of how men received it. We are not saying that Paul did not accommodate himself to the culture in which he lived, for we know that he did (1 Corinthians 9:19-23). Nevertheless, whether Paul was with those who had the Law or was with those who did not have the Law, Paul remained under the law of Christ (9:21). He did not compromise his faith or his teaching as he moved from culture to culture.

Some bring up relevance, but perhaps the relevance of the gospel of Christ is not the question at all. Perhaps we should remember some heart soil is hard, some is rocky, and some is thorny. Jesus sowed the same seed to all four. Paul preached the same gospel to Jew and Gentile, to legalist and libertine, to men and women, and to Greek and Barbarian. He did not preach a Stoic gospel in one place and an Epicurean gospel elsewhere. He knew there are simply some eternal things which supercede culture, language and mindset. By the grace of God, Jesus tasted death for every man (Hebrews 2:9), and He expects His disciples to tell the story of the cross and the empty tomb to every person. Jesus intended for His converts to conform to His image, to salt the earth, to give light to the world. The gospel must turn the world upside down, changing people's lives and attitudes. Churches which become like the world may think they are relevant, but such relevance robs them of the power to make lasting change. Their lamps grow dim, and their salt loses its taste. Only when the message preached clings to the cross does it remain powerful and effective.

Paul told Timothy, "Pay close attention to yourself and to your teaching; persevere in these things; for as you do this you will insure salvation both for yourself and for those who hear you" (1 Timothy 4:16). Rather than be distracted by the changing fads of our time, we too must stay with the task of sound teaching. We cannot win the world for Jesus Christ through faddish entertainment but through the straightforward preaching of the gospel. God chose to save those who believe through the preached message (1 Corinthians 1:21). God so designed the gospel that it would prick and pierce the hearts of men to bring them to salvation. To suppose man can develop anything that could substitute for or replace the gospel is to invite arrogance and presumption.

Paul admonished Timothy, "Retain the standard of sound words which you have heard from me, in the faith and love which are in Christ Jesus" (2 Timothy 1:13). Why would he say that? Did Paul not know he would soon die, and Timothy would preach to a new generation? Yes, Paul knew that. He also knew that Timothy's real success could only come by staying the course of the gospel. He must retain the sound teaching; Timothy must never get off to the right or the left but remain in the narrow way. We too must listen to

Paul's inspired advice to the young preacher. Our power to change the world comes from staying with the Word. Nothing else has the power or the blessing of God.

Discussion Questions

1. How have Christians become intimidated by the sciences of psychology and sociology?

2. How has the desire for church growth affected the theology of churches of Christ?

3. How has "church shopping" and "church hopping" affected the way leaders make decisions in churches of Christ?

4. What is "relevant" preaching, and how has the demand for relevance affected mainline denominations?

CHAPTER 11

Keeping Heart
WE HOLD ON TO HIS HAND IN THE STORMS

*"Watch over your heart with all diligence,
For from it flow the springs of life" (Proverbs 4:23).*

We cannot stop the rain or hold back the wind. The storms of life rage around us as long as we live; we cannot avoid them. I grew up in Oklahoma where Tornado Alley remains alive and well. I have spent anxious hours with my loved ones in a storm cellar or closet waiting for the tempest to pass. Nevertheless, there is more to consider than the mere storm. I remember as a small child clutching my Bible for security as I feared the hail and wind. I learned to hold to the hand of God through the fiercest winds. We all need to remember God is with us. Through the years I have faced all kinds of storms and trials with my loved ones and with my church family. I have found God to be true to His promise: "Do not fear, for I am with you; Do not anxiously look about you, for I am your God. I will strengthen you, surely I will help you, Surely I will uphold you with My righteous right hand" (Isaiah 41:10). David said, "But let all who take refuge in Thee be glad, Let them ever sing for joy; And mayest Thou shelter them, That those who love Thy name may exult in Thee" (Psalm 5:11).

God is with His people, and we must remember His help and comfort through our confusions and weaknesses. Our present storm comes in the form of postmodernism. By means of accusations, postmodernists seek to replace confidence with indecision, conviction with uncertainty, and trust with doubt – accusing anyone who has convictions of arrogance and conceit. They label as "mean-spirited" anyone who takes a stand on the Word of God. Not wanting strong preaching, postmodernists do not want to hear about righteousness, self-control or the judgment to come. They rail against anyone who would move them from their state of comfort. Assailed by this storm of peer pressure and stereotyping, Christians who take their stand with the Lord must watch their attitudes.

Because the worst taboo of our time is to judge or criticize others, Christians must exercise self-control in their approaches to nonbelievers. The accusation of being "arrogant" or "mean-spirited" has in some cases proven true. In any discussion there are two levels of competition. The first level is logical and determines who is more correct according to the facts and the validity of the argument. The second is one of attitude and respect. One may win in the first category and lose in the second. This is especially true today because respect has come to be more valuable to some than the truth. People quit listening and begin condemning the person they believe shows little respect to others, in spite of how right he may be. More than being right in our beliefs, we must also treat others the right way. We must guard our hearts and attitudes to avoid throwing up a barrier we cannot remove.

Some years ago I attended a debate, between a member of the church and a man from another background, on the necessity of baptism to salvation. The second man spoke with such bias and ugliness, slandering members of the church of Christ, that his own people were ashamed and refused to attend the later portions of the debate. I told my preaching brother he had won the debate in the hearts of the listeners. He apparently won the logical side as well, for some who previously held the other view obeyed the gospel and were baptized for the remission of their sins. Attitude matters because love matters. Paul urged us to speak the truth in love (Ephesians 4:15). He reminded Timothy: "the goal of our instruction is love from a pure heart and a good conscience and a sincere faith" (1 Timothy 1:5).

People must know that we love them before they will listen to our message. We must keep our hearts, our hands and our lives busy with loving others so that we can open the doors of their hearts to the gospel.

Attitudes Toward God

When the lawyer tested Jesus by asking what the great commandment was, Jesus answered, " 'You shall love the Lord your God with all your heart, and with all your soul, and with all your mind.' This is the great and foremost commandment. The second is like it, 'You shall love your neighbor as yourself.' On these two commandments depend the whole Law and the Prophets" (Matthew 22:36-40). Christians today need an all-consuming love for God; He must be first in their hearts, souls and minds. Jesus demands a love for Himself greater than any other love. Christians must put away their selfishness and allow their love for Him to control their minds and behavior. Paul spoke of his consuming love for Christ in sacrificial terms when he said, "I have been crucified with Christ; and it is no longer I who live, but Christ lives in me; and the life which I now live in the flesh I live by faith in the Son of God, who loved me, and delivered Himself up for me" (Galatians 2:20). This crucifixion means that we die to ourselves so that we can live for our Lord. He is our first and last thought; He is our breath and food. We ought to sing with our lives as well as our lips, "He is my everything, He is my all."

To truly, fully love God, we must possess a deep intimacy with Him. We must take the time to listen to His Word, to pray to Him, to meditate on His ways, and to see His hand of providence in our lives. If we are to speak meaningfully of God to the postmodern world, then we must enjoy a deep relationship with Him. We must know God. We must know how He loves us, His will for our lives, and His plan for our future. We must know how He deals with us in our successes and our failures. We must know Him as our Father, our Lord, our Creator, our Savior, and our Sustainer. Like Paul our desire should be to "comprehend with all the saints what is the breadth and length and height and depth, and to know the love of

Christ which surpasses knowledge, that you may be filled up to all
the fullness of God" (Ephesians 3:18-19).

Attitudes Toward the World

We are not of this world but are strangers and aliens, looking for
a city with foundations whose builder and maker is God. We are not
to love this world. John said,

> Do not love the world, nor the things in the world. If any-
> one loves the world, the love of the Father is not in him.
> For all that is in the world, the lust of the flesh and the
> lust of the eyes and the boastful pride of life, is not from
> the Father, but is from the world. And the world is pass-
> ing away, and also its lusts; but the one who does the will
> of God abides forever (1 John 2:15-17).

Although we cannot leave this world, we must never love its ways
to the point we cease to love our God. James upbraided those to
whom he wrote for trying to make friends with the world, "You
adulteresses, do you not know that friendship with the world is hostility toward God? Therefore whoever wishes to be a friend of the
world makes himself an enemy of God. Or do you think that the
Scripture speaks to no purpose: 'He jealously desires the Spirit which
He has made to dwell in us'?" (James 4:4-5). God wants you, and
He is not willing to give you up to the lusts and the pride of this life.
He knows how those things will destroy you; and the Father is too
good to give you up that easily.

How are we to live in this world? We cannot leave this world, nor
can we leave the ungodly people who are here. How can we maintain our identity in a world that does not understand or appreciate
us? The answer lies in keeping our minds focused on God. Paul said,
"do not be conformed to this world, but be transformed by the renewing of your mind, that you may prove what the will of God is,
that which is good and acceptable and perfect" (Romans 12:2). We
change to be like God by renewing our minds each day in His will.
We continually probe and meditate on God's will. By renewing our
thinking we change our behavior; and our behavior says to this world,

"This is what God wants! God's will is good! God's will is acceptable! God's will is perfect!" The most effective way to communicate what we believe is to live it. We are to salt the earth with ourselves by godly living; we are to light the world by allowing God's will to shine through us. People will appreciate and glorify God when they see His ways in us. If we cannot "tell" the world what we believe, perhaps we can demonstrate our faith to them. We can show the superiority and the divine wisdom of the Christian life.

We are not to conform to this world. If we sell out our faith to identify with the world, we will have little ability to persuade the world to be like us. Why should they become like us? We have already moved to become like them. If we lower our standards, how can ask them to raise theirs? In the end we are the worse for it, and they are not better. We did not salt them; they salted us. Dimming our lights does not lead them to rid themselves of darkness. We can hardly ask people to repent if we join their disobedience.

Here someone asks, "But didn't Paul identify with the people around him? Didn't he do all he could to win people to the Lord?" Indeed he did. Paul said,

> For though I am free from all men, I have made myself a slave to all, that I might win the more. And to the Jews I became as a Jew, that I might win Jews; to those who are under the Law, as under the Law, though not being myself under the Law, that I might win those who are under the Law; to those who are without law, as without law, though not being without the law of God but under the law of Christ, that I might win those who are without law. To the weak I became weak, that I might win the weak; I have become all things to all men, that I may by all means save some. And I do all things for the sake of the gospel, that I may become a fellow partaker of it (1 Corinthians 9:19-23).

Paul lived like the people around him in order to win their souls to Christ. This is wise and good strategy, but Paul never forgot he was under the law of Christ. He did not give up what he believed;

he was living among them to prove what the will of God is. Paul went among them to win them to Christ, not to leave them in ignorance. To the postmodern mindset there is no reason to win anybody to anything; everyone is okay the way he is and does not need saving. Paul's love for the lost obligated him to preach and persuade. He did what he did for the sake of the gospel. Far from compromising, he further says, "I run in such a way, as not without aim; I box in such a way, as not beating the air; but I buffet my body and make it my slave, lest possibly, after I have preached to others, I myself should be disqualified" (1 Corinthians 9:26-27). Paul would not allow himself to do anything whereby his own soul was at risk. He knew where he was going and where he wanted to take others. He was not content to leave people where they were.

Evangelists who buy into the postmodern mindset undoubtedly do not follow in the steps of the apostle Paul. Men who give the lost a false sense of assurance are unworthy to be called "gospel preachers." Those who refuse to speak the truth and leave the lost in darkness – the denominationalists in their denominations, the sprinkled in man-made precepts, the instrumentalists in their presumption, or the untaught in their perverted gospels – have abandoned the work of the Lord. Gospel preachers cannot leave the lost as they find them. They cannot look the other way and leave the impression that everything is acceptable to God. Gospel preachers must "preach the word; be ready in season and out of season; reprove, rebuke, exhort, with great patience and instruction" (2 Timothy 4:2). While we do not know if those who hear will obey, we must preach the truth. We must love people enough to give them what they need the most not what they want the most.

What, then, do they need? People need the whole gospel. Paul did not neglect to teach the whole counsel of God (Acts 20:27). They need to know how God loves them, how He gave His Son for their sins, and how He has planned a home in heaven for them. They need to know there is only one God and only one Savior, Jesus Christ. They need to know God created the heavens and the earth and sustains us each day by His power. They need to know humans are made in God's image with purpose and are not products of chance. They need to know God saves them by His grace, and no one can earn salvation. They need to know God hates sin because sin is an offense to Him and destructive to His people.

They need to know God expects people to respond in faith, love and obedience. They need to know God regards our obedience as the means by which we love Him. They need to know God expects us to repent of our sins by forsaking them and turning to Him. They need to know baptism is the time when God forgives our sins, adds us to His church, causes us to be born again, and gives us His Spirit. They need to know God expects faithfulness and obedience for a lifetime. They need to know Jesus wants us to observe all that He has commanded. They need to know they can lose their salvation if they forsake the Lord for immorality or false teachings. They need to know Jesus built only one church, has only one gospel, recognizes only one baptism, and teaches only one faith.

They need to know God will care for them, will hear their prayers, will strengthen them, and will comfort them. They need to know Jesus is coming again and will judge them according to His Word. They need to know the penalty for sin is spending an eternity in hell with the devil and His angels. They need to know God wants them to spend eternity with Him in heaven. There are surely other truths vital to our understanding of God and His will for our lives, but these fundamentals are necessary to know if we are to please God.

In addressing the world, Paul told the Colossians, "Conduct yourselves with wisdom toward outsiders, making the most of the opportunity. Let your speech always be with grace, seasoned, as it were, with salt, so that you may know how you should respond to each person" (Colossians 4:5-6). There is never a place in Christianity for rudeness or ugliness in our attitudes. We must speak with kindness in our words and in our tone of voice. Unfortunately evangelists sometimes send double messages. When the tone of voice or body language conflicts with the words they speak, listeners can become confused. Communication experts say messages are 7 percent the words we speak, 38 percent tone of voice, and 55 percent body language. The kindest words of salvation spoken through clenched teeth will hardly portray the glad tidings of the gospel. People tend to believe what they see in the body language and what they hear in the tone of voice more than the spoken words. Soul-winners should take time to watch and listen to themselves so as to perceive the total message they are sending.

Using an appropriate approach matters in reaching the lost. Because we represent the Lord Jesus, we ought to consider how we want the world to see Him. Our world often views "Christians" as hypocrites, as mean-spirited people, or as radicals. The cults, the liberal denominations, and popular television Christianity have left a bad taste in the mouths of many who would like to find real Christianity. We have a great opportunity to present unpolluted New Testament Christianity to a world searching for a genuine faith. In order to get a hearing in the world, the words of Paul seem more relevant than ever. The world we speak to in the coming century is very much like the world Paul spoke to in the first century. For this reason we ought to pay special attention to the inspired apostle's counsel to Timothy:

> And the Lord's bond-servant must not be quarrelsome,
> but be kind to all, able to teach, patient when wronged,
> with gentleness correcting those who are in opposition,
> if perhaps God may grant them repentance leading to the
> knowledge of the truth, and they may come to their sens-
> es and escape from the snare of the devil, having been
> held captive by him to do his will (2 Timothy 2:24-26).

We will not be able to argue people into the kingdom. Although people used this method at one time in churches of Christ, it will not work in the postmodern era. Postmodern people tend to throw up a barrier against anything emotionally negative. If we expect to get any hearing at all, we must express ourselves with kindness and gentleness.

We must be shrewd as serpents and yet innocent as doves (Matthew 10:16). We must have wise strategies to communicate the gospel, but we must do it an innocent way. Despite the fact that the gospel is good news, there is a challenge in the gospel to repent. Worldly people must be confronted with sin and the coming judgment and condemnation. The gospel is good news because sin brings bad news. We need to point people lovingly to heaven. Occasionally I hear stories of evangelists who tell their listeners they are "going to hell." I heard one lady describe a preacher as a man "who preached me into hell and was glad I was going there." It never occurs to some evangelists the harm they can do to others by thoughtless cruelty. It is not preaching on hell that is objectionable; rather, it is the attitude with which it is preached. We are calling here for balance. We cannot pervert the gospel, as some have done, by neglecting to preach on sin and hell. Neither can we preach on hell with such an ugly attitude that we build barriers. Instead we must preach lovingly with broken hearts, warning people of the wrath to come.

Those who evangelize need to stop and consider how others perceive what Christ is asking them to do. We are asking lost people to forsake their ways, to leave their old lifestyles, and to begin a new walk with the Lord. We are asking them to bear a cross, to crucify themselves with Christ. This momentous change demands much from new converts. Converting the lost to Christ is far more complicated than selling a box of soap, and Madison Avenue methods will not be sufficient to the task. In evangelism, our most important assets are love and credibility. We must earn the right to speak to people about the most important aspects of their lives. We can no longer assume we have earned that right simply because we speak in the name of Jesus Christ. We must demonstrate to them our love and concern for their souls. We must personally invest ourselves in their lives – enough to earn the right to talk to them about sin and salvation. The cliché, "People do not care how much you know, until they know how much you care," rings especially true today.

James reminds us, "the wisdom from above is first pure, then peaceable, gentle, reasonable, full of mercy and good fruits, unwavering, without hypocrisy" (James 3:17). We must fill our lives with these winning characteristics. People of the world will notice the difference between what we have to offer and what others offer, and the godliness of our message will speak loudly to their hearts. Christianity conquered the thinking of pagan Greece and Rome because the common people could see the contrast between a real God and the emptiness of their idols. They realized the genuine hope Christianity offered compared to the empty promises of man-made religion. They saw purity, peace, gentleness, kindness and genuineness in the lives of Christians who were willing to die for their faith. As we move into an era increasingly more pagan, we must respond by developing lives that are increasingly more spiritual and devoted to Christ.

Attitudes Toward False Teachers

False teachers present a number of particularly difficult problems for the church. How do we deal with a false teacher? How do we treat those who have compromised their faith? Shall we fellowship nearby congregations who have bought into postmodern thinking? How can we avoid becoming radical in our objections to error? What can we do to minimize the polarizing between various factions of the church? These suggestions may prove helpful:

We must love the brotherhood (1 Peter 2:17). Every child of God is our brother; there are no stepchildren in the family of God. Being all too human and weak, even Christians can fall into the traps of jealousy, suspicion, unfounded rumors, or power ploys. Some, overcome by these traps, have granted themselves permission to deal unfairly, cruelly or rudely with their brothers. Some are quick to accuse or to believe accusations. Unsubstantiated rumors and gossip can ruin reputations and can create stumbling blocks. Before we speak about a brother, we must ask ourselves if we love that brother's soul. Have we prayed and mourned for our brother? We must look deep into our own motives to be sure we are not acting spitefully or with malice. Like the prodigal son's older brother, we are often all too ready to end relations with our brethren.

Remarkably, Paul lists eight works of the flesh dealing with relationships: enmities, strife, jealousy, outbursts of anger, disputes, dissensions, factions, and envying. He forewarned "that those who practice such things shall not inherit the kingdom of God" (Galatians 5:20-21). Paul wrote these to the church, and brethren should realize they can be tempted with these soul-destroying sins. John reminds us, "Beloved, let us love one another, for love is from God; and everyone who loves is born of God and knows God. The one who does not love does not know God, for God is love" (1 John 4:7, 8). Love is the first characteristic of the Spirit's work in our lives. When we fail to love our own brethren, we provide evidence of our unwillingness to walk by the Spirit. Paul said, "Now those who belong to Christ Jesus have crucified the flesh with its passions and desires" (Galatians 5:24). Loving the brotherhood means crucifying those passions and desires that break down relationships and destroy others.

In our homes, our congregations, and the brotherhood we need to restore the practice of reconciliation. We have lost in great measure our sense of what sin is. The consequence to this loss of sin consciousness is the loss of confession and sorrow for sin. No reconciliation can take place with God or with a brother as long as pride and indifference keep us from confessing our sins and apologizing. The phrase "I have sinned" is found only a handful of times in all of Scripture, and it is just as rare today. People seem to have an inborn distaste for admitting their sins, and godly sorrow for sin is even more rare. No wonder we strain our relationships! Add to this the "get even" mentality, and the whole church gets hurt. Some offended brethren simply find it hard to forgive and forget. They hold grudges and punish their brothers and sisters without end. It would do the whole church good to practice more apologizing and forgiving.

Paul said, "Let your forbearing spirit be known to all men. The Lord is near" (Philippians 4:5). Christians need to cultivate within themselves a "sweet spirit of reasonableness." Sadly, some brethren have cultivated a reputation of unapproachability. No one can reason with them. They need to grow beyond hypersensitivity and grouchiness. Some have become so suspicious of others they see problems where none exist. Others with incomplete facts rush to judge, to blame, and to slander. Like Diotrephes they have become lords over their congregations and have booted out sound brethren.

We need to cultivate a different attitude, an attitude of patience and understanding. God will judge us the way we judge others. Closed spirits will close the heart of God against us. Anyone who wants to follow in the steps of Jesus ought to develop a gracious spirit of forbearance and compassion. Paul reminds us:

> And so, as those who have been chosen of God, holy and beloved, put on a heart of compassion, kindness, humility, gentleness and patience; bearing with one another, and forgiving each other, whoever has a complaint against anyone; just as the Lord forgave you, so also should you. And beyond all these things put on love, which is the perfect bond of unity (Colossians 3:12-14).

We must avoid arrogance. Inspired by the Holy Spirit, Paul observed, "Knowledge makes arrogant, but love edifies" (1 Corinthians 8:1). Pride is a terrible troubler of the church. It prevents fellowship, promotes rebellion, and produces sectarianism. Like the Paulites, Apollosites and Cephasites of Corinth, some have gathered under the banner of some school or publication. Not content to be merely Christians, they must be some brand of Christian. Arrogance cries out, "I am right, and you are wrong! I am good, and you are bad!" Such attitudes split the church and make the Lord's body a laughing stock to the world.

Arrogance leads to an unteachable spirit. Some apparently have learned all there is to learn and need not know anything more. Others apparently feel they have such superior knowledge they look down upon others as ignorant. There is hope for a naive person because although he is unaware of much, he is open to new truth. The arrogant and unteachable person, however, has little hope for growth because he does not recognize his remaining ignorance. Some in ignorance have arrogantly and unfairly labeled others as false teachers. Preachers and elders who rush to judgment against anyone who does not use a preferred version, for instance, often know little about the original languages or the translation process. Some who like their preferred version simply will not learn from anything else or listen to anybody else. We find no fault in having preferences, but we find great fault in making laws where God has not made them. Arrogance leads to exalting opinions and judgments to the point one quits listening; that spiritual malady can even shut an ear and heart to God.

Perhaps we all need to re-enroll in the school of humility. Paul advises, "Be of the same mind toward one another; do not be haughty in mind, but associate with the lowly. Do not be wise in your own estimation" (Romans 12:16). Humility reminds us of our own weaknesses and limitations. In a world fixated on the value of self-esteem, we may have lost sight of the value of humility. Not content to be anything less than first, we may have forgotten the value of being a servant and of obedience. The first beatitude points to the value of being poor in spirit (Matthew 5:3). The Lord knew He could do nothing with a man until that man saw his utter poverty and utter need for God. As long as a person is arrogant, he finds little need for anyone but himself. We need God and each other as brethren.

We must discipline the factious. Paul listed "factions" as one of the works of the flesh. Those who practice "such things shall not inherit the kingdom of God" (Galatians 5:19-21). The word "faction" comes from the Greek word from which we get the word "heresy." The faction, or division, arose from the dissension over a false teaching. Factions are doubly dangerous to the body of Christ; they not only lead their adherents away from the truth but also cause splits. Heresies are self-chosen teachings, and heretics pull people away into a self-chosen party or sect. Paul gave clear instructions to Titus, "Reject a factious man after a first and second warning, knowing that such a man is perverted and is sinning, being self-condemned" (Titus 3:10-11).

The word for warning is perhaps better understood as "admonition." An admonition is an instruction which warns and expects correction. After two such warnings, the church must "reject" the heretic, i.e., dismiss him, or remove him from fellowship. The church must take such radical action, not only because of the false teaching but also because of the obstinacy of one who would refuse two warnings. The church must stop those who pervert the apostles' teaching by promoting a self-chosen teaching to the splitting of the body.

Divisive doctrinal error brings about sin, and those who promote it condemn themselves. Jesus dealt decisively with Jezebel and her children because He knew her false teaching would destroy the church at Thyatira. Paul warned of the Judaizers saying of their doctrine, "a little leaven leavens the whole lump" (Galatians 5:9). Elders must not allow false teachings to permeate and ruin congregations. Elders, shepherding the church, must not only feed but also protect the flock from the dangerous wolves who will not spare the flock (Acts 20:28-31). Here Paul warned the Ephesian elders of savage wolves "speaking perverse things, to draw away disciples after them." Paul knew the importance of what people teach. What one teaches and what people believe do matter. When church leaders back off from "doctrinal issues" with a *laissez-faire* attitude, they forsake their God-appointed duty as protectors. Churches fall away from the truth when elders allow the preaching of error. Paul warned Timothy:

> Be diligent to present yourself approved to God as a work-man who does not need to be ashamed, handling accurately the word of truth. But avoid worldly and empty chatter, for it will lead to further ungodliness, and their talk will spread like gangrene. Among them are Hymenaeus and Philetus, men who have gone astray from the truth saying that the resurrection has already taken place, and thus they upset the faith of some (2 Timothy 2:15-18).

Talk, unchecked and unrefuted, will lead to lost faith and lost souls. Gangrene kills and so does false teaching. In a climate that denies absolute truth and promotes pluralism, the church faces an incredible threat of apostasy. Elders must be doubly alert to the teachings of their preachers and teachers. We must call for elders and preachers to stand firm against the postmodern mindset and discipline heretics who divide the body.

Attitudes Toward Compromise

When churches compromise the truth, they always lose. We do admit, however, that life is filled with give and take. The Bible clearly teaches Christians should forbear one another and not judge one another in matters of expediency. Anyone who lives with others must yield his desires in order to keep harmony. There are some things, however, not for sale; and truth is one of those things. Solomon said, "Buy truth, and do not sell it, Get wisdom and instruction and understanding" (Proverbs 23:23). Truth and wisdom are commodities of great value because they come from God. Foolish is the man or the church who sells out the truth for some lesser gain.

Jesus prayed for unity among His people (John 17:20-23), but the disciples' unity came from their sanctification in the truth (17:17-19). Jesus never considered a unity devoid of the truth of His Word. The word of truth brought them their identity (John 8:31) and their freedom (8:32). The present notion of setting aside the truth in order to maintain unity or to increase the membership contradicts everything Jesus came to accomplish. Jesus brought grace and truth to mankind (John 1:18). He is the way, the truth, and the life (14:6). Jesus came to bear witness to the truth (18:37), and those who reject Him and do not receive His words will be judged by the words He spoke (12:48). Jesus demanded that His people buy the truth and not sell it. To sell out the truth for numbers defeats the purpose. Compromising the word will never strengthen the church; it dilutes the church's ability to be the pillar and support of the truth (1 Timothy 3:15).

Solomon learned the bitter fruits of compromise. He loved many foreign wives "from the nations concerning which the Lord had said to the sons of Israel, 'You shall not associate with them, neither shall they associate with you, for they will surely turn your heart away after their gods.' Solomon held fast to these in love" (1 Kings 11:2). Perhaps he thought he was strong enough to resist their charms and their gods, but time would prove otherwise. "For it came about when Solomon was old, his wives turned his heart away after other gods; and his heart was not wholly devoted to the Lord his God, as the heart of David his father had been" (11:4). Solomon compromised his love and devotion toward God in order to love his foreign wives. He began worshiping foreign idols and ultimately built high places to Chemosh and Molech. He offered sacrifices to the gods of his wives and "turned away from the Lord, the God of Israel, who had appeared to him twice" (11:9). In time, small compromises of the truth turn the heart away from God. One cannot embrace those who hold error and not be touched by it. Solomon ultimately loved his wives more than he loved the Lord.

Some have compromised in the same way by learning to love people or things more than they love the Lord. Jesus demanded a love greater than parents, spouses, brothers, sisters or children (Matthew 10:37). Why would He do that? Jesus demanded our ultimate loyalty because He knew our loved ones could be the enemy of our souls. We are sometimes told "people are more important than rules." This sounds reasonable at first, but it is shortsighted. The rules are God's rules; and when we break the rules for the sake of people, we start turning our hearts away from God and giving people first place. God will never tolerate being second to anyone or anything.

Some today are not wanting to affirm baptism as necessary to salvation because they would rather hold to people than say their beliefs are in error. Solomon knew there was but one God, but he could not say no to the wives he loved. Loving God more than anyone means saying no to those who would draw us away from Him and His Word. Satan has schemed to make us choose between the people we love and God. Some of the changes we face in the church fall into the same category. How can we be so "mean-spirited" as to tell women they cannot lead? We choose to tell them the truth because of our greater love for God. Of course, telling people the truth is also a means of loving them and their souls. How can we coldly forbid people to play the instrument in their worship? We choose to sing a cappella and refuse the instrument out of a greater love for the Father's instructions than for man-made worship. We love God by listening to Him and doing only what He teaches us to do.

Devotion to God means His will always wins out in our lives. We obey Him out of a surpassing love. We will not allow desire for our own way or affection for loved ones to come between God and ourselves. An all-consuming love for God will never permit compromise of His truth because every compromise means we love God less. Secularism wants to dethrone God; compromise does not treat

Him that way. Rather, it demotes Him by giving Him one vote among many. Compromising truth permits men to outvote God when they want to. It says to God, "We'll listen to You; but we'll only take Your teachings under advisement." In compromise God gets to make His point, but He does not get to make the decision. Compromise is a terrible insult to God because it fails to respect Him as God. Because Jesus is the one and only Lord, compromise is not an option.

Discussion Questions

1. Cite some examples of God's holding to your hand when you faced the storms of life.

2. How did Paul identify with the Jews and the Gentiles?

3. In our preaching, what are the things people need most?

4. What responsibility does the church have toward divisive false teachers?

5. How did Solomon's compromises with his wives hurt Israel?

CHAPTER 12

Pointing the Way
EVANGELIZING THE POSTMODERN MIND

"Always be ready to make a defense ... for the hope that
is in you, yet with gentleness and reverence" (1 Peter 3:15).

As the postmodern mindset saturates our culture, we must adjust our approaches to people in order to persuade them with the eternal gospel of Jesus Christ. We must be listening to their doubts, their questions, and their way of dealing with life issues. Our traditional approaches may not fit the times because the presuppositions of this present time are unlike that of previous generations. At one time we could assume that people believed in the authority and inspiration of Scripture; we cannot assume that today. At one time we could assume most people believed Christianity was the one true religion; but we cannot assume that today. We can no longer assume people will regard truth as absolute, objective and unequivocal, i.e., understandable in only one clear way. The privatizing of faith (designing our own religion) and the pluralizing of Christianity (accepting conflicting beliefs) clash violently with the biblical teaching that there is one Lord, one faith, and one baptism.

With this in mind we must ask ourselves the question, "How will we ever be able to speak meaningfully and authoritatively to a people who are convinced of such uncertainty?" The answer is not an easy one. Privatization is an individualistic endeavor and may require individualized approaches to reach many people. Nevertheless, there are some general principles of life that can apply broadly. Although people do not want to hear about their sins, each person does still have a conscience. People remain vitally interested in religion even if they do not know God. People still want to know where they came from, who they are, and where they are going. People still want a purposeful and meaningful life. While the world is caught up in theological relativism, people want some absolutes – even if they do not realize they want absolutes. Those who have set their hearts on the sea of uncertainty will someday tire of drifting and wish for something more substantial to hold onto. We must hook into these desires.

There is a difference between drifting and a journey. The human soul will not be satisfied forever with an endless disconnection to reality. He will demand that he become somebody going somewhere for some reason. That desire is the nature of being human. James Patterson and Peter Kim, in the book *The Day That America Told the Truth,* reveal that there is a price to pay for the individualism characterizing our country. When a person's rationalizing means he can no longer tell right from wrong, "It also raises fear and doubt, which often leads to depression: Did I do the right thing? Does it matter anymore? Does anything matter?"[1] This fear, doubt and depression must not be taken lightly. An amoral world is a dark, lonely and fearful place. When each one has his own morality, how can we trust anyone or anything?

To set ourselves adrift from a moral and theological foundation may seem pleasant for awhile, but what will we do when the waters are troubled? What will we do when the wind blows, and we do not have an anchor? There are no ports on the sea of uncertainty. When there are no foundations, there are no real securities or havens. The sea of uncertainty with all of its freedom also lacks substance and is painful. Postmodernism has no firm answers or promises for the widow at the cemetery. It cannot point the rebellious youth back to morality. It cannot assure a fetus of its right to life. It gives no hope for repentance because it gives no demand for change. Uncertainty robs us of all the blessings of hope and trust; it casts us

PHIL SANDERS

into an absurd and insane life. The price of absolute doctrinal and moral freedom, which rids us of God and absolute truth, is far higher than many people realize.

In practical terms, life is not lived in a relative world. We do not fully apply the uncertainty of today's morals and theology to the way we live our practical lives. Bank accounts hold exact amounts of money and not relative figures. A check written on insufficient funds, however close to the actual amount, can have serious consequences. Let a bank forget to include your deposit in its calculations, and you will correct them quickly. You demand fairness when you are cheated. When people go to the shoe store, they learn that just any size shoe will not do. When people go to the pharmacist, they realize that just any drug will not cure their problem. Those who deal with computers realize that older MacIntosh programs will not work in Windows-based computers. We realistically live by standards and measures in every aspect of our lives. Olympians are often judged by hundredths of a second. While each of them would love a medal, each one knows there is a difference between gold, silver and bronze. Dialing a number close to being right will not secure a telephone connection to the party we desire. This practical exactness that permeates our lives cannot be ignored. Relative accuracy does not count in the real world. We must seize on this point of connection.

It is through life itself that we can show points of connection with people who have a postmodern mindset. We can touch them by living our lives with confidence and hope. Although they may claim absolute moral and doctrinal freedom, they cannot live their lives without some rules, some laws, or some values. They are not willing to grant anyone the freedom to sexually molest their children, to steal from them, to kill their friends, or to sleep with their spouses. Their resolute desire for life without foundations breaks down when they themselves become the victim of an evil. All of a sudden the freedom they so longed for is not so attractive! Indeed, it is frightening! When a postmodernist is pressed, he will have to admit that there is right and wrong. Here is a point of connection.

Another connecting point is in the reality of death. The old saying "there is nothing certain except death and taxes" has particular relevance here. There is a certainty about our eventual demise; no one can live on this earth forever. Christians must sometimes look their neighbors in the eye and remind them of their own mortality. When Paul spoke to the godless Felix about righteousness, self-control and the judgment to come, Felix became frightened. Although Felix became frightened and would not listen, there was a point of connection. One does not get frightened over that which has no meaning. The Hebrew writer said, "It is appointed for men to die once and after this comes judgment" (Hebrews 9:27). David noted our dependence on God in Psalm 22:28-29:

> For the kingdom is the LORD'S, And He rules over
>   the nations.
> All the prosperous of the earth will eat and worship,
> All those who go down to the dust will bow before
>   Him,
> Even he who cannot keep his soul alive.

In God's presence man is still weak and powerless. In the end every knee will bow and every tongue will confess Jesus as Lord to the glory of the Father (Philippians 2:10-11). One may jettison morality, but one cannot so easily throw out accountability, either to other people or to God. Death reminds one of his accountability in stark and undeniable terms. The Word of God is living and powerful; it really is sharper than a two-edged sword. It can cut deep into the heart of an unbeliever, for he knows down deep – however much he may deny it – that there is truth in God's Word. Christians must find the points of connection.

We must show in just such practical means that Jesus is the Christ, the Son of the Living God. Mohammed, Buddha or Confucius simply cannot do for you what Christ can do. They simply do not have the objective, historical evidence behind them that Jesus Christ has. No one has ever died for your sins but Jesus Christ. Only the tomb of Jesus Christ is empty. There is a real difference. To suggest that in theological realms all distinctions become moot and all religions are alike contradicts reality. Genuine belief in Jesus must come to grips with His exclusive nature. There is no other name under heaven whereby we must be saved (Acts 4:12); no one can come to the Father but by Him (John 14:6).

Nor should we think Christianity the only exclusive religion. Judaism is itself exclusive; orthodox Jews still make distinctions between themselves and Gentiles. The Islamic faith is exclusive; there is no God but Allah for them. They do not regard Jesus as the Son of God but as a prophet. They regard the gospels of the New Testament as inspired of God but corrupted of man and untrustworthy. For them, Mohammed is the prophet of Allah. Christians who reject Mohammed cannot be accepted into the Islamic faith.

The pluralism of our time cannot stand, for it of necessity contradicts itself. It leads to a meaningless belief system full of contradictions and compromise. Nothing is ever settled because no one can know the truth. There can be no convictions because as soon as a person speaks out, he must take it back. The many religions of the world may share some moral traits, but a closer examination will reveal how mutually exclusive they are. When postmodernists expect everyone to accept every religion, they create enormous confusion. By nature, people do not want such pervasive confusion; they want to make some sense of life. Christian evangelists can help people to rise above the confusion and meaninglessness of theological pluralism.

We must stress the uniqueness and the originality of Jesus. He is an historical reality, and we must remind them of His unique fulfillment of ancient prophecies. To suggest that Jesus is one great, moral teacher among many does not stack up with the evidence. The impact of Jesus goes far beyond moral teaching; He demands utter allegiance to His way. More than that, He declares the severest judgment on any who fail to do the will of God (Matthew 7:21-23; John 12:48; Revelation 20:11-15). We must ultimately look to Jesus, however, because of Who He is as a Person. Mohammed claimed to be a prophet, but he never said he was the Son of God. We must look to Christ and realize that He is in a category all to Himself.

At some time we must confess with Paul that in Christ are "all the treasures of wisdom and knowledge" (Colossians 2:3). James D. Bales observed concerning Christianity and other religions that there are similarities, but there are also profound differences:

> It is well to remember that there are similarities between a man and a donkey, and a woman and a monkey, but all of us, I am confident will say: There are vast differences, and long live the differences! We misrepresent man and woman if we ignore the differences. We misrepresent Christ if we ignore the differences between Him and other religious leaders. These things make it clear that even when Jesus taught some truths which others had taught, He presented them in their greatest height, their deepest depth, and their widest breadth. But what is more significant is who Jesus was and is.[2]

With this in mind, we move to these fundamental questions: 1. Who is Jesus Christ (to me)? and 2. Why should I believe in Him?

The first question must be taken in two parts. It is one thing to ask who Jesus Christ is, and it is another to ask who Jesus is to me. The former part is an objective question, while the latter is personal and subjective. What Jesus is in reality may not be who Jesus is in my mind. Occasionally I hear people speak of Jesus or God in terms of what they think He would or would not do. Some think that God or Jesus would never send anyone to hell because their perception of Him is such; but this perception of God ignores the biblical revelation of God. Their perception of God and the biblically revealed God are very different. Our world today is not so unlike the first century when Gentiles did not know God (1 Thessalonians 4:5). They may know what they wish God was like, but this is not "knowing" God. The single greatest problem of our time or any time is that people do not know God.

Although we accept the notion that each believer must come to own his own faith, this is not the same thing as manufacturing one's own faith. An objective faith believes truth is outside and bigger than one's self, whereas a subjective faith believes in an inwardly determined truth. Objective truth is founded upon facts and historical realities outside ourselves, whereas subjective truth is founded upon feelings, thoughts and beliefs within ourselves. Objectivity means that one relies on outside realities; subjectivity means that one relies on inside perceptions.

That perceptions are faulty is obvious from life and from history. No matter how much man has relied on his perception that the earth is flat, the objective truth is the earth is round. No matter how one perceives the sun to revolve around the earth, the objective truth is the earth revolves around the sun. No matter how dark a shadowed stop sign appears, the sign is painted red and white. Whatever one may see in the mirror, there is no world on the other side of the glass. What we think, feel, believe or perceive does not change physical reality. We may deceive ourselves with our perceptions; and we may even act boldly on the basis of those perceptions. But our perceptions of reality may or may not be in line with the truth. Optical illusions are just that – illusions. Since perceptions are faulty, the idea that we can manufacture truth from our perceptions leads to a faulty faith.

What we perceive, believe, think or feel is the will of God may or may not be in line with the truth of God's Word. Truth, then, is not determined by what we think but by what God says. What God says is a constant; but what we perceive religiously may or may not change, since we are influenced and colored by our experiences. A lie may color our perceptions of the truth, but a lie will not change the truth itself. Even if we confirm our perceptions with the testimony of other people, this does not change what stands written by God in His Word. We must bring our personal faith in line with His eternal Word. Who Jesus is to me must come into line with who Jesus is in reality; otherwise, my faith is in an imaginary Jesus of my own manufacturing.

It is precisely here that Christianity presents a stumbling block for many postmodernists. The postmodernist devotes himself to a personalized, individualistic religion. He wants nothing less than to manufacture his own faith rather than inherit it from some source outside himself. He wants to reinvent Jesus in a likeness that suits him. He prefers a church in which he can determine the rules and traditions. He is not content to adapt to what he finds; the postmodernist feels that he must be a change agent. He honestly feels that the traditional church cannot survive without his expertise and guidance. He sees the future as the end of Christianity as it has traditionally been known. It never occurs to him that the church has survived for thousands of years through a wide variety of challenges (and all without his guidance and counsel). We can be sure New Testament Christianity and the church will survive postmodernism.

The postmodernist considers evangelism arrogant and intolerant, because it stands in judgment of someone else's unique experience and culture. Many people in the emerging generation no longer consider Christianity as an option for them. They do not reject the Christ because there is no historical evidence or because He does not have something to offer. They reject Him because He claims to be universally and objectively true. He claims to be true for everybody in every culture and in every time. This claim violates the carefully cultivated disbelief in anything absolute or objective. The offense of Christianity is that it does not allow absolute freedom to the individual to determine his own faith. Consequently, the postmodernist asks the question, "What does Christ mean to me?" He must come to understand that there is something in the universe bigger than himself. There is something bigger than self-made religion. A self-made Christianity is no better than a self-made idol. It cannot do what biblical Christianity can do. If everybody has the privilege of manufacturing his own Christianity, who is Christ really? He is but an imaginary Lord. On the other hand, if Jesus Christ is real and objective, He must be taken on His terms and not ours. If He is Lord, only He has the right to set His terms. Whatever humans may think or dream up is merely an illusion.

The second question is: "Why should I believe in Him?" The evangelist to a postmodern world must also be an apologist, i.e., a defender of his faith. Peter reminds us that we should "always be ready to make a defense ... for the hope that is in you, yet with gentleness and reverence" (1 Peter 3:15). An acquaintance with the historical proofs of Jesus' existence, the facts surrounding the resurrection, and the prophecies about and by Jesus will help anyone who wishes to give a reason for his hope in Christ. Christians must be able to show the unique place that Jesus Christ has in this world and why one should be exclusively devoted to Him. We must once again make a case for Jesus Christ.

Gary R. Habermas in *The Historical Jesus* provides 129 distinct facts about Jesus Christ from 45 ancient sources outside of the New Testament. These evidences reveal a solid base for our trust in Jesus of Nazareth. Concerning Him, Habermas said,

> There can be little doubt that this is a substantial amount of pre- and non-New Testament material for Jesus' existence and for numerous facts about his life. In light of these reports we can better understand how groundless the speculations are that deny his existence or that postulate only a minimal amount of facts concerning him. Much of ancient history is based on many fewer sources that are much later than the events that they record, as we have seen. While some believe that we know almost nothing about Jesus from ancient, non-New Testament sources, this is plainly not the case. Not only are there many such sources, but Jesus is one of the persons of ancient history concerning whom we have a significant amount of quality data. His is one of the most mentioned and most substantiated lives in ancient times.[3]

Such evidences cannot be ignored or denied by honest people. There is a substantive difference between a real Jesus and a questionable Buddha or Confucius, about whom we know very little. Jesus is not a myth or fairy tale. He is not a manufactured Messiah but a real Messiah. Those who followed Him died for His cause because they believed in Him. Men do not make such commitments for what they know is fake. Those who lived and knew Jesus best testified with their lives that He was really the Son of God. They had undeniable convictions that they would not take back even under the threat of beatings and death. There is a genuineness underlying such convictions that cannot easily be laid aside. Jesus was real; men do not die for empty hopes.

Scholars through the ages have given painstaking scrutiny to the events surrounding the resurrection of Jesus Christ. Through the years some have suggested swoon theories, hallucinations and body snatching. Such theories contradict the available evidence in the gospels and testify more to the imagination of the authors than to the gospel facts. The prophecies of the Old Testament predicting the coming Messiah provide a powerful testimony to the unique Son of God. No other person in all of history could have fulfilled the prophecies Jesus fulfilled. Human beings cannot plot the prophecies of their own births. They cannot plan the amount of their betrayal, nor can humans successfully predict their own resurrections. Jesus did, and by so doing He declared with power that He was the Son of God (Romans 1:4).

Jesus' own prophecies and the remarkable events of His life speak loudly as to His genuineness. Jesus could never have gotten the following He had in Palestine had He not been able to fulfill His predictions. When one considers some of the remarkable things Jesus did, it is no wonder that He had so many disciples. If Jesus, however, had failed with some of His short-term prophecies, He certainly would not have maintained the loyalty of His disciples. Jesus once told Peter to go fishing. Peter's first catch was to have four drachmas, exactly enough to pay for the temple tax of Jesus and Peter (Matthew 17:24-27). What if there had been no coin in the mouth of that fish? How would Peter have ever trusted Jesus? If Jesus' words had not proven true early on, the disciples would never have continued to follow Him.

Jesus told friends or family members that their loved ones had already been healed, sometimes at great distances from the discussion. Can you imagine the anger and the charges there would have been against Jesus had he failed to heal the loved ones of these people. The centurion (Matthew 8:13) or the royal official in Capernaum (John 4:50-53) would certainly have imprisoned Jesus had his prophesied healings been phony. They would have done every-thing they could to prove Jesus a fraud. Instead, Jesus warned those He healed not to tell everyone about the healings. If Jesus had nev-er really healed these and thousands of other people, everyone would have known it. Jesus made predictions about the future that no per-son would have dared to make, unless the power of God was with them. Nicodemus said of Jesus, "Rabbi, we know that You have come from God as a teacher; for no one can do these signs that You do unless God is with him" (John 3:2). The things that Jesus did were not done in a corner (Acts 26:26).

In these days of uncertainty, evangelists must know what they be-lieve and why they believe it. We must renew our study of the de-fense of our faith. We must give our world a reason for the hope that is within us, providing a justification for our faith.

Some Crucial Questions Postmodernists Ask

Why do we even need God now that we have modern science? Modern science can tell us the whats of life, but they cannot tell us whys. Science was never intended to answer metaphysical ques-tions. There are realms beyond the scope of what science is designed to consider. Science cannot do everything. It can make life last a lit-tle longer, but science cannot stop death. Science can tell us what our universe is like, but it cannot determine what power holds it to-gether. Many of the questions God asked Job still remain unan-swered.[4] It is often man's arrogance, not his knowledge, that caus-es him to ask such a thing.

Scientists may analyze, but they cannot fulfill the hunger in man to adore that which is greater than himself. Man is incurably reli-gious, and science cannot fill the restlessness within us. Many years ago Augustine said,

> You are great, O Lord, and greatly to be praised: great is your power and to your wisdom there is no limit. And man, who is part of your creation, wishes to praise you, man who bears about within himself his mortality, who bears about within himself the testimony that you resist

the proud. Yet man, this part of your creation, wishes to praise you. You arouse him to take joy in praising you, for you have made us for yourself, and our heart is restless until it rests in you.[5]

The hunger of the soul is universal in time and culture; such hunger cannot so easily be dismissed by those who have worship at the altar of science. That man-made altar is insufficient to fill the greater needs of man.

Who says there is such a thing as "truth" anyway? People in all societies throughout the centuries have believed in truth. This is why there are laws on the books against perjury and bearing false witness. This is why men from every era have despised injustice and hypocrisy. Someone who finds out that he has been deceived suddenly has a new appreciation for the truth. Few people go to the doctor with a serious disease in order to remain uninformed; they do not want to be told that no one knows what disease they have. No, they want the truth. They realize that their physical life can only be sustained if they treat the true problem. Theoretically, people like to say there is no such thing as truth; but they will take this pessimism back in real life. In life they want the truth. What we must do is show the contradictions between the postmodern mindset and real, everyday life. The fact is, a postmodern world is a fantasy.

If you are a Christian, a postmodernist might say to you, "Hey, since you choose a Christian lifestyle, why can't I choose the lifestyle that's right for me?" Everyone has the right to choose whatever lifestyle he pleases, but everyone must understand that there are consequences to his choices. A long time ago, a younger son chose to live an ungodly life in a country of his choosing. He discovered life without the stable foundations of home and faith could be bitter, empty and lonely. It is a shame that many people have to discover that lesson for themselves. Solomon said to the young men of his time:

> Rejoice, young man, during your childhood, and let your heart be pleasant during the days of young manhood. And follow the impulses of your heart and the desires of your eyes. Yet know that God will bring you to judgment

for all these things. So, remove vexation from your heart and put away pain from your body, because childhood and the prime of life are fleeting (Ecclesiastes 11:9-10).

God gave His laws for our good (Deuteronomy 6:24; 10:13). He has never wanted anything but what is best for us. God gave His laws to us to bless us and to protect us from evil. It is a basic mis-understanding of God to resent the laws He has given us. John said, "For this is the love of God, that we keep His commandments; and His commandments are not burdensome" (1 John 5:3).

How can you say that Jesus is the ONLY way to God? Today if you tell many people "God loves you," they are likely to respond, "Which God are you talking about?" Most people love and respect someone who does not believe in Jesus Christ. Many cannot imag-ine their nonbelieving loved ones being lost. Rather than face the painful reality of their spiritually lost condition, many prefer to re-vert to some form of universalism – believing everyone is saved. For them, God surely will not send anyone to hell. Again comes the crunch. The Bible teaches that those who do not believe in Jesus as the Christ are lost (Mark 16:16; John 3:18; 2 Thessalonians 1:7-9). The faithful Christian must make a choice either to place His trust in Christ's teachings or his own thinking. It is, after all, Jesus who said He was the only way to heaven. Christians believe that, because they believe Jesus. It is confidence in the person Jesus that leads to confidence in the words of Jesus.

How can I believe in a God I cannot see? As limited human be-ings we sometimes need to ask ourselves if we have seen every-thing. How much do we really know? You might ask, "What per-cent of all knowledge do you possess?" Perhaps he will say, "Less than one percent." Then ask, "Is it possible that the knowledge of God lies outside of your limited knowledge?" A true postmodernist can never say he knows God is just a myth. A postmodernist can-not know anything. He may think he knows. If truth is not absolute, he can never make any final statement about anything. Whatever he says, he must take it back. The postmodern mindset is the high-est form of agnosticism.

Valid Questions Christians May Ask

If postmodernism is a worldview or mindset, then evangelists and teachers must not only teach facts but also teach their students how to think Christian. It is not enough to know about apologetics, Bible doctrine, and God. We must teach people to have the mind of Christ within themselves and to see life itself through a Christian worldview. Fran Sciacca in *Generation at Risk* spoke of connecting with teenagers in his senior Bible class by contemplating 10 key questions. He was looking at these questions from both a biblical and a secular worldview, trying to find a legitimate answer.[6]

> Individuality: Who or what am I?
>
> Meaning: What's the point of it all?
>
> Values: How am I to make moral choices?
>
> Truth: Is it possible to know the truth about ourselves and the universe?
>
> Love: What is love, and where can it be found?
>
> Suffering: Why is there suffering, and how can we live with it?
>
> Death: How am I to face death? Is there life after death?
>
> Hope: What hope is there for the human race?
>
> Reality: Is there anything more than the physical world?
>
> Evil: Is there any hope in fighting evil and injustice?

The gospel of Jesus provides the answer to these fundamental and relevant questions. Christian evangelists do not merely have one answer among many; they ultimately have the only answers that matter. We must not allow ourselves to be intimidated by the bullies of political correctness. They have sold their convictions to gain power, but a power without foundations cannot last. Christianity survived the dominance of pagan Rome, and it will surely survive the postmodern mindset. We cannot afford timidity at this time; we must be willing privately and publicly to speak boldly and faithfully. Christians must preach the gospel at all times, realizing that the teachings of Christ will always offend the world. Worldly powers have never wanted to hear teaching against sin, but this should not keep us from our task. We must not be intimidated into thinking that because many reject our message, everyone will. Paul told Timothy, "God has not given us a spirit of timidity, but of power and love and discipline" (2 Timothy 1:7).

The gospel possesses God's power; this is why the world fears and despises it. God has not left us ill-equipped in this or in any society to do the work He has called us to do. He has given us His armor, to equip us for the challenges ahead. Paul said,

> Therefore, take up the full armor of God, that you may be able to resist in the evil day, and having done everything, to stand firm. Stand firm therefore, having girded your loins with truth, and having put on the breastplate of righteousness, and having shod your feet with the preparation of the gospel of peace; in addition to all, taking up the shield of faith with which you will be able to extinguish all the flaming missiles of the evil one. And take the helmet of salvation, and the sword of the Spirit, which is the word of God. With all prayer and petition pray at all times in the Spirit, and with this in view, be on the alert with all perseverance and petition for all the saints, and pray on my behalf, that utterance may be given to me in the opening of my mouth, to make known with boldness the mystery of the gospel, for which I am an ambassador in chains; that in proclaiming it I may speak boldly, as I ought to speak (Ephesians 6:13-20).

As Christians we are not going into this challenge of worldviews unable to defend ourselves or unable to pierce the hearts of the unbelieving. Righteous and loving people who speak the truth will always gain a hearing with good and honest hearts. The story of the cross, a story of love and sacrifice for helpless and sinful man, still has persuasive power. God Himself said through the prophet Isaiah, "So shall My word be which goes forth from My mouth; It shall not return to Me empty, Without accomplishing what I desire, And without succeeding in the matter for which I sent it" (Isaiah 55:11). The gospel has God's power behind it. If God could speak the world into existence, surely His word is powerful enough to touch today's hearts.

When I traveled on campaign into Minsk, Belarus, in 1992, I found a country dominated by communism for 70 years. The former Soviet Union forced every college graduate to take at least two years of class in Atheism. The government had trained the people to believe Karl Marx's axiom, "Religion is the opium of the people." Marx hated religion; and the socialism he espoused sought to banish the opportunity to have a faith. I do not believe that Marx understood how greatly his philosophies robbed the very hearts and souls of the people. The unbelief of the country had left people empty of God and empty of hope (Ephesians 2:12). They were incredibly hungry for truth, for righteousness, for love, and for hope. The gospel fed them what they needed. Belarus reminded me of the words of Amos:

> "Behold, days are coming," declares the Lord God, "When I will send a famine on the land, Not a famine for bread or a thirst for water, But rather for hearing the words of the LORD. And people will stagger from sea to sea, And from the north even to the east; They will go to and fro to seek the word of the LORD, But they will not find it" (Amos 8:11-12).

Whether men realize it or not, they need God's Word as much as they need air and water. As evangelists we must help people realize their hunger and God's provision for them. The hunger is already inside each of us; we must help people who are without God awaken to their emptiness.

The gospel is not an opium; it is the bread of life. The gospel does not blind and enslave; it opens our eyes and sets us free. Jesus said, "It is written, 'Man shall not live on bread alone, but on every word that proceeds out of the mouth of God' " (Matthew 4:4; Deuteronomy 8:3). These words were true in Moses' day and in Jesus' day, and they will be true to the end of time. Men need the Bible to live. Jesus said, "the words that I have spoken to you are spirit and are life" (John 6:63). The gospel, more than anything else, is the Word of Life. We must realize God's purpose in us to take light and freedom, hope and love, righteousness and promise to a world darkened and deceived by sin. God called Paul to preach to the Gentiles – "to open their eyes so that they may turn from darkness to light and from the dominion of Satan to God, in order that they may receive forgiveness of sins and an inheritance among those who have been sanctified by faith in Me" (Acts 26:18). God still calls us to this work in the postmodern era. We must understand the mindset of our time, but we must also reassure our hearts that we have the gospel answer to the problems and the confusions. The gospel will remain long after postmodernism falls. The church will survive the postmodern era; therefore, let us not lose heart.

Discussion Questions

1. What are some of the fruits of uncertainty?

2. What "points of connection" can we make with postmodern people?

3. What is the difference between the questions "Who is Jesus?" and "Who is Jesus to me?"

4. What evidences do we have of the uniqueness and Deity of Jesus?

5. How does the removal of religious foundations affect people?

CHAPTER 13

Go in Faith, Go in Hope, Go in Love

AN OPTIMISTIC VIEW FOR FAITHFUL CHURCHES OF CHRIST

What of the future? What can we expect for ourselves as we grow older? What can we expect for our children and our grandchildren? How serious a threat is postmodernism? It seems as if Satan has been saving up every evil scheme to throw at the 21st century church all at once. Declining morals, eroding foundations, and dying faith have left our society religiously bankrupt. Each year we lose some sacred right to our religious freedom, and we find the "prince of this world" winning battles against the truth. We must even fear our brethren at times, since the phrase "church of Christ" does not guarantee what we will find anymore.

The postmodern mindset of political correctness will continue to dominate the 21st century. Political correctness lends itself easily to theological correctness, and this means serious problems for committed Christians. As postmodernism and the desire for change gain philosophical momentum, the belief in absolute truth seems more and more out of step. One might worry the day will come when Christianity will be obsolete. We look at European countries whose secularized morals and empty churches prophesy a post-Christian society for America. Should we dwell on such matters, we would surely become depressed and discouraged.

We might ask, "Will the church, the kingdom of Christ, endure?" The answer is an unqualified yes. The church will surely endure. Daniel said that while other kingdoms would fall, the Messianic kingdom "will itself endure forever" (Daniel 2:44). The angel told Mary concerning the baby in her womb:

> He will be great, and will be called the Son of the Most High; and the Lord God will give Him the throne of His father David; and He will reign over the house of Jacob forever; and His kingdom will have no end (Luke 1:32-33).

Jesus Himself said, "upon this rock I will build My church; and the gates of Hades shall not overpower it" (Matthew 16:18). If Jesus' death did not stop Him from building His church, nothing can keep it from enduring.

We do not face a more serious threat to our faith than did Christians in other centuries. The book of Revelation proclaims loudly that the Lamb will overcome His enemies. However powerful, popular, or organized Satan may be, he will surely fall to the Lamb. The glory of Rome and the power of Caesar had challenged the faith of the frightened Christians of Asia Minor. Rome would persecute and kill some for their faith. They had already witnessed the loss of their brothers and sisters to Rome's cruelty. They needed reassurance and to see the bigger picture. Revelation pictures the surpassing power and glory of "Lord Christ" over "lord Caesar." John told them, "These will wage war against the Lamb, and the Lamb will overcome them, because He is Lord of lords and King of kings, and those who are with Him are the called and chosen and faithful" (Revelation 17:14). We too need a fresh vision of the King of kings and the Lord of lords. We need to see Him seated in Heaven, lofty and mighty. By faith we need to see the One whom we serve. He reigns undefeated in grandeur and glory. He is the true Son of God.

We must not take our eyes off the facts. We may ignore or deny the foundations God has laid for us, but our attitudes toward them do not remove them. When you are traveling, you may come upon a sign warning "Dangerous Curve Ahead." Those who posted the sign did so to get your attention. They are pointing you to reality and warning you of an impending danger. You, however, have some options in how you will react to that sign. First, you can take its warning, slow down, and drive with caution. Second, you can ignore the sign and risk traveling at the same rate of speed. Third, you can scoff the sign, tempt fate, and see how fast you can take the curve. Regardless of what you think or do, the dangerous curve is still there. It remains unchanged. Your attitude does not affect its angle, does not widen the road, and does not remove the ditch or the trees. If you violate the law of that curve, you will suddenly face its harsh reality. You simply cannot cheat reality. You can ignore it, deny it, defy it, or despise it; but reality returns. Reality is not dependent upon consent – personal or public.

The postmodern mindset does not remove reality. It may proclaim with force its commitment to anti-foundationalism, to theological correctness, and to nonjudgmentalism; but this does not change reality. The one true and living God rules heaven and earth. He exists, and all our posturing to get along with others cannot remove that reality. Those who have tried through the centuries to destroy the Word of God found it impossible. The Word of God is settled in heaven and indestructible on earth. It has its eternal foundation in God Himself. Jesus said, "Heaven and earth will pass away, but My words shall not pass away" (Matthew 24:35). God's truths remain as "the" reality, whether or not men recognize them. Although postmodernism may gain temporary strength in the coming century, it will not stand the tests of reality. God's word has survived every scheme planned against it, and it will survive this mindset as well.

Paul reminded the Galatians, "Do not be deceived, God is not mocked; for whatever a man sows, this he will also reap. For the one who sows to his own flesh shall from the flesh reap corruption, but the one who sows to the Spirit shall from the Spirit reap eternal life" (Galatians 6:7-8). Apparently some Galatians had deceived themselves by thinking they could live after the flesh and not suffer for it. Paul wanted to wake them to reality: "you cannot thumb your nose at God." Postmodernists think they can dismiss God with the wave of their hands; their commitment is to absolute moral freedom. In time they will wake to the harsh realities of God's moral laws. The freedoms postmodernists boast have not made their lives richer or better. Despite condoms, social diseases remain epidemic. The cur-

221

rent experiments with replacements for marriage have yielded renewed poverty and fatherless children. Each time men increase their lawlessness, they also increasingly find themselves victims of their own sins. Reality will not go away. Paul said of ancient men:

> For even though they knew God, they did not honor Him as God, or give thanks; but they became futile in their speculations, and their foolish heart was darkened. Professing to be wise, they became fools, and exchanged the glory of the incorruptible God for an image in the form of corruptible man and of birds and four-footed animals and crawling creatures. Therefore God gave them over in the lusts of their hearts to impurity, that their bodies might be dishonored among them. For they exchanged the truth of God for a lie, and worshiped and served the creature rather than the Creator, who is blessed forever. Amen (Romans 1:21-25).

Postmodernists exchange the truth of God for their own truths. They profess wisdom in their theological correctness but end up fools. Although they do not form idols of animals, they make themselves into gods. Is it any wonder that impurity dominates our society?

The message of the book of Revelation is simply, "we win!" In this current battle of worldviews and mindsets, we will not win everyone; but we will win with the Lord. We have enjoyed in our lifetime the privilege of standing with a moral majority. The tide of popular belief has turned from the truth and from morality to uncertainty and amorality. These changes mean we will more and more be an obstacle in the way of an ungodly agenda. Our children and grandchildren may face stiff opposition to their faith. Satan has always despised the light, and he will despise us for exposing his wicked schemes. The day may come when he will attack us freshly with persecution, imprisonment and death. If we are to win eternally, we must cling to the King of kings and Lord of lords, who is able to deliver us from the hand of the evil one.

We must renew our resolve to stand firm in our faith, to fix our hope on Him, and to love the Lord with all our hearts. Faith, hope and love remain when all else fails (1 Corinthians 13:13). Whether those outside the body of Christ know it or not, what they most need are faith, hope and love. The most important thing we can do in response to the changing mindset of our time is to take our Christianity seriously. We must be lights in a world dominated by darkness. The worldly will not appreciate us, but those searching for the truth will seek us out. Let us not set our hope on ruling the world but on entering heaven. John reminds us, "We know that we are of God, and the whole world lies in the power of the evil one" (1 John 5:19). Let us be who we are! That is our best hope of holding onto God and of reaching those who are outside.

Our Need for Faith: A North Star to Guide

Acts 27 tells the story of Paul's ill-fated voyage to Italy. From Fair Havens in Crete Paul sailed in an Alexandrian ship with 276 passengers and crew in the hope of reaching Phoenix. For 14 days the northwest wind Euraquilo violently battered the ship. Luke, who was on board with Paul, remarked, "since neither sun nor stars appeared for many days, and no small storm was assailing us, from then on all hope of our being saved was gradually abandoned" (Acts 27:20). The ship's captain and crew had no reference point, no North Star, to guide them. The storm kept all of them at its mercy. So despondent were the men, they did not eat. In the midst of their hopelessness Paul received a vision from God. He told his fellow passengers:

> Men, you ought to have followed my advice and not to have set sail from Crete, and incurred this damage and loss. And yet now I urge you to keep up your courage, for there shall be no loss of life among you, but only of the ship. For this very night an angel of the God to whom I belong and whom I serve stood before me, saying, 'Do not be afraid, Paul; you must stand before Caesar; and behold, God has granted you all those who are sailing with you.' Therefore, keep up your courage, men, for I believe God, that it will turn out exactly as I have been told (Acts 27:21-25).

In our own despair, adrift on a sea of uncertainty, we too have a God who can lead us through the storm. Paul proclaimed, "I believe God." We too need a sure faith in God, who will keep His promises and do just as He has told us. Just as all 276 people survived the storm in Paul's day, so we today can survive the uncertain storms we face if we hold fast to our faith.

And what kind of faith is necessary for these times?

We need an informed faith. We must know what we believe and why we believe it. The word of God itself remains the basis of any Christian faith. Paul said, "faith comes from hearing, and hearing by the word of Christ" (Romans 10:17). Christians would do well to read God's Word daily to strengthen their hearts for the challenges to come. The 21st century evangelist needs continuous preparation on a wide variety of issues. He must not only know why he believes in God; he must also know God. He must know the evidences for God's existence, for the inspiration and inerrancy of the Scriptures, for the uniqueness of Jesus Christ, for Christianity as the one and only saving faith, and for the importance and necessity of the church. The Word of God has power to touch hearts and make changes in people's lives. We must know the Word and put confidence in its ability to bring people to a saving knowledge of the Lord.

He must also understand the disjointed thinking of our postmodern times – how people have begun to think in a format like picture albums or slide shows. In times past we have trained our evangelists to reason and to think in a logical procession. The postmodern mindset rejects logic and teaches the coming generation to think in terms of a loosely connected set of facts. These facts do not need to be consistent and may contradict each other. Those beyond the age of thirty would do well to spend an hour watching and listening to MTV, not for its morality but to see how it communicates to the younger generation. Generation X has learned to make sense of what is otherwise confusing, rapid-fire images. Evangelists in the future will need to be more visual in their presentations of the Word of God. They may need to present the gospel of Jesus with more graphics and stand-alone word pictures.[1] While we can never change the message, we must learn effective ways of presenting the old story.

We need an effective faith. The times ahead demand conviction. The world will hardly take our faith any more seriously than we do. We cannot share a faith we do not possess. Some churches have moved so far from sharing their faith, they hardly do more than keep house. Whether they are afraid, indifferent or lazy, we do not know; but we do know they are ineffective. Paul told Philemon:

> I thank my God always, making mention of you in my prayers, because I hear of your love, and of the faith which you have toward the Lord Jesus, and toward all the saints; and I pray that the fellowship of your faith may become effective through the knowledge of every good thing which is in you for Christ's sake. For I have come to have much joy and comfort in your love, because the hearts of the saints have been refreshed through you, brother (Philemon 4-7).

We too need a faith of such character that when people are with us, it rubs off on them. Our lives, our attitudes, our faith, and our love ought to make people want to be Christians. Philemon refreshed the hearts of people around him, and we can do the same. The most attractive person in any room is not the best looking but the most loving and attentive. We too must cultivate in our lives the spirit of Christ, so the world will come to love the Christ who lives in us.

We need a bold faith. We must not allow the world to intimidate us into silence. The worst thing we can do is adopt a strategy of passive neutrality. We cannot afford to sit silently as spectators while the world speaks loud and long of the death of God. John revealed, "many even of the rulers believed in Him, but because of the Pharisees they were not confessing Him, lest they should be put out of the synagogue; for they loved the approval of men rather than the approval of God" (John 12:42-43). Bold faith puts its trust in God over the objections of men. Like Peter, it cries out, "We must obey God rather than men" (Acts 5:29). Churches who compromise to get along with religious neighbors are saying they want the approval of men more than they want the approval of God. In their own way they are contributing to current trends of pluralization and privatization. They are saying each man can have his own faith and each view is as good as another's. If this be true, where is the Lord's authority? Bold faith is willing to stand with the Lord and against the tide of popular belief. Bold faith is willing to take the consequences of believing; it is willing to die for Christ and with Christ.

Paul asked the Ephesians to pray for him at all times "that utterance may be given to me in the opening of my mouth, to make known with boldness the mystery of the gospel, for which I am an ambassador in chains; that in proclaiming it I may speak boldly, as I ought to speak" (Ephesians 6:19-20). Christianity has some hard things to say to lost people. It is never easy to speak of sin, repentance, or the consequences of disobedience. We cannot know how people will react to our message, and we fear their rejection. Any preacher who speaks the truth will find someone getting up and walking out on him. No one likes rejection, but faithfulness to God demands the courage to speak the truth. We need a faith like Daniel, who prayed to the Lord in spite of the king's law. We need a faith like the three Hebrew children, who would gladly enter the fiery furnace whether God delivered them or not. We need a faith like Elijah, who in the midst of hundreds of false prophets called for fire from heaven. We need faith like John the Baptist, who spoke out against sin at the cost of his head. We need faith like Paul, who challenged the philosophers of Athens with the resurrection.

We need an active faith. Peter admonished the brethren of his time to "Keep your behavior excellent among the Gentiles, so that in the thing in which they slander you as evildoers, they may on account of your good deeds, as they observe them, glorify God in the day of visitation" (1 Peter 2:12). Faith without works is dead toward God and unfruitful with men. James said, "You believe that God is one. You do well; the demons also believe, and shudder. But are you willing to recognize, you foolish fellow, that faith without works is useless" (James 2:19-20)? The church must do more than speak; it must act out its faith. Good deeds matter to the postmodern world; people still react favorably to love and attention. Kindness characterized the church of the early centuries and won countless converts.

The Roman historian Suetonius mistakenly spoke of Christ with the word "Chrestus" instead of "Christus."[2] "Chrestus" means kind, and the mistake was not all that unintentional, for early Christians were known for their kindness. In a world not listening to much else, kindness may be the unanswerable argument for Christianity.

We need a morally pure faith. James describes "pure religion" as "keeping oneself unstained by the world" (James 1:27). Many Christians have made incredible moral compromises in the last few decades. The dramatic increases in ungodliness in media, R-rated movies, legalized abortion, widespread gambling, no-fault divorce, and unwanted pregnancies have left our country morally neutral. We are afraid to speak out against sin because we all know people close to us who are facing moral dilemmas. By adopting an approach of nonjudgmentalism, we have unwittingly encouraged amorality, i.e., the lack of a sense of right and wrong. Christians who pattern their lives after the Lord learn to live above the level of the world. Paul said,

> This I say therefore, and affirm together with the Lord, that you walk no longer just as the Gentiles also walk, in the futility of their mind, being darkened in their understanding, excluded from the life of God, because of the ignorance that is in them, because of the hardness of their heart; and they, having become callous, have given themselves over to sensuality, for the practice of every kind of impurity with greediness. But you did not learn Christ in this way, if indeed you have heard Him and have been taught in Him, just as truth is in Jesus, that, in reference to your former manner of life, you lay aside the old self, which is being corrupted in accordance with the lusts of deceit, and that you be renewed in the spirit of your mind, and put on the new self, which in the likeness of God has been created in righteousness and holiness of the truth (Ephesians 4:17-24).

There is a difference in the way genuine Christians live and in the way those who do not know God live. The world itself sees this difference and appreciates it. The church regularly get calls from companies and employment agencies looking to hire Christians. Why do they call the church? They want workers they can trust – who will not steal and who will give an honest day's work. Many companies want Christian workers because Christians have a work ethic tied to their faith. Christian workers do what is right because God and Christ expect them to. The more amoral our society becomes, the more difficult it will be to find good employees.

When postmodernism suggests the removal of the foundations of religion and morality, they also lose the benefits of those foundations. As long as Christians maintain pure and honest lives, they will maintain a practical attractiveness in the world. Although the world theoretically wants to rid itself of moral restraints, it demands something better for itself. Many people value absolute moral freedom until they become the victim of someone else's morality.

What people believe matters. Christians need to develop a strong and mature faith, which will guide them through the roughest storms in the coming years. In the Bible they have the directions to the everlastingly safe harbor, heaven. They need not be uncertain when God's word has been proven true over and over again. They need not remain lost when the Bible gives them the guidance to know where they came from, who they are, where they are now, why they are here, and where they are going. Yes, what people believe matters.

Our Need for Hope: An Anchor to the Soul

We are not the first generation to face an unknown enemy who frightens and confuses us. The history of the Bible reveals the continuing challenges of those who believed. Each generation has had its Goliaths to conquer, its temptations to avoid, and its hardships to suffer. Peter reminded the persecuted brothers to whom he wrote:

> Beloved, do not be surprised at the fiery ordeal among you, which comes upon you for your testing, as though some strange thing were happening to you; but to the degree that you share the sufferings of Christ, keep on rejoicing; so that also at the revelation of His glory, you may rejoice with exultation. If you are reviled for the

name of Christ, you are blessed, because the Spirit of glory and of God rests upon you (1 Peter 4:12-14).

Because the Lord's people have always been tested, we should not expect to escape it. Although our testing may differ from the persecution of early times, it is nevertheless the time for us to stand with God and against the forces of evil.

In generations past we enjoyed the favor of popular opinion; we called our country a "Christian" nation. For a time America modeled its laws and ways after the morals written in God's Word. Alexis de Tocqueville (1801-59), a French statesman and political philosopher, came to America in 1831 to examine this country after 50 years of democracy. In 1835 and 1840 he wrote his famous book *Democracy in America*, describing the American system. Tocqueville said, "America is great because she is good; and if America ever ceases to be good, America will cease to be great." Tocqueville's prophecy proved to be true. The Supreme Court, breaking from its long history, separated the church from the state by ruling against prayer and Bible reading in school. We have watched in the past four decades the demand for more and more freedom from religion. God was dethroned from the law of the land. Today, while the Ten Commandments hang upon the walls of our high courts, we censure our judges who use the Bible to make legal decisions. The prince of this world, our enemy, has reared his ugly head.

At ease for so many years, we have found ourselves ill-prepared for the rapid changes of popular belief that both test and confuse us. We have awakened to find all those bedrock beliefs missing from our courts and our schools. In the midst of a storm, we are forced to look to God. Perhaps, by the will of God, we needed this testing to remind us of our hope. When tumultuous change surrounds us, we pay more attention to Him who does not change. He is our anchor in times of storm, and there is no other.

We should not think that this is the first generation to be intolerant of intolerance. The church of the first three centuries encountered an incredible prejudice because they believed in one God. The world has hardly ever tolerated the kind of conviction in one God the early Christians displayed. Pagan emperors tried every scheme imaginable, tortured in every way possible, and used every power conceivable to root out Christianity; but they failed. The blood of the martyrs became the seed of the kingdom. For every death, two became Christians. Paul reminds us, "And indeed, all who desire to live godly in Christ Jesus will be persecuted" (2 Timothy 3:12). Persecution, however, does not end the story; God says more. The last chapter of the story of our lives has not yet been written. Peter gave this encouragement, "And after you have suffered for a little while, the God of all grace, who called you to His eternal glory in Christ, will Himself perfect, confirm, strengthen and establish you" (1 Peter 5:10). We should not face the current trends against us with sadness but with resolution as an opportunity to stand for our faith. After we have passed through our testing, God Himself will "perfect, confirm, strengthen and establish" us. This promise gives us hope.

From time to time, God prunes the branches of His vine. We are perhaps entering just such a time. God Himself will chop away the spiritually dead and unfruitful branches and will prune clean the living ones. Unfruitful branches, however luxurious and leafy, rob the vine of its vitality for the productive branches; and God demands fruit. The unfruitful branches are more concerned with their own welfare than in doing the will of God. We become clean through the Word Jesus has spoken to us (John 15:3). God's Word distinguishes between genuine disciples and people who think they are disciples (John 8:31-32). Our Lord Jesus said, "If you keep My commandments, you will abide in My love; just as I have kept My Father's commandments, and abide in His love" (John 15:10). Abiding in Jesus means we keep His commandments; obedience is God's measure of our love toward Him.

When progressive inclusivists argue for the acceptance of perverted gospels, they do not lead people to keep the commandments or to abide in the love of God. Rather, they lead to selfish and unfaithful religion, which compromises with the world. How, when and under what circumstances God removes branches remains in the hands of God; we do not presume to stand in God's place. We grieve over the loss of branches that fail to be productive, but we rejoice that God prunes productive branches so that they may be more productive. We pray that God will count us faithful and fruitful. We could only wish those who are arguing for change would spend less time listening to the selfish demands of people and more time with God's Word.

We possess hope in God because God keeps His promises. His trustworthiness and dependability provide a constant source of truth and promise for us. Postmodernism's desire for absolute freedom comes at the cost of hope and promise. Postmodernism has no reason for hope, for it does not know what the future holds. He has no assurance that he can depend on the future. Commitment to absolute liberty evolves into chaos and absurdity. It leaves men uncertain, confused, hopeless and depressed. In the uncertainty of our times, people long for some sense of security; postmodernism has no means of satisfying this spiritual yearning. It offers no expectation life will improve. Remember, whatever postmodernism offers, it must take back. Ultimately, the postmodern mindset believes nothing; it can offer no hope because it finds no reliable promise. Such is the high price of denying absolute truth. Man needs hope, and the day will come when he will long for more than what postmodernism has to offer. He will tire of the sea of uncertainty and will seek the shore of truth. Fredrich Nietzsche, the German philosopher who espoused the view "God is dead," expressed his disappointment with life. He asked, "Where is my home? For it do I ask and seek, and have sought, but have not found it. O eternal everywhere, O eternal nowhere, O eternal – in vain!"[3] The postmodernist will ask why we have hope, and we can share our hope with him. Peter said, "but sanctify Christ as Lord in your hearts, always being ready to make a defense to everyone who asks you to give an account for the hope that is in you, yet with gentleness and reverence" (1 Peter 3:15).

We have in Christ the one hope the world seeks. The offer of hope gives us a powerful point of connection with an empty world. We offer what no one else can offer – a better future. We offer a better future through the good teaching of Christ, which brings an abundant life (John 10:10). We offer a moral and servant life patterned after Jesus Christ. We offer a life freed from the guilt and punishment of sin. We offer purpose and direction – something worth living and dying for. We have relationship and intimacy with our Creator and Savior. We offer an eternal dwelling place with God (John 14:1-3). The empty tomb of Jesus may be dismissed by the postmodernist, but it matters when we must lay our loved ones to rest at the cemetery. The postmodernist who drifts in uncertainty has little to offer the grieving. His philosophies offer little more than the stale fragrance of an empty perfume bottle. They smell nice at first but have no substance. A generation lulled to sleep by the postmodern mindset will one day awaken to find itself incredibly hungry and thirsty. Adrift on the sea of uncertainty, it will hunger for a port to find the spiritual realities it needs to make some sense of life. It will long to come home to God. Men often do not understand what they have until they have lost it. We must be there to gently, lovingly point them to the one great hope we have in Christ Jesus.

As committed Christians we have no reason to despair, whatever happens in this life. We must learn to be content in any circumstances with the grace given so freely to us. We need to imitate the attitude of Paul who said of his own life, "we are afflicted in every way, but not crushed; perplexed, but not despairing; persecuted, but not forsaken; struck down, but not destroyed" (2 Corinthians 4:8-9). Satan can beat us up, but he cannot rob us of our hope. We can confidently expect a better life than we now possess; we have heaven.

Our Need for Love: A Rudder to Steer

While I was a student at Harding Graduate School of Religion, I wrote my guided research paper, "Evangelizing the Thorough-going Empiricist." In the process of research and discussing how to reach those who only believed what they saw and heard, I met a fellow student during a break in class. I had never met him before, and I have never seen him since. I wish I knew his name. During a brief conversation I learned he had been an atheist, having studied science in a major university in California. He revealed the training his unbelieving professors had given him to deal with Christians. He believed he could answer whatever argument a Christian could throw at him. Nevertheless, he met a godly Christian girl who stole his heart. She influenced him to attend church with her, and she would not miss services. Early on, he found himself debating with those who taught faith in Christ. In his mind he could easily answer the Christian evidences presented at the church.

What he never prepared for was the love and joy he saw in that church. He knew they had something he did not have. He was educated but empty, missing the love and joy of faith in Christ. Their faith had given them a well-roundedness that science could never have offered. He saw first in his fiancée and later in the church a godly warmth for which his soul hungered. Love and warmth conquered his soul in a way reason and logic could not. The atheist in him died of spiritual hunger, and he was born again in Christ. I learned a valuable lesson from that experience – a lesson I saw repeated often in my trips to the former Soviet Union. Love will do what logic and argument cannot do. It pierces areas of the heart and soul that reason cannot touch.

Over and over in Belarus and Ukraine I saw atheists and agnostics come to faith in Christ. Each college graduate in the former Soviet republics had taken the compulsory two years of study in atheism. They had grown full of doubts and questions outwardly, but inwardly they suffered for it. They wanted to believe but did not always know how. They knew the emptiness of having no relationship with the God who created them; they longed to know Him and to love Him. In the message of the cross, they learned about the depth of His love for them. They learned that love for God was not "the opium of the masses," as Karl Marx claimed; it was wholesome and healthy. Faith in Christ brought them life and joy, and they experienced a love they had never enjoyed before. The love of the gospel changed their lives forever.

Our world today desperately needs to know the overwhelming love of God. Even the church needs to take a long and close look at the cross of Christ. We need to see once again the nails that pierced

His hands and feet, the crown of thorns upon His head, the torn flesh upon His back, the bruises upon His face, and the agony of His death. We need to hear Him weeping in prayer in the garden, asking for His killers' forgiveness at the nailing, crying out at His forsaking, and commending His spirit into the hands of the Father. We need to recall the soldiers mocking Him and spitting upon Him. Once again we need to listen to an intolerant crowd calling for His blood, accusing Him with lies and falsehoods, and taunting Him with sarcasm and shame. We need to feel with Him the excruciating pain in bearing the crucifixion, struggling in bitter agony for every breath, and realizing the weight of the world's sins upon His soul. Only then can we begin to know what great love the Father and the Son have for mankind. The real message of Christianity must start and end with the cross. Paul "determined to know nothing ... except Jesus Christ, and Him crucified" (1 Corinthians 2:2).

If we are to restore ourselves to a proper perspective, we must stop focusing on ourselves and look long and hard at the cross. We must see His passion, remember His sacrifice, and imitate His love. The world needs to know the love of God more than anything else. Love will cure our arrogance and curb our rebellion. Love will turn the selfishness of our spoiled times into selflessness and sacrifice. The love of the cross will overcome cynicism and skepticism. Love will renew our passion and revive our zeal. The love of Christ will bind us together in perfect unity and correct our attitudes.

The postmodern mindset grows so full of selfishness it has no room for God. The cross of Jesus provides the answer to our soul-sick society. We need the heart of Paul who said, "I have been crucified with Christ; and it is no longer I who live, but Christ lives in me; and the life which I now live in the flesh I live by faith in the Son of God, who loved me, and delivered Himself up for me" (Galatians 2:20). The church does not need to change in order to be like the world; the church needs to let Christ live in it. Christ can never live in His church until those who are in His church are willing to be crucified with Him. This love, as a rudder, steers our lives; it is our mindset.

The church can go in faith, in hope, and in love when it carries the cross. It can survive an unfriendly world, reach into the hearts of the searching, and radiate joy and peace. As long as we cling to the cross, we can resist the chaos and confusion of our times. The church need not be set adrift on the sea of uncertainty; we have foundations that cannot be removed. We must hold firmly to them. The cross and the empty tomb unfailingly point us back to the Father and the foundations we so desperately need. Like Dorothy in *The Wizard of Oz*, we must awaken from an imaginary world and come back to reality. Of the inspired, inerrant and unchanging Word of God, we too say, "There's no place like home."

Discussion Questions

1. What may we expect of postmodernism in the future?

2. What kept the church in existence through the persecutions early in its history?

3. What kind of faith will Christians need to face in the 21st century?

4. What hope does the Christian have in a postmodern world?

5. What difference has the love of God made in your life?

End Notes

Chapter 1

1. Op. cit. from *God's Word, translation of God's Word to the Nations Bible Society* (Grand Rapids, Mich.: World Publishing, 1995).

2. George Barna, *The Frog in the Kettle: What Christians Need to Know about Life in the Year 2000* (Ventura, Calif.: Regal Books, 1990), p. 123.

3. David F. Wells, *God in the Wasteland: The Reality of Truth in a World of Fading Dreams* (Grand Rapids, Mich.: Eerdmans, 1994), p. 114.

Chapter 2

1. D. Martin Fields, "Postmodernism" in *Premise*, 11 (Sept. 27, 1995), pp. 5-6.

2. Gene Edward Veith, Jr., *Postmodern Times* (Wheaton, Ill.: Crossway Books, 1994), pp. 19-20.

3. George Barna, *Absolute Confusion: How Our Moral and Spiritual Foundations Are Eroding in This Age of Change* (Ventura, CA: Regal Books, 1993).

4. Robert L. Simon, "The Paralysis of 'Absolutophobia,' " *The Chronicles of Higher Education* (July 27, 1997): pp. B5-B6. See in the same issue Kay Haugaard, "Suspending Moral Judgment: Students Who Refuse to Condemn the Unthinkable," pp. B4-B5.

5. Data is based on a poll conducted by the Roper organization commissioned by the Family Research Council. Two thousand adult men and women from all walks of life, geographic regions, and political persuasions were included. This data appeared in the January 1995 issue of *American Family Association Journal.*

6. Gene Veith, *Postmodern Times* (Wheaton, Ill.: Crossway Books, 1994), p. 51.

7. Veith, *Postmodern Times*, p. 22.

Chapter 3

1. Dennis McCallum, ed., *The Death of Truth* (Minneapolis, Minn.: Bethany House Publishers, 1996), p. 282.

2. Derrick Sherwin Bailey, *Homosexuality and the Western Christian Tradition* (Harlow: Longmans, Green 1955), p. 4.

3. Letha Scanzoni and Virginia R. Mollenkott, *Is the Homosexual My Neighbor?* (New York: Harper & Row, and SCM, 1978), p. 111, quoted by John R. W. Stott, in *Involvement: Social and Sexual Relationships in the Modern World* (Old Tappan, NJ: Fleming H. Revell Co., 1985), p. 226.

4. Robert Williams, *Just As I Am* (New York: Crown, 1992), p. 42, cited in F. LaGard Smith, *Sodom's Second Coming* (Eugene, Ore.: Harvest House Publishers, 1993), p. 128.

5. The listing of these trends are based on the work of William E. Jones, *Forces At Work* (Searcy, Ark.: Resource Publications, 1991).

6. Friedrich Nietzsche, *The Joyful Wisdom*, No. 343, found in *The Complete Works*, ed. Oscar Levy (Allen and Unwin, 18 vols., 1909-1913).

7. Corliss Lamont, *The Philosophy of Humanism* (New York: Frederick Ungar Publishing, 1982), p. 145.

8. "Scholars enlighten the masses – reject the divinity of Christ, replace initials B.C., A.D.," in *AFA Journal*, Nov./Dec. 1997, p. 13, quoting from an article found in *U.S. News & World Report*, Aug. 4, 1997.

9. William E. Jones, *Forces At Work: External Influences Affecting the Mission of Churches of Christ* (Searcy, Ark.: Resource Publications, 1991), pp. 115-116.

10. Robert Wuthnow, *Christianity in the Twenty-first Century: Reflection on the Challenge Ahead* (New York: Oxford Univ. Press, 1993), p. 105.

11. David F. Wells, *God in the Wasteland* (Grand Rapids, Mich.: Eerdmans, 1994), p. 27.

12. George Barna, *If Things Are So Good, Why Do I Feel So Bad?* (Chicago: Moody Press, 1994), p. 88.

13. Os Guinness, *The Gravedigger File: Papers on the Subversion of the Modern Church* (Downers Grove, Ill.: InterVarsity, 1983), p. 93, quoted in William E. Jones, *Forces At Work* (Searcy, Ark.: Resource Publications, 1991), p. 116.

14. Harold O.J. Brown, "Evangelicals and Social Ethics," in *Evangelical Affirmations*, ed. Kenneth S. Kantzer and Carl F. H. Henry (Grand Rapids: Zondervan/Academie, 1990), p. 279.

15. Barna, *If Things Are So Good, Why Do I Feel So Bad?*, pp. 176-177.

16. J. Richard Middleton and Brian J. Walsh, *Truth Is Stranger Than It Used to Be: Biblical Faith in a Postmodern Age* (Downer's Grove, Ill.: Intervarsity Press, 1995), pp. 4-5.

17. Elmer J. Thiessen, "Truth in a Pluralist World," *Mennonite Brethren Herald* 36:4 (Spring/Summer Encounter).

18. George Barna, *If Things Are So Good, Why Do I Feel So Bad?* (Chicago: Moody Press, 1994), p. 91.

19. See Walter Bauer, *A Greek-English Lexicon of the New Testament and Other Early Christian Literature*, 2d ed., rev. William F. Arndt, F. Wilbur Gingrich, and Frederick W. Danker (Chicago: University of Chicago Press, 1979), pp. 71-72.

Chapter 4

1. George Barna, *The Barna Report: What Americans Believe* (Ventura, Calif.: Regal Books, 1991), pp. 83-85.

2. See Pauline Marie Rosenau, *Post-Modernism and the Social Sciences: Insights, Inroads and Intrusions* (Princeton: Princeton Univ. Press, 1992), p. 128; Huston Smith, *Beyond the Post-Modern Mind* (Wheaton, Ill.: Theosophical, 1989), p. 233.

3. Walter Truett Anderson, ed., "Introduction: What's Going On Here?", in *The Truth About The Truth: De-Confusing and Re-Constructing the Postmodern World* (New York: Putnam Books, 1995), p. 8, citing Richard Rorty, *Contingency, Irony, and Solidarity* (New York: Cambridge Univ. Press, 1989), p. 3.

4. See Richard T. Hughes, *Reviving the Ancient Faith* (Grand Rapids, Mich.: Eerdmans, 1996), p. 2; Douglas A. Foster, *Will the Cycle Be Unbroken?* (Abilene, Tex.: ACU Press, 1994), pp. 43-65. To be fair, in both books the concept of being a denomination is more in line with the sociological model developed by German theologian Ernest Troeltsch. However, the implication that the theological change is also taking place cannot be ignored.

5. See for instance, Deuteronomy 30:11-14; Luke 1:1-4; Ephesians 3:4; 1 John 5:13.

6. The context of Paul's statements not only encompasses the story of Jesus' death and resurrection but also includes the requirements of the gospel. Indeed, the book of Galatians at length discusses what the requirements of Christianity for salvation are. In that book it is stated clearly that the faith of a child of God is one that presupposes baptism.

7. Norman Geisler and Ronald M. Brooks, *Come, Let Us Reason: An Introduction to Logical Thinking* (Grand Rapids, Mich.: Baker, 1990), p. 16.

8. For a more complete discussion of this point, see "Covenant Obedience" in my book, *Let All the Earth Keep Silence* (Ft. Worth, Tex.: Star Publishing, 1989), pp. 17-33.

9. For more detailed study on this, see "Jesus and Silence" in my book, *Let All the Earth Keep Silence*, pp. 35-52.

10. While there is some controversy as to whether the genitive in 2 John 9 is subjective or objective, the question is really moot as far as the doctrine of silence is concerned. If the phrase "doctrine of Christ" has a subjective genitive, then the idea is that no one should go beyond what Christ has taught. If the phrase "doctrine of Christ" contains an objective genitive, then the idea is that one should not go beyond the doctrine of Christ. In either case, it is the act of going beyond the teaching (and so not listening to God's Word) that causes the perversion and error. Even if we limit the error to the narrow objective genitive, by example we are teaching that one cannot go beyond what is taught and remain approved of God. Certainly if this is true of the deity of Christ, it is likewise true of many other fundamental doctrines. For instance, one who goes beyond and does not abide in the teaching that there is one church, certainly perverts Bible teaching. Those who go beyond and do not abide in the teaching that there is one baptism have sinned just as greatly as those who would dismiss the deity of Jesus. While some have abused

2 John 9 by applying it to their pet opinions, others have abused it just as much by restricting the point of the passage to such a narrowly defined doctrine that it is irrelevant to today's thinking.

Chapter 5

1. Robert L. Simon, "The Paralysis of 'Absolutophobia,' " in *The Chronicle of Higher Education* 43 (June 27, 1997): pp. B5-B6.

2. Benjamin B. Warfield, *Selected Shorter Writings of Benjamin B. Warfield*, ed. John E. Meeter (Nutley, N.J.: Presb. & Ref., 1970), I:47; II:221.

3. cf. Exodus 34:26; Deuteronomy 14:21.

4. For a detailed argument on prohibitive silence, see my book *Let All the Earth Keep Silence* (Ft. Worth, Tex.: Star Publishing, 1989).

5. William J. Bennett, *The De-Valuing of America* (Colorado Springs, Colo.: Focus on the Family, rev. ed. 1994), preface to the updated edition. For another valuable book on this subject, see Robert H. Bork, *Slouching Toward Gomorrah: Modern Liberalism and American Decline* (New York: HarperCollins/ReganBooks, 1996).

6. Richard C. Trench, *Synonyms of the New Testament* (Grand Rapids, Mich.: Eerdmans, 1880), 13.

Chapter 6

1. Victor L. Hunter, "Some Thoughts on Theology and Mission," *Mission* (March 1972): p. 6.

2. Rubel Shelly and Randall J. Harris, *The Second Incarnation* (West Monroe, La.: Howard Publishing Co., 1992), p. 62.

3. Alexander Campbell, "The Ancient Order of Things, No. 1," *The Christian Baptist*, Vol. 2, No. 7 (Joplin, Missouri: College Press, 1988), p. 128.

4. Campbell, "A Restoration of the Ancient Order of Things. No. 2," *The Christian Baptist,* p. 133.

5. Raymond C. Kelcy, "The Restoration Principle," Abilene Christian College Lectures, p. 119.

6. Kelcy, "The Restoration Principle," Abilene Christian College Lectures, p. 119.

Chapter 7

1. The Martyrdom of Polycarp 9:1,2, in *The Apostolic Fathers*, trans. J.B. Lightfoot and J.R. Harmer, ed. and rev. Michael W. Holmes, 2nd ed. (Grand Rapids, Mich.: Baker, 1989), pp. 138-139.

2. Rubel Shelly, "What Is Your Church's Name?", *Lovelines*, Vol. 24, No. 5, Feb. 4, 1998.

3. William Barclay, *The Gospel of John*, vol. 1, in *The Daily Study Bible Series*, rev. ed (Philadelphia: Westminster Press, 1975), p. 229.

4. Peggy Sanford, "Cookies to Communion: Changing Roles of Women in the Church of Christ," *Integrity*, Vol. 4, No. 5, pp. 82-87.

5. Robert H. Schuller, *Self-Esteem: The New Reformation* (Waco, Tex.: Word Publishing, 1982), p. 35.

6. Don Matzat, "Guiltless good news," *Modern Reformation*, Nov/Dec 1997, Vol. 6., No. 6, pp. 18-21.

7. Schuller, *New Reformation*, p. 45.

Chapter 8

1. This information is based on a series of articles by *Star* Religion writer, Carol Elrod, which appeared in the *Indianapolis Star* in July and August 1989.

2. Alexander Campbell, "Any Christians Among Protestant Parties," in *Millennial Harbinger*, September 1837, pp. 411-414.

3. Ibid., November 1837, p. 506f.

4. Ibid.

5. In addition to Caleb and Joshua, the Levites also were thought to be able to enter the promised land. Generally, there are two supposed reasons for this. (1) The Levites did not send up a spy as did the other tribes. (2) The Levites did not take up arms to fight. Since the Levites were not included in the numbering found in chapter one, it is inferred that they did not enter into this matter at all.

6. Edward T. Hiscox, *The Standard Manual for Baptist Churches* (Philadelphia: The American Baptist Publication Society, 1890; reprint, 1931), pp. 20-21. "Baptism is not essential to salvation, for our churches utterly repudiate the dogma of 'baptismal regeneration.'; but it is essential to obedience, since Christ has commanded it. It is also essential to a public confession of Christ before the world, and to membership in the church which is his body. And no true lover of his Lord will refuse these acts of obedience and tokens of affection." In the section called "Christian Baptism," Hiscox further says, "We believe the Scriptures teach that Christian baptism is the immersion in water of a believer in Christ, into the name of the Father, and Son, and Holy Ghost; to show forth in solemn and beautiful emblem his faith in the crucified, buried, and risen Saviour, with its effect, in his death to sin and resurrection to a new life; that it is a prerequisite to the privileges of a church relation, and to the Lord's Supper" (pp. 69-70). J.E. Cobb in *A New Manual for Baptist Churches* (Little Rock, Ark.: Baptist Publications Committee) says, "Baptism is not a procurative, but a declarative ordinance; it is a public declaration of the believer's separation from the world and unto the life in Christ. It is the visible line of demarcation between believers and unbelievers. ... In the second place, baptism is a picture of the gospel. Baptism is not the gospel, nor any part of the gospel, but it is the picture of the gospel" (p. 43). Again, "baptism declares the fact of the remission of sins. It does not actually remit sins, but it declares remission. In Acts 2:38 Peter commanded his hearers to be baptized in the name of Jesus Christ for the the remission of sins. Not in order to remit their sins, but because their sins had been remitted" (p. 44). "Baptism is an outward sign of an inward work ... It is plainly evident that baptism is not in order to obtain salvation from the simple reason that the Scriptures tell us that it is not by works that we are saved. Baptism is the performance of a good work; therefore, it is not es-

sential to salvation, but it is the voluntary submission of a child of God to the will of his Lord and Master – Jesus," (p. 45).

7. Wayne Detzler, *New Testament Words in Today's Language* (Wheaton, Ill.: Victor Books, 1986), p. 290.

8. Note the statement of Jesus about His teachings in John 12:49-50: "For I did not speak on My own initiative, but the Father Himself who sent Me has given Me commandment, what to say, and what to speak. And I know that His commandment is eternal life; therefore the things I speak, I speak just as the Father has told Me." The teachings of Jesus were not His own but those the Father "told" Him. Note how conscientious Jesus was to listen and to pass on exactly what the Father told Him to say. He said what He was supposed to say in the way He was supposed to say it. We can be grateful for that, for His listening and speaking assures us that we truly know the Father's will.

9. Walter Bauer, *A Greek-English Lexicon of the New Testament and Other Early Christian Literature*, 2d ed., rev. William F. Arndt, F. Wilbur Gingrich, and Frederick W. Danker (Chicago: University of Chicago Press, 1979), p. 229. Joseph Henry Thayer, *Thayer's Greek-English Lexicon of the New Testament* (Marshalltown, Del.: National Foundation for Christian Education, 1889), p. 94.

10. Everett Ferguson, *Early Christians Speak* (Austin, Tex.: Sweet Publishing, 1971), p. 38.

11. Martin Luther, "On Baptism," *The Large Catechism*, IV:110-117.

Chapter 9

1. *Webster's New Universal Unabridged Dictionary*, Deluxe second ed. (New York: Dorset & Baber, 1983), p. 2109.

2. Ibid., p. 607.

3. Ibid., p. 1332.

4. For a valuable study of this, see Dan Chambers, *Showtime: Worship in the Age of Show Business* (Nashville, Tenn.: 21st Century Christian, 1997).

5. Jimmy Jividen, *Worship in Song* (Ft. Worth, Tex.: Star, 1987), p. 19.

6. Everett Ferguson, *Early Christians Speak* (Austin, Tex.: Sweet Publishing, 1971), p. 160.

7. Ibid., p. 161.

8. *Hom.* xi, vol. xii; and *Hom.* xxxvi. in 1 Corinthians vol. x. See "Christian Music" in *Cyclopedia of Biblical, Theological, and Ecclesiastical Literature*, ed. John McClintock and James Strong (Grand Rapids Mich.: Baker, 1876, reprint 1969), Vol. VI, pp. 757-758.

9. Ferguson, *Early Christians Speak*, p. 161 citing Egon Wellesz, A History of Byzantine Music and Hymnography (Oxford: Clarendon Press, 1961), p. 35.

10. *Early Christians Speak*, p. 84.

11. McClintock & Strong, *Cyclopedia*, VI:758b.

12. H.E. Dana and Julius R. Mantey, *A Manual Grammar of the Greek New Testament* (Toronto: Macmillan, 1955), p. 131.

13. A.T. Robertson, *A Grammar of the Greek New Testament in Light of Historical Research* (Nashville: Broadman, 1934), p. 692.

14. Everett Ferguson, *A Cappella Music in the Public Worship of the Church* (Abilene, Tex.: Biblical Research Press, 1972), p. 17.

15. ομοθυμαδον, Walter Bauer, *A Greek-English Lexicon of the New Testament and Other Early Christian Literature*, 2d ed., rev. F. Wilbur Ginrich, and Frederick W. Danker (Chicago: University of Chicago Press, 1979), p. 566.

16. Ferguson, *A Cappella Music*, p. 34.

17. Jividen, *Worship in Song*, p. 22.

18. McClintock & Strong, *Cyclopedia*, VI:758.

Chapter 10

1. John F. MacArthur, Jr., *Ashamed of the Gospel* (Wheaton, Ill.: Crossway Books, 1993), p. 49. MacArthur cites George Barna, *Marketing the Church* (Colorado Springs, Colo.: NavPress, 1988), pp. 33, 45.

2. D.A. Carson, *The Gagging of God: Christianity Confronts Pluralism* (Grand Rapids, Mich.: Zondervan, 1996), p. 508.

3. George Barna, *Evangelism That Works* (Ventura, Calif.: Regal Books, 1995), pp. 141-142.

4. Mounce, NICNT, Revelation, p. 98.

5. John F. MacArthur Jr., *Ashamed of the Gospel* (Wheaton, Ill.: Crossway Books, 1993), p. 81.

6. Note the lengthy arguments by Robert Schuller on the dignity of man and how Christians should evangelize today in *Self-Esteem: The New Reformation* (Waco, Tex.: Word Books, 1982), pp. 11-40.

7. James Davison Hunter, *Evangelicalism: The Coming Generation* (Chicago: University of Chicago, 1987), p. 40.

8. Transcripted from an interview between Robert Schuller and Billy Graham, May 31, 1997 found in Texe Marrs, "Billy Graham is a Great Deceiver," *Flashpoint 98,* May 1998, pp. 1-3.

9. D.A. Carson, *The Gagging of God: Christianity Confronts Pluralism* (Grand Rapids, Mich.: Zondervan, 1996), p. 476.

Chapter 12

1. James Patterson and Peter Kim, *The Day America Told the Truth* (New York: Prentice Hall Press, 1991), p. 31.

2. James D. Bales, *The Originality of Jesus Christ* (Searcy, Ark.: Bales, n.d.), p. 33.

3. Gary R. Habermas, *The Historical Jesus* (Joplin, Mo.: College Press, 1996), p. 251.

4. See Job 38:1-40:2.

5. Augustine, *The Confessions of Augustine*, trans. John K. Ryan (Garden City, N.Y.: Doubleday & Co., Inc., 1960), I:1:1,2.

6. Fran Sciacca, *Generation at Risk* (Chicago: Moody, 1991), pp. 169-170. The original list of these 10 questions appear in Colin Chapman, *The Case for Christianity* (Grand Rapids, Mich.: Eerdmans, 1981), pp. 9-36.

Chapter 13

1. The literature of the four gospels presents Jesus in the form of stand-alone narratives or teachings in the form of pericopes. Gordon D. Fee and Douglas Stuart encourage students of the gospels to "think paragraphs." *How to Read the Bible for All Its Worth* (Grand Rapids, Mich.: Zondervan, 1982), p. 110. While we do not want to deny the unity of the gospels, we do want to see the whole as a collection of units. The wisdom literature of the Old Testament also lends itself to this kind of thinking. Ecclesiastes presents many seemingly disjointed snapshots of life, which are loosely connected by the major premise of the book. The pithy statements in Proverbs often stand alone in their own context. We are not here suggesting that all preaching should take this form. We are saying preachers need to be sensitive to the changes taking place in the coming generations and find ways to communicate effectively.

2. Suetonius, *Life of Claudius* (25:4). Suetonius says of Christ, "As the Jews were making constant disturbances at the instigation of Chrestus, he expelled them from Rome."

3. Fredreich Nietzsche, *Thus Spake Zarathustra*, trans. John Common, The Modern Library (New York: Boni and Liveright, Inc., 19170, 274, quoted by Batsell Barrett Baxter, *I Believe Because* (Grand Rapids, Mich.: Baker Books, 1971), p. 76.

Recommended Reading on Postmodernism

Highly Recommended

Chambers, Dan. *Showtime: Worship in the Age of Show Business.* Nashville, Tenn.: 21st Century Christian, 1997.

Dockery, David S., ed. *The Challenge of Postmodernism: An Evangelical Engagement.* Wheaton, Ill.: BridgePoint Books, 1995.

Jones, William E. *Forces At Work: External Influences Affecting the Mission of Churches of Christ.* Searcy, Ark.: Resource Publications, 1991.

MacArthur, John F. Jr. *Ashamed of the Gospel: When the Church Becomes Like the World.* Wheaton, Ill.: Crossway Books, 1993,

McCallum, Dennis, ed. *The Death of Truth.* Minneapolis, Minn.: Bethany House Publishers, 1996.

Nash, Robert N. Jr. *An 8-Track Church in a CD World: The Modern Church in the Postmodern World.* Macon, Georgia: Smyth & Helwys Pub. Co., 1997.

Sheerer, Jim and Williams, Charles L. *Directions for the Road Ahead: Stability in Change in the churches of Christ.* Chickasha, Okla.: Yeomen Press, 1998.

Sproul, R.C. *Choosing My Religion.* Grand Rapids, Mich.: Baker Books, 1995.

Veith, Gene Edward Jr. *Postmodern Times: A Christian Guide to Contemporary Thought and Culture.* Wheaton, Ill.: Crossway Books, 1994.

Current Thoughts and Trends, NavPress, PO Box 35004, Colorado Springs, CO, 80935-9937.

Other Valuable Works

Armstrong, John H., ed. *The Coming Evangelical Crisis.* Chicago: Moody Press, 1996.

Barna, George. *If Things Are So Good, Why Do I Feel So Bad.* Chicago: Moody Press, 1994.

_____. *The Future of the American Family.* Chicago: Moody Press, 1993.

_____. *Virtual America: The Barna Report 1994-1995.* Ventura, Calif.: Regal Books, 1994.

Bennett, William J. *The De-Valuing of America.* Colorado Springs, Colo.: Focus on the Family, 1994.

Blamires, Harry. *The Postchristian Mind.* Ann Arbor, Mich.: Servant Publications, 1999.

Bloom, Allan. *The Closing of the American Mind.* New York: Simon and Schuster, 1987.

Bork, Robert H. *Slouching Toward Gomorrah: Modern Liberalism and American Decline.* New York: HarperCollins Publishers, 1996.

Burnham, Frederic B., ed. *Postmodern Theology: Christian Faith in a Postmodern World.* San Francisco: Harper, 1989.

Copan, Paul. *True For You, But Not For Me.* Minneapolis, Minn.: Bethany House, 1998.

Downs, Tim. *Finding Common Ground.* Chicago: Moody Press, 1999.

Hunter, James Davison. *Culture Wars: The Struggle to Define America.* New York: Basic Books, 1991.

Kreeft, Peter. *The Journey: A Spiritual Roadmap for Modern Pilgrims.* Downer's Grove, Ill.: InterVarsity Press, 1996.

Naisbitt, John and Aburdene, Patricia. *Megatrends 2000: Ten New Directions for the 1990's.* New York: William Morrow and Co., 1990.

Noebel, David A. *Understanding the Times: The Religious Worldviews of Our Day and the Search for Truth.* Eugene, Ore.: Harvest House, 1991.

Packer, J.I. *Truth and Power: The Place of Scripture in the Christian Life.* Wheaton: Ill.: Robert Shaw Publishers, 1996.

Patterson, James and Kim, Peter. *The Day America Told The Truth.* New York: Prentice Hall Press, 1991.

Phillips, Timothy R. and Okholm, Dennis L. *Christian Apologetics in the Postmodern World.* Downer's Grove, Ill.: InterVarsity Press, 1995.

Sciacca, Fran. *Generation at Risk.* Chicago: Moody Press. Rev. ed., 1991.

Smith, F. LaGard. *The Cultural Church.* Nashville, Tenn.: 21st Century Christian, 1992.

_____. *Who Is My Brother?* Malibu, Calif.: Cotswold Publishing, 1997.

Wells, David F. *God in the Wasteland: The Reality of Truth in a World of Fading Dreams.* Grand Rapids, Mich.: Eerdmans, 1994.

Glossary of Terms

Absolutism: The belief that truth and values are objective and universal. "Objective" means that truth exists outside of the individual, and "universal" means that truth applies to every person in every place at every time.

Exclusivism: The belief in the need to reject those who differ theologically.

Existentialism: The attempt to create meaning and personal identity out of a meaningless universe by the exercise of free will.

Foundationalism: The belief that knowledge may be based on first principles or immediately justified beliefs.

Inclusivism: The belief in the need to include those who differ theologically.

Modernism: Another term for enlightenment thought; modernist thought centered on a belief in human progress, reason as the ultimate source of authority; human autonomy.

Objective Truth: Truth that exists independent of human thought rather than truth that depends on human thought or experience.

Paradigm (archetype or pattern): A model. In postmodernism, a paradigm is a way of looking at reality specific to one social group. The rules of thought and consistency apply within a given paradigm, but cannot be applied to another.

Pattern Theology: The belief that the New Testament has certain forms or patterns to which God demands our careful attention and obedience.

Pluralism (Christian): The state of things that permits several competing, alternative theologies with the belief that such a state is not only approved by God but also healthy.

Postmodernism: Is not a distinct set of doctrines or truth claims but:

*a mood – a view of the world characterized by a deep distrust of reason, not to mention a disdain for the knowledge Christians believe the Bible provides.

*a methodology – a completely new way of analyzing ideas.

*a movement – a fresh onslaught on truth that brings a more or less cohesive approach to literature, history, politics, education, law sociology, linguistics, and virtually every other discipline, including science.

*a metamorphosis – transforming every area of life.

Precision Obedience: The practice of obeying commands precisely and conscientiously. It is the application of John 8:31; 2 Timothy 2:15; and 2 John 9 to the forms and patterns found in the New Testament.

Privitization: The process whereby religion is made a purely private matter where concerns for ends apply only to individuals. "Do-it-yourself religiosity." "Pick-and-choose Christianity."

Progressive Inclusivists: A description of those in the churches of Christ who believe the church should fellowship people who are members of denominational churches. The basis of this fellowship comes from belief and love of God, with the notion that doctrinal differences do not limit the grace of God.

Relativism: The belief that there are no absolutes. "Truth is not fixed by outside reality (God) but is decided by a group or individual for themselves. Truth is not discovered but manufactured. Truth is ever-changing, not only in insignificant matters of taste or fashion, but in crucial matters of spirituality, morality and reality itself.

Secularization: Life lived without significant religion, making God and service to Him undesirable for society. This is similar in meaning to worldliness (1 John 2:15-17).

Skepticism: The belief that one should doubt or suspend judgment on philosophical questions.

Subjective Truth: Truth that is "true to me," as opposed to truth that is truly independent of our thought or experience.

Subjectivism: In ethics, the belief that there are no objective, universal principles of conduct. Challenging normlessness is the great heresy.

Syncretism: The reconciliation of union of conflicting beliefs. The joining together of different views, especially religious views, often blending even contradictory religions into one.

Worldview: A philosophy of life. A worldview is a set of interrelated basic beliefs.